PENGUIN BOOKS
HOLY MOTHER

Gabrielle Donnelly was born in Muswell Hill, London, one of a large Roman Catholic family. She studied English Literature at London University, after which she became a magazine and newspaper journalist, contributing to *Options*, *Woman's Realm*, *Woman's World*, *Woman* and *The Times*. She now lives in California but continues to write for British magazines and newspapers.

HOLY MOTHER

Gabrielle Donnelly

PENGUIN BOOKS

PENGUIN BOOKS

Published by the Penguin Group
27 Wrights Lane, London w8 5tz, England
Viking Penguin Inc., 40 West 23rd Street, New York, New York 10010, USA
Penguin Books Australia Ltd, Ringwood, Victoria, Australia
Penguin Books Canada Ltd, 2801 John Street, Markham, Ontario, Canada l3r 1b4
Penguin Books (NZ) Ltd, 182–190 Wairau Road, Auckland 10, New Zealand

Penguin Books Ltd, Registered Offices: Harmondsworth, Middlesex, England

First published in Great Britain by Victor Gollancz 1987
Published in Penguin Books 1988

Copyright © Gabrielle Donnelly, 1987
All rights reserved

Made and printed in Great Britain by
Richard Clay Ltd, Bungay, Suffolk

To Richard Barber
and Judith Hall
with love and thanks

HOLY MOTHER

Anne always sang at the Friday-evening Mass, her pure voice rising from her dumpy form as effortlessly as the soul of a saint rising to heaven, her gooseberry-coloured eyes shining behind their plastic-rimmed spectacles.

'Hallowed be thy name,' she sang as she had sung every week through the long London winter, moulding the ancient words from Israel to the West Indian tune that was so new. 'Lead us not into temptation, hallowed be thy name; but deliver us from all that is evil, hallowed be thy name; hallowed be thy name.'

Her tune hung shivering in the air for a moment before Father Bob's masculine voice tramped in. 'Deliver us, Lord,' he said, 'from every evil, and grant us peace in our day. In your mercy keep us free from sin, and protect us from all anxiety, as we wait in joyful hope for the coming of our Saviour, Jesus Christ.'

Stephen wound his uncomfortably long legs around the rickety legs of his chair, looked at Anne, and, as he seemed to have been doing hourly in the four weeks since she had become his wife, marvelled at his good fortune. His Faith had brought him up among miracles, among visions of saints and inexplicable healings of sicknesses, and daily changing, as he had just witnessed, of the bread and wine into the Eucharist, the very body and blood of the living Son of God. But none of them, in his mind, could compare with the miracle of Anne's love for him. Positively greedy it seemed to ask, on top of that, to be kept free from sin and protected from anxiety. He smiled at his dumpy love, who smiled back at him, and, generous in his happiness, sent up a prayer for those less blessed than he.

'For the kingdom, the power, and the glory are yours, now and forever,' they replied.

Maureen caught the secret look that passed between Anne and Stephen, and frowned, drawing her heavy brows down over her eyes. It was simple for them, unfairly so. They were good people who genuinely liked each other, genuinely liked being Catholic, even, extraordinarily, apparently liked Maureen herself. Maureen, laden

9

with the burden of being that self, found it difficult to like, as she found it difficult to like the God who had created it, as she found it, at times, impossible to like the Catholic Faith which her grandparents had so infuriatingly brought with them when they had crossed St George's Channel all those years ago. But more infuriating still was that, years and fury notwithstanding, it was her own Faith, too, as innate and unchosen a part of her as her fuzzy black hair or her raspberry-coloured cheeks. Detaching herself from the proceedings —there would, after all, be nothing said that she had not heard before and would not, God willing, live to hear again—she allowed herself to drift into a favourite fantasy of atheism.

'Lord Jesus Christ,' said Father Bob, 'you said to your apostles, I leave you peace, my peace I give you; look not on our sins, but on the faith of your Church, and grant us the peace and unity of your kingdom, where you live for ever and ever.'

'Amen,' they replied.

Not even to Maureen, to whom he felt probably as close as to any living soul, would Denis dream of expressing exactly what Mass meant to him. It was peace, pure, simple, and comforting as clean sheets, probably the most peaceful thing there was. It was at Mass that he could release himself, briefly, from his life sentence of playing the fool, could lose himself, briefly, in the one act that was, under all normal circumstances, unquestionably right, unmitigatedly good. It was at Mass, too, that he could, if not forget—how could he ever forget?—the other thing, then at least accept it, because it didn't matter, really, nothing in this world mattered, really. What mattered was God, and the Mass.

'The peace of the Lord be with you always,' said Father Bob.

'And also with you,' they replied.

Having known peace all his life, Geoffrey could never understand why others set such store by it. Geoffrey was pure English, a convert; he stood slightly apart from the others, tall, fair, relaxed with a familiar assurance, here in his own land, that the others, children and grandchildren of immigrants, could never attain. His race had seen nothing but peace, on its own soil, at least, for a full three hundred years; he therefore assumed it, viewed it casually, with a simple clarity. Peace was knowing what must be done, and having the strength to do it. God had blessed him enough to show him the way when He had pointed him towards the Catholic Church; since strength of purpose had never for him posed a challenge, the rest had been easy. The result was the peace of God that passed all understanding. Geoffrey bowed his head, and thanked God for the gift.

'Let us offer each other the sign of peace,' said Father Bob.

The sign of peace was Kate's favourite part of the Mass, especially when it was the kind of Mass where you knew everyone. Of course, every Mass could not be quite so intimate, and it was true that it was another kind of joy, in a large church, to shake the hand of the perfect stranger next to you, kid-gloved dowager at Our Lady of Kensington, or Aer Lingus hostess when you popped into Warwick Street at lunch-time, and say, in effect, I don't know you, but God bless you, anyway. But that joy could never compare with this, the mingling of sharing the love of God with just a few people you also knew and loved for themselves, and sharing it, too, not with a cold handshake, but with proper hugs, so that you actually felt the different warm softnesses of Maureen and Anne, the harder expanses of Bob and Geoffrey, the spideriness of Stephen, and the narrowness of Denis, who was really not so much bigger than she was. Kate looked forward all week to Friday's sign of peace.

The group was rather grandly referred to in the *Westminster Year Book* as the Our Lady of Sorrows (Soho) Parish Society of St Thomas Aquinas. It was a religious discussion group, the brainchild of Father Bob Power, who had been curate of the parish for the last year, and, in his eyes, was one of his most successful institutions. A young priest who prided himself on his relaxed attitude to the trappings of the ministry, he was blessed with optimism which made him quite simply blind to the growing numbers of people who every year drifted away from the Church, focusing only, and with triumphant precision, on those who stayed in. It depressed him not in the slightest that, of the thousands of baptised people who flocked into the centre of London every weekday, just half a dozen should be interested enough in their Faith regularly to spend a Friday evening discussing it. They were a half-dozen of whom he was proud: of whom, he was sure, anyone would be proud.

They were a diverse group, admittedly, having on the whole little in common with each other besides their Faith, and that in so many shades of belief and practice that they could scarcely be said to share it at all. It was, in fact, not so much religious devotion which drew them together, as a more human herding instinct. To be Catholic in

England was to be subtly outside the rest of the community. England was above all a Protestant country, and Catholics, as every Catholic knew, were more different from Protestants than Protestants realised. To Protestants, religion was essentially a private affair, to be sorted out individually, mentioned rarely and never without respect. To Catholics it was public, an integral part of the fabric of everyday life, its symbols hung casually on living-room walls and around necks, its heroes easily invoked and its villains repudiated, its music whistled daily on the street. This held nothing extraordinary for them: it was how they had, all but Geoffrey, been brought up, how their mothers and aunts and grandmothers had been, how the priests and the nuns at school had taught them to be themselves. How they had indeed been, until they had gone into society: Protestant society.

They had all adapted. They had adopted, more or less slowly and with more or less success, the protective colouring of this alien land that was the land of their birth. They had hidden their plaster statues in drawers and their Leonardo Madonnas in the backs of cupboards; had forced themselves not to mention if it was St Joseph's day or the feast of the Assumption; had disciplined themselves not to cross themselves when lightning flashed or to bow their heads at the name of Jesus, or ask St Anthony to help find lost keys, and never ever, if humanly possible, to let slip the fact that they went regularly to Mass. For the most part, they succeeded; for the most part those around them, friends and colleagues, were aware of their Catholicism dimly if at all, certainly had no idea of the breadth of the chasm that lay between the way they seemed to be and the way they were. Among their own kind, however, the pretence could be dropped. And it was the luxury of being with their own kind which, as much as any spiritual benefit, was the benefit of the Society of St Thomas Aquinas.

Meetings were held in a basement off Soho Square lent to them by an intellectual Catholic society, a cheerless room with chilly white walls, broken high up by the lower halves of sternly uncurtained windows, glaring onto Soho's sin-filled winter night. The one attractive feature of the basement was that it held a small bar, where, Mass and discussion over, they would fortify themselves for the journey home with drink and chat.

'I have never,' said Denis—they were discussing Anne and Stephen's flat-warming party the previous Saturday—'in all my born days seen one bloke—even a priest—put back so many sausage rolls in one evening.'

'You have never,' returned Father Bob, 'had Mrs Herlihy as a housekeeper.'

'And I certainly,' continued Denis unheeding, 'would not have believed that one man, and he an Englishman, could have put away quite so much wine and yet remained more or less standing.'

Geoffrey raised an eyebrow with a faint smile. He was a young man of few words, and unconscious of the advantage this gave him over those around him.

'You had a good time, then?' said Anne.

'Terrible,' said Maureen instantly. 'Hated every minute.'

Kate flushed. 'I had a lovely time,' she said.

'Did you?' said Stephen. He smiled at her; he liked Kate. 'Good.'

'Didn't feel so bloody good at Mass the next morning,' said Denis.

'Who went to Mass?' said Maureen. She looked hard at Bob. 'I didn't.'

Bob said nothing. Maureen's soul and conscience were her own affair, and for himself, he had long given up trying to establish whether she could or could not, even in these liberal days, properly be described as a practising Catholic. He turned instead to Stephen and Anne. 'It was a splendid evening,' he said. 'Really splendid. We should do it more often.'

It was a casual comment, but it struck a chord in Stephen. He edged his chair closer to Anne's, so that their knees were touching. 'Let's,' he said. 'We don't see enough of each other socially. We should.'

'OK.' Denis rubbed his hands. 'Tomorrow evening, eight o'clock sharp. What are you cooking?'

'I mean it,' said Stephen. He did. It was through the group that he and Anne had met, and he could not think of a single group of people for whom he felt less complicated an affection. 'We should.'

'I'll tell you what we should do, now you mention it,' said Bob. He nodded approvingly at Stephen. 'One day we should go on a pilgrimage.'

'God.' Maureen shuddered. 'Can you imagine Denis on an aeroplane?'

'An English pilgrimage,' said Bob. 'Just for the day. Let's not forget that we are, after all, English Catholics.'

'Ah, Father.' Denis dropped into the stage brogue which, London born and bred though he was, came to him more naturally than cockney. 'We are that, so we are, praise be to God.'

Nevertheless, the idea was taking hold.

'There must be English shrines,' said Stephen.

Geoffrey stroked his beard, fuller and fairer than Stephen's, thought of Chaucer, and said nothing.

'There's Canterbury,' said Anne.

'Bit crowded.'

'Walsingham?'

'It's Anglican.'

'Is it?'

'Of course not.'

'Yes, it is.'

'There's always Aylesford.'

Everyone turned to the speaker, Kate, who blushed.

'It's in Kent. I was at school near there. It's very pretty.'

'I've been there,' Maureen added. 'The nuns were always dragging us. Maureen Callaghan ees ze naughtiest girrl in ze class. Nice place, though. Carmelite, old. Didn't someone see Our Lady there? Simon Stock.'

'We could go on St Patrick's day,' said Denis. 'That'd be ironic for us, wouldn't it? That's—what?—six weeks this Saturday.'

And so it was decided. On St Patrick's day, they would go to Aylesford.

Anne and Stephen sat at the little kitchen table of their spanking new flat, eating toast and marmalade, and contemplating the joy of a whole Saturday together.

'It's going to rain,' said Stephen. 'Let's not go out at all.'

'And eat what?' said Anne.

'Baked beans?'

'Let's hear you say that at supper-time.'

'I mean it.' He brushed a crumb from his beard. 'I don't want to go out. I don't ever want to go out. Anywhere.' He reached for her slice of toast.

She slapped his hand away, and dropped two slices of bread into the toaster. 'And this is the man who yesterday was organising the whole group on pilgrimages up and down the country.'

'Oh, that. That was a good idea, wasn't it? We should socialise more with each other. Catholics. We're not like other people, are we?'

'Aren't we?' She shrugged; her father was Protestant.

'Well, I don't think so. They're a funny old lot, that group, aren't they? They should all get married, I can recommend it most highly.'

She looked at the wedding-ring gleaming on her stubby finger. 'I never thought I'd get married. I don't suppose anyone ever really does. But I never did.'

'They should all get married,' he repeated. 'It's just their tough luck that the best wife's already spoken for.'

'Maureen should get married,' she said. 'Calm her down a bit.'

'Maureen!' He frowned in uncharacteristic disapproval. 'Who'd put up with her?'

'Oh, she's OK.' The toast popped up, and she handed him a slice.

'Yes, she's OK, but . . .' He shook his head. 'She's never happy, that one.'

She pounced, remembering one of their first evenings out together, to see *HMS Pinafore*.

'What, *never*?'

'Well . . .' he responded, '*hardly* ever . . . *I'm* happy, Anne. I'm very, very happy.'

She looked at him, and, unasked, passed the marmalade. 'Good,' she said.

Maureen and Jonathan were fighting. Rather, Maureen was fighting: Jonathan did not fight. He sprawled on the shabby old sofa in the impossibly small sitting-room of Maureen's impossibly small flat in West Hampstead, watching her in mild and totally unconcealed amusement.

'If I have told you once,' she was saying, 'I have told you a hundred thousand times. Don't call me Fighting Irish.'

'And if I,' he replied, 'have told you once, I have told you thirty thousand million times. Don't exaggerate.'

Maureen ground her teeth. It was not supposed to be like this. They were opposites, she and Jonathan, opposites in race and opposites in temperament, they were even doing postgraduate studies on opposite subjects, he on chemistry, she on Spanish literature. Opposites were supposed to complement, to fulfil each other, everyone said so. It was not supposed to be like this.

'I just wish,' she said, 'you'd stop assuming that simply because I'm Catholic, I'm therefore riddled with guilt.'

'I wasn't assuming,' he said. 'My sweet dove of peace. Actually, I thoroughly enjoyed myself, and you, if you don't mind my mentioning it, seemed to be doing the same. Why spoil it with assumptions? My gently cooing lovebird.'

'Don't be sarcastic,' she snapped.

The trouble was, she realised, staring glumly out of the window at the rain torrenting on the dirty pavement far below, that of course, she was riddled with guilt. Crawling with it, like a corpse with maggots. Guilty unfairly, unnecessarily, because—why? Because earlier that afternoon she and the young man behind her had lain in each other's arms, enjoying themselves, as he said, thoroughly? Because the previous Sunday she and the same young man had drunk coffee and laughed over newspapers and enjoyed each other then, too, instead of standing grimly separated in a draughty church? No crime had been committed, no wrong done to one or other, nothing at all done that was not being done everywhere, down the street, through the city, across the country. Why, then, the guilt that sat like a black crow on her shoulder, that beat its wings against her face, and would not fly away?

In the street below, a respectably shabby old couple stumbled into the dusk, huddling together under a greenish-black umbrella. She turned from the grey window to the lamp-lit room and handsome, sensible Jonathan laughing at her from the sofa.

'Well, don't just sit there grinning like an idiot,' she said. 'I've got to cook a casserole for these bloody friends of yours.'

It was a joke: the dinner guests who were arriving that evening were her own friends. He went along with it, following her into the even smaller kitchen, thanking her profusely while she chopped onions, carrots, and beef. After a while she began to feel better, as she always did when she was cooking. She poured them red wine from a large bottle.

'I can't see you on Monday,' she said. 'That school friend I told you about, Alison, the public relations person in Los Angeles? Well, she's back. And she's coming to supper.'

He heaved a melodramatic sigh. 'Cast aside. Like an old glove.'

He glanced out of the window at the silvery rain in the night. 'You cook her something warm. She'll be feeling the cold.'

He was kind, was Jonathan, so much kinder than she. Here he was, charming and cheerful to her, here he would be, charming and cheerful to her guests tonight. He even had a considerate word for Alison, who had just spoiled his plans for Monday evening. He was good for her, everyone agreed: he cheered her up and was, they all said, a stabilising influence. The question to which, search herself as she might, she could never find an answer, was, why he put up with her. Looking at his calm face across the table, she doubted whether she would ever know.

Denis was a popular dinner guest, which was convenient, since his own cooking skills were limited. It was not, perhaps, a particularly imaginative choice for a Saturday evening to spend it with the other half of the features department of the weekly *Sentinel*; but then, journalists were notoriously clannish, and besides, it was not Philip who had issued the invitation, but his girlfriend Ruth, who not only was an accountant rather than a journalist, but also happened to be an accomplished cook.

'I like cohabiting friends,' he remarked, passing his plate willingly for extra chicken. 'Especially when one of them cooks like this.'

'Thank you,' said Philip. 'I do my poor best.'

'I can recommend cohabiting,' said Ruth. 'You should try it yourself.'

Denis sighed. 'Ruth,' he said, 'you have but to say the word.'

'I mean it,' said Ruth. 'When are you going to find someone?'

'Ruth!' said Philip.

Denis clutched the table in outrage. 'And live in sin,' he thundered, 'like the pair of you?'

'Really, Denis,' said Ruth. 'There are lots of nice girls around. What's stopping you?'

'Ruth!'

'Oh, shut up, Philip. Honestly, you men.' She waved an exasperated serving spoon at the two of them. 'You share an office all week, and I bet you never even talk about anything important. No wonder you all have heart attacks.'

'Heart attacks?' Denis furrowed his brow. 'So that's where you were last Wednesday.'

'It's the time of year,' agreed Philip. 'I've had one pretty well non-stop since Christmas.'

'My advice to you, chum, is vitamin C tablets.'

'You big babies,' said Ruth.

Denis had fielded the question with such practised skill that he had hardly even noticed himself doing it. Of course he could never as Ruth said, 'find someone'; given the situation, it was completely out of the question even to consider it. He had long ago resigned himself to that.

'Ruth,' he said now, scraping from his plate the last remnants of chicken sauce, 'when are you going to leave Eejit Features here, and come and live with me?'

It was Monday morning. Geoffrey sidled with accomplished ease through the crowd of tourists who even on that raw February day were cluttering the entrance to the House of Commons, and went in through the smaller private door. He showed his pass to the doorman, and walked unseeing up stone steps and through endless, gaudy, mock Gothic passages to the offices of Francis Upton, MP, where he worked as research assistant.

Francis was not so much leader of the party, as the party itself. He had started it in disgust with the larger parties some years previously; had watched with pride as, at first, its elected membership had swelled to ten; and with greater pride—declaring that the mark of an idealist was his unpopularity—as, over the years, it had gradually dwindled to three. He worked long, hard, and was much hated in the House.

Geoffrey was not, as he congratulated himself, a man given to undue admiration of his fellow men, but in the case of Francis, he made an exception. For one thing, Francis was extremely rude, and Geoffrey had always appreciated rudeness. For another, Francis was a Catholic, not a convert like himself, not bog Irish or mad foreign like most of the Catholics you met, but a real English Catholic, one of a family that in the bad old days had hidden priests and sent sons to Tyburn, a descendant, in an unbroken line that twitched romantically at something buried deep in Geoffrey's English soul, of the original converts, the *non Angli sed angeli*, the golden-haired barbarians whom Pope Gregory had sent Augustine from Rome to lead to Christ. Above all, Francis was a righteous man. Geoffrey was constantly aware of his privilege in working for him.

He opened the door from the cold corridor into the cheerful little set of offices, nodded good morning to the motherly woman who was Francis's secretary, and climbed the rickety stairs to the small attic chamber he shared with the two other assistants. As usual, he was the first to arrive; as usual, he relished the opportunity to pursue his work in peace. He sat down at his small, scrupulously tidy desk under the television screen, opened the government paper on which he had been making notes on Friday afternoon, and immediately set to work.

He was hard at it when the telephone rang. He picked it up, cursing the interruption.

'Geoffrey Johnson.'

It was a woman's voice, educated, brusque, no longer young.

'Francis Upton, please.'

Geoffrey wished the girls on the switchboard would do their job and leave him free to do his.

'I'm afraid you have the wrong extension,' he said. 'This is his research assistants' office.'

'Bloody hell,' said the voice genially. 'That young ass there? Mr Simpson or Timpson?'

'Who is speaking, please?'

'Name's Bellweather. Margaret Bellweather.'

Geoffrey raised his eyebrows. Margaret Bellweather was a familiar name in political circles; as the young wife of a prominent Foreign Minister of forty years ago, she had been reputed to have known more about the inner workings of Parliament than the Prime Minister himself. Widowed now and surely in her seventies, she had retired from social life, and Geoffrey wondered, with a slight twinge of annoyance, just how his colleague Nigel—an ass, in Geoffrey's view, of the most asinine if ever there were one—had made himself known to a woman like her.

'I'm afraid,' he said, 'Mr Simmonds is in a meeting.' A lie, but it would not do to let Margaret Bellweather, of all people, know that one of Francis's assistants had not arrived in the office by 10.30 of even a traditionally quiet Monday morning.

A snort travelled down the telephone line. 'Still in bed, you mean.

So's Buggerlugs Upton, probably. Well, I'll try him later. Never know your luck, eh?'

So that was Margaret Bellweather. Geoffrey was replacing the receiver on a part, albeit minor, of British political history when Big Ben sounded the half-hour and footsteps on the stairs told him that either Nigel or the other research assistant, Sue, was finally putting in an appearance. As it turned out, they arrived together, two healthy young animals, handsome, well dressed, and at the moment laughing hard at some joke of their own.

They fell silent as they entered the room, and Geoffrey knew they had been discussing Sue's birthday party on Saturday, to which he had not been invited. This last disturbed him not at all. He had taken the job not to enhance his social life, but to do a decent job of work: and if as a result his relations with his peers were at times strained, well, that, unfortunately, appeared to be the price you paid in this office for taking your work seriously. Francis approved of him, and that was the important thing.

'Morning,' said Nigel.

'Good morning,' replied Geoffrey, icily polite. He glanced at the clock, and out of the corner of his eyes, caught them exchanging a glance of their own.

'Good weekend?' asked Sue. He knew he made them both uneasy, and was not above taking satisfaction in it.

'Sue,' he said, 'Mr Douglas from the library has been looking for you for half an hour.'

'Heavens.' She clutched her heart. 'Mr Douglas from the library! How can I stand the excitement?' She collapsed against Nigel.

Geoffrey smiled briefly. Then he returned to his notes. 'And you,' he told Nigel, abstracting himself to disguise his curiosity, 'had a telephone call. From Margaret Bellweather. She wanted to speak to either you or Francis.' And withdrawing his attention so sharply that he completely missed another, very different exchange of glances between his two colleagues, he immersed himself in his work.

Rather, he tried to: it was hard, to work with Nigel and Sue in the room. They made coffee, amid a great deal of clattering. They made telephone calls, Sue to her flatmate to remind her to pay the electricity bill, Nigel to a girl he had apparently met at Sue's party. They discussed their telephone calls. At last, at long last, silence fell, and Geoffrey, who had been keeping his eyes fixed sternly on his notes, allowed himself to look up. They were both reading the morning paper.

It was a mystery, he decided, looking at their two bent heads. Could they really not see that there was work—the party's work, ultimately the country's work—to be done?

Geoffrey was a patriotic young man, his love of his country if anything sharpened by exposure to the mixed bag of nationalities into which his conversion to Catholicism had so unexpectedly thrust him. He would, he had no doubt, called upon, die for his country; he genuinely could not understand how Nigel and Sue, colleagues and compatriots both, could not do for her even a diligent day's work.

'Oh, listen,' said Sue. 'My horoscope. "A strange man will influence your life." I wonder who?'

'Probably Francis,' said Nigel. 'They don't come much stranger.'

Geoffrey was hit by a wave of depression. It was so empty, this trivial chatter here in the building where the state of the nation was decided, there was no place in it for one such as himself. He liked to regard himself, on the whole, as being above such self-indulgent emotions as loneliness. But suddenly he found himself craving the companionship of his own kind. He decided to call Denis.

Wary as he instinctively was of his fellow man, he had long ago decided that Denis was a nice chap. Down-to-earth, unusually so for an Irishman. Decent in an old-fashioned, straightforward sort of a way. He was not a friend, exactly: Geoffrey did not need friends; and besides, living as he did in his fly-by-night world of journalism, Denis could not possibly fully understand the pressures of doing what Geoffrey was doing in the situation in which he was doing it. But he was a nice chap all the same, and the two got together for a drink really quite surprisingly often.

Reaching the phone, he caught Nigel's eye and withdrew his hand, deciding to wait until he was alone in the office. It could not, God knew, be too long.

'Oh, God,' thought Denis, with a flash of intuition. 'Don't let it be Geoffrey.'

He let the telephone ring a couple of times, deciding on his line. Tonight? *Sorry*. Office bash, someone's birthday. (That it happened to be true, assuaged the guilt not in the slightest.) God knows how long, you know how these things run on. (A sudden, horrible thought: he very possibly didn't.) Tomorrow, no. Dinner party miles away. But look, I'll see you on Friday, OK? (End on upbeat note.) Don't work too hard, OK? Please, God, don't let it be Geoffrey. He picked up the receiver.

'Denis O'Leary.'

'Denis.'

Shit.

'This is a voice crying in the wilderness.'

Double shit: Geoffrey never made jokes.

'It's crying, how about a drink tonight?'

'Tonight?' Triple shit. '*Sorry*. Office bash. Someone's birthday.'

'Oh. Well. Just a thought.'

'You know how these things run on.'

'Oh, yes. Yes, I know.'

He didn't know.

'But look.' Denis took a deep breath. Quadruple shit squared. 'I don't have to stay forever. I could buy my round and be out by seven, if you'll still be around.'

A pause.

'No. No, it was just a thought.'

'Well.' Squared, cubed and multiplied by pi. 'If you'll be around.'

'Actually, I might be working late, as it turns out.'

'OK, then.' And it would have been a good booze-up. 'The Clachan. Seven. And either of us might be a few minutes late, OK?'

'If,' remarked his editor, not unkindly, as he passed, 'you persist in knocking your head against that desk, you might just accidentally shake a few brain cells into action. And that would never do, now, would it?'

Geoffrey towered over Denis in the pub, his presence accentuating the other's thin nervousness. Denis actually had to lift his chin to look him in the eye.

'I really wouldn't worry about it,' he was now saying for the third time. 'If they don't want to work hard, that's their decision.'

'It's a question,' said Geoffrey for the fourth time, 'of a public duty, which they are shirking.'

Denis put down his Guinness, and squinted up at him in something approaching exasperation. They had been there for a full hour, had been chasing the same subject around in a circle, and as far as he could see were full set to chase the same subject around the same circle until closing orders. And it had been such a promising booze-up, too. Patiently, he prepared to go over it just the once more.

'Listen,' he began again. 'I honestly don't see that it's your responsibility. So these two people are acting ... not very professionally. Francis's problem. Their problem, in the end. But, really, not yours. Is it?'

Geoffrey sighed. He had known that Denis would not understand. 'I am sharing an office,' he said, 'with two people who accept a salary they have not earned. Don't you see? I am sharing an office with two petty crooks.'

'Petty crooks.' Geoffrey was really going too far: the atmosphere would simply have to be lightened. 'I always like the sound of petty crooks: do you think they quarrel about who's going to wear which stocking over his head?'

It was a mistake. 'I said,' said Geoffrey, frostily, 'petty crooks. And I meant petty crooks.'

And the split second of hurt disappointment that flashed across his eyes before they froze was more than Denis could bear. So they sat there, and Denis, wondering vaguely how many years you got off Purgatory for missing a good booze-up, prepared to go through it yet again.

Maureen was always slightly rude to Alison, possibly because she had admired Alison ever since she could remember. Meeting Alison, in fact, was almost her first concrete memory: the first day at school, a bright morning with late-summer sunshine lying in blocks over pristine blackboard and desks as yet unstained with ink, and herself and two dozen others, bewildered in gym slips two sizes too big, identifying themselves to mad Mother Mary Berthe: Geraldine Farrell, cheerful with a faceful of freckles; Angela Mancuso, dark and skinny; Bozhena Padowska, on the lumpish side. And suddenly from the back of the class, dropped among the North London immigrant voices like a crystal teardrop among pebbles, had come Alison's. 'My name is Alison Beck.' Everyone had turned to look at her. And mad Mother Mary Berthe had turned to Mother Mary of the Redeemer, standing unimaginably old and ugly under the statue of the Little Flower, and said, 'Ah. Ze daughteur of Docteur Beck.' And both had beamed.

Alison was the child of converts, blonde, even aged five defined of features, and possessor, it had seemed to the secretly overawed Maureen, of perpetually clean fingernails. How exactly the two had become friends was lost in the mists of childhood; but friends they had become, and friends they had, slightly to the surprise of both of them, remained. It had not been for years a friendship based on close physical proximity; when the two girls were both eleven, Alison's parents had taken her from the rough Breton peasant women of St Joseph's ('My nuns were French,' Maureen would sometimes say now, airily, and snigger to herself should anyone appear impressed), and sent her away to a more genteel order of pale-faced aristocrats; since then, college careers, Maureen's study trips to Spain, and Alison's worldwide travels for her public relations firm, had meant they were rarely in even the same country for long. Despite or because of this, the friendship had survived; and now here they were, slumped and easy with two decades of comradeship, sitting in Maureen's absurdly small kitchen, wrapping themselves, in the yellow glow of the electric light, around absurdly large amounts of spaghetti bolognese and cheap red wine.

'So.' Alison helped herself to wine without ceremony. She had grown into an attractive young woman, with fine bones and the sort of blonde colouring that was set off admirably by a suntan. 'How's the love life?'

Across the table, Maureen shrugged, the eloquent shrug that she was not even conscious the nuns had taught her.

Alison nodded sympathetically. 'Still the same old Jonathan?'

'Who told you about him?'

'You did. In a letter full of typing mistakes.'

'Did I? Oh, yes.' She shrugged again. 'Yes, still the same old Jonathan. How's your love life, anyway?'

She was sure that the answer would depress her: Alison was always lucky in love.

'Mine? Give me a chance, woman, I'm barely through Customs.'

This, in a corner of Maureen of which she was well aware and as deeply ashamed, was better news than she had hoped.

'What about that man with the silly name?'

'J.J? Nice guy. Nice guy. But . . .' She left the sentence unfinished and picked at her salad. 'If you're jolly old English, you know, you're jolly old English.'

She smiled, heart-free and at perfect ease with herself. Maureen looked at her, envying, not for the first time, her ability to extract from her surroundings the best, and only the best, that they had to offer. From Paris, she had returned with silk scarves and an expensive taste in shoes; in Hong Kong, she had become a passable Chinese cook; and now here she was back from California, all out-of-season tan and silver and turquoise jewellery, and already as happily at home as if she had been away for the weekend instead of a year. Maureen, whose last long Spanish sojourn had left her with pierced ears and an inner image of dusty roads lined with olive trees which had hurt her for weeks and could, if she let it, hurt her still, was stabbed by a sudden envy. She covered it by pouring more wine.

'*Slàinte*,' she said.

'How is your religion, anyway?' asked Alison.

'Oh, doddering on.' It was their custom to speak of Maureen's faith as of a somewhat cantankerous elderly relative; Alison had long made peace with her own.

'Going to Mass these days?'

'Nah. Well, sometimes. Actually, yes.' She had forgotten about the group Mass which, since it was on a Friday, did not fulfil the Sunday obligation. Nor somehow had she mentioned the group in any of her letters. 'Believe it or not, I've started going to a discussion group.'

Alison raised a polite eyebrow. 'A what?'

'Discussion group. Religious, you know. Just like RE at school.'

'Oh, yes. I remember how much you enjoyed RE at school.'

Maureen had forgotten what a skilful straight woman Alison could be. 'It's quite like school actually. We sit and talk about transubstantiation, and everyone thinks I'm a heathen.'

'Surely not.'

'We all sit there, and everyone else says, "I believe in God," and I say, "I don't," and they say, "But you've got to," and I say, "Why?", and they say, "Because God tells you to."'

Alison laughed. 'And you say, "But I don't believe in God . . ."'

'And they say, "But he's in the Bible," and I say, "I don't believe the Bible . . ."'

'And they give you two order marks, and make you stay behind afterwards to clean the chapel.'

Quite without warning, Maureen's mood changed. There was

nothing in the last remark that was so very different in tone from the few preceding it, but it had nevertheless caught her somehow on the raw. Very well for Alison to laugh, she whose parents had slid gracefully into the Church, and who herself, to all appearances, had slid as gracefully out of it. There was nothing graceful or easy in Maureen's faith; and little that was laughable, either. 'Actually,' she said coldly, 'it's often quite interesting.' She decided to make trouble. 'You should come.'

'Me?' Rather gratifyingly, Alison dropped her fork. 'A religious discussion group? Just like an RE lesson?'

'Yes.' Maureen stared stonily at her, not playing. 'You.'

Alison picked up her fork, wound spaghetti around it, and said nothing. Maureen watched her, angry now. How dare she sit there, so cool and polite, not losing her temper, she who had been so ready to laugh at the whole idea?

'Why not?' she asked, needling, as she often found herself doing with Alison. 'There's a meeting on Friday night, lots of interesting people. Why not come?'

'All right,' said Alison suddenly.

Maureen was stopped in her tracks. 'What?'

'I said all right.' She swallowed her spaghetti, and grinned at her. 'Friday. I'll come on Friday. All right?'

'All right,' said Maureen.

As soon as Alison had gone, Maureen poured the meagre glass of wine which remained, dropped into the only comfortable chair in the sitting-room, and, for neither the first, nor, she was well aware, the last time in her life, cursed her gargantuan mouth. Because of course it was not all right, could not be further from all right, was headed with all the accuracy of the sinking *Titanic* towards the most unmitigated of disasters.

The truth was that she had been rather looking forward, now that for the first time they were two adults living in the same city, to introducing Alison to her friends. To waving a casual hand of introduction towards her, and standing back, basking in the revelation that this was the sort of person whom lumpen, argumentative Maureen had for an oldest friend. But that was to her other friends. To Jonathan, of course. To Roger and Teresa in the Department. To Ros, with whom for eighteen ridiculous months a couple of years ago she had shared a flat hardly bigger than this. To friends who would appreciate Alison, whom Alison would like. Not—and she covered her face with a cushion and groaned aloud at the prospect —dear God, not to the whole of the Friday-night crowd. Friday night swam, suddenly and in merciless technicolour, into her mind. Bob at his most banal she saw, and Stephen and Anne exchanging their most lovesick glances across their sixteen-inch height difference, flanked by silent Geoffrey, and poor, colourless Kate; and Denis, in sharp contrast, cracking joke after joke that became steadily more feeble as the tension in the atmosphere strengthened. And in the middle of it all—she groaned again—Alison. Alison impassively watching, her mask of good manners hiding what Maureen knew to be her amusement, her disdain, her, yes, pity for Maureen, who, she would be convinced and nothing would ever shake that conviction, could find nothing else to do in this glittering city on a Friday night than sit in a draughty cellar with others who had nothing else to do than sit in a draughty cellar and talk, earnestly and without notable articulacy, about, God help us, the power of prayer.

Under her cushion, Maureen prayed, hopelessly, for the end of the world to arrive before Friday night.

At 3.30 precisely, the bell rang, and twenty small faces erupted in unsuppressed glee.

'Good afternoon, children,' said Anne.

'Good afternoon, Miss Dowse,' they chorused.

Anne raised her eyebrows, and titters were heard. 'Good afternoon, Mrs Collins,' they corrected.

'That's better,' said Anne. 'Run along home now.'

In thirty seconds flat, the classroom was empty.

She was home herself half an hour later, sitting with her feet up on the brand-new sofa they would be paying for for years, a cup of tea and a plate of forbidden chocolate biscuits to hand, enjoying what had already come to be two precious hours of privacy before Stephen returned home, bursting with conversation from his silent accountants' office.

They were not supposed to be married yet: the wedding had originally been planned for the Sunday after Easter at Anne's childhood church in the West Country. But this flat that was so perfect had come up suddenly, and they could not begin to afford a mortgage as well as two separate rents. So they had married hastily in

London in a quiet and, to the private relief of Anne's father and public disappointment of her three younger sisters, extremely simple ceremony at Our Lady of Sorrows. There had not even been time to arrange a honeymoon, unless you counted as honeymoon those first few days at the flat before Anne's school term began, days of much laughter and excited discovery of a marvel that would, everyone said, grow more marvellous still, days on which, she already found herself looking back with a wistfulness, almost a nostalgia.

It went without saying that she was happily married. Stephen was a good man, she knew it, and had loved him from the start. And it was a given that, as she loved him, he worshipped her, devotedly, unchangingly, forgiving her faults, accepting her, allowing nothing that she did or said to diminish his worship, because whatever she did was Anne, and what was Anne was, for him, unalloyedly adorable.

She was lucky. People told her she was lucky, and she knew she was. For all the many people in the world who had no love, unremarkable she had so much and from so sweet a source. Daily she thanked God for her good fortune.

And occasionally in the quiet afternoon with the reading lamp throwing a bright circle of light against the gathering dusk, half-asleep between a cup of tea and a book, she would wonder whether there were anything on earth that she could possibly do that would make him actually dislike her.

And then she would hear his key in the door, and her heart would turn over with love.

If you had asked Alison why she had agreed to accompany Maureen that Friday night, she would have been hard put to it to reply. It was partly mischief, of course, since the invitation, mischievous itself, had so clearly not been intended to be taken seriously. Partly, too, it was a childish reflex left over from the St Joseph days, of not refusing a dare. And partly, and this not the least considerable part, it was a genuine, and half-shameful curiosity.

Maureen had from the start been to Alison something of an enigma. She had been an unremarkable child, just clever enough to satisfy the nuns when she happened to be interested, just naughty enough to please her classmates when she did not. But through it all, then as today, she had remained herself somehow uninvolved, her allegiance with neither one side nor the other, but somewhere else entirely, somewhere where no one—certainly not Alison, of whose preoccupations a major one was to be as cordially accepted as possible by as many people as possible—appeared able to follow.

Take, for instance, her Catholicism. Alison had, it was true, been baptised into the same church as had Maureen; but there, it often seemed, the religious similarity stopped. Alison's religious associations were of the sunny variety, of an old golden brick school set in rolling lawns, where the hockey team—a couple of Protestants, a couple of European aristocrats, the odd Waugh—was one of the best in the county; of the parish priest occasionally dropping in at home for sherry; of gigglingly glorious school trips to Lourdes, Rome, or Fatima; of a faith taken lightly, and certainly not dwelt on unless one were very old, slightly eccentric, or a nun. She now thought of herself, when she thought in those terms at all, as a Catholic after a fashion; that is, she believed firmly, if vaguely, in a higher being, scribbled RC when necessary on official forms, tried hard to live a good life, and rather liked the idea that if she were ever rushed to hospital, bleeding to death after some horrible accident, a priest would be on hand to give her the last rites.

Of Maureen's faith she had no comprehension at all. 'You're not a Catholic,' Maureen was fond of assuring her, her tone a mixture of envy and scorn, and in Maureen's terms she apparently was not, although in Maureen's terms, Maureen herself, who missed Mass, slept with her boyfriends, and regularly proclaimed her lack of faith in any god at all, mysteriously was. Alison could not see that it much mattered either way, having a dimly approving memory of Jesus saying something to the effect that you'd know them by their fruits; but to Maureen, it clearly did, and burningly. So much so, it seemed, that she chose to spend her Friday evenings, that most precious evening of the working week, perching on an uncomfortable chair in a coldly lit cellar, earnestly discussing the very faith that she railed against. It was a mystery. But then much of Maureen was, even after this time, a mystery to her. Meanwhile, Alison sat straight and convent girl demure on her rickety chair, repressed a grin at the memory of what she and J.J. had been doing exactly two weeks (give or take the eight-hour time difference) ago, and prepared, for the first time since the Christmas before last, to hear Mass.

'There you go.' Mass and discussion were over, and the small one with the bony Celtic face, who seemed to be the unofficial barman, poured her a glass of white wine. 'Thank you right kindly pardner, and here's looking at you, kid. Maureen says you've been in the States.'

'Los Angeles.' She knew he found her attractive, and liked the knowledge. 'Do you know it?'

'Never been there. I've got cousins in San Francisco.' Of course, she remembered, Catholic families had cousins everywhere. 'What did you think of the discussion?'

'It was . . . interesting.' She began to laugh. 'Is Maureen always like that?'

'Tonight,' he said seriously, 'she was a young ewe lamb.'

They looked across to the corner where Maureen, face growing redder and gestures wilder by the moment, was expostulating to a tight-lipped Father Bob.

'Ah,' the small one wagged his head, his bearing slipping from that of an educated young Englishman to that of an elderly farmer in a Kerry pub. ''Tis the fightin' d'you see. 'Tis in the blood.' Without warning, he burst into off-key song.

'My father's anger softened, and he shared my boyish fun—
"Ah, well," says he, " 'tis in your blood, like that oul'
Fenian gun." '

'Denis!' The girl who had sung at Mass clapped her hands to her ears.

Alison turned to her. 'You have a beautiful voice,' she said.

The girl turned pink, and the lanky one who had been introduced as her husband beamed.

'Thank you,' they said, together.

Across them, Alison caught the eye of the quiet rather attractive one, and both smiled. The approval was electric in the air. Slightly to her surprise, Alison realised she was enjoying herself.

Maureen could hardly believe what she saw out of the corner of her own eye. It seemed, incredibly, to be going quite well. Alison was genuinely laughing at something Denis was saying, Geoffrey was hovering on the edge of the conversation appearing positively friendly, and even Kate, if not actually speaking, was at least looking as if it were not inconceivable that she might. And this was the disaster she had so confidently predicted. Her spirits rose: it was no disaster at all, but simply a group of perfectly nice people having a perfectly pleasant conversation—a conversation, now she thought of it, that was probably considerably more pleasant than the one she was engaged in herself.

'Come on,' she said, abruptly cutting off Bob's defence of the charismatic movement. 'Come and talk to Alison.'

She led the way over and laid a proprietary arm, sturdy in red Shetland wool, over Alison's elegantly narrow shoulders. 'This is my friend,' she announced smirkingly, hamming up her pride to conceal it.

'Strange,' mused Denis. 'She seemed quite normal.'

They all laughed harder than usual, the stranger a charming catalyst among them, making them like each other better, as they wanted her to like them. For a brief moment Maureen knew the grateful sensation of having done something, albeit something so trivial as bringing Alison this evening, that was in the group's eyes, unadulteratedly right.

'A drop more of the wine for ye, Missus Callaghan?' said Denis.

'I will that, sir,' she replied. 'No, hang on, I won't.' She was to visit her parents the next day. 'I've got to go home and wash some socks.'

'I'll go too,' said Alison. With impeccable convent manners, she extended a slim brown hand to Father Bob. 'Thank you very much, Father, it's been fascinating.'

'Bob,' corrected Bob, taking the hand. He was, Maureen realised, and instantly avoided Denis's eye, trying hard not to goggle.

'Bob,' Alison agreed with a smile.

Maureen led her out in a positive sunburst of reflected glory.

Kate woke up, pushed away the cold hot-water bottle, and felt her heart sink. It was Saturday morning, and Kate dreaded Saturday mornings. It was not that she so much enjoyed going to work: on the contrary, it was rather pleasant to lie in in the morning instead of fighting her way through the rush hour to the dark little office behind the bookshop, where she squandered a perfectly good History degree on a job that was that of a barely glamourised clerical assistant. It was even pleasant to get up, as she did, slowly and lazily, to treat herself to something nice for breakfast, and not to get dressed, if she felt like it (and if, of course, she had not gone home for the weekend), until after midday. No, to Saturdays as such, Kate had not the faintest objection. She dreaded them because of what they represented: a week, a whole, dreary, endless seven days until the next meeting of the group.

Kate loved the Friday-night group: she loved the Mass, loved the discussions, and, especially, loved all the members. She thought about them off and on throughout the week: wistfully on Saturday, nostalgically on Sunday, and through the long weekdays with an anticipation that grew to a scarcely containable crescendo of excitement as the golden hours of Friday evening approached, magically were on her, and then, devastatingly, were gone. She dreamed sometimes, her dreams lately grown fat on the memory of Anne and Stephen's party and the promise of Aylesford to come, of being friends with them, not Friday-night friends, or even friends in Christ, but proper friends, the sort who chatted on the phone, and dropped in on each other for coffee. She daydreamed, as others dream of fame or fortune, of dinner parties at Anne and Stephen's flat; of rowdy lunch-time drinks with Maureen; of tea at the House of Commons; of anywhere or anything at all with Denis, because Kate had been in love with Denis since shortly after she had met him.

She sighed, and slowly, because she was growing bored with lying in bed, began to get up. She slid her feet into her comfortable old bedroom slippers, wrapped around her the pale pink quilted dressing gown she had bought at Harrods' sale last year, and sat down at the dressing table to remove the old-fashioned curler she wore every night to keep her thick gingery hair from flopping into her eyes in the morning. She looked at her reflection with neither pleasure nor displeasure, scarcely seeing the small, tidy features that had looked the same ten years ago and would look the same ten years hence, the humorously upturned nose balanced by a mouth that, were she not careful, could appear almost disapproving, the deep blue eyes that, if their expression were not one of constant anxiety, could be striking, almost beautiful. She patted her hair into place and let her gaze wander over the roof-tops of South Kensington, wondering what she would do. There was always a bath and a Georgette Heyer, Kate's passion for whom was a burningly shameful secret. Or maybe she would simply tidy the flat. At least she would be alone, since

Caroline, her flatmate, had gone away for the weekend, taking with her, thank God, the naval lieutenant with the disturbing tendency to fondle Caroline's breasts during the *Nine O'Clock News*.

Kate's demon was uncharitable thoughts. She fought it, constantly, as best she could, knowing as she did that without charity anything else was sounding brass and tinkling cymbals. But there it was: she was not a charitable person, and, train herself as she might, simply could not prevent herself from noticing, for instance, the loudness of the naval lieutenant's laugh, or the glazed expression in Caroline's eyes when he repeated a favourite story time after time. It was a fault, a grave fault, and all she could do was to fight it. At least she could congratulate herself that she had never uttered a single uncharitable thought aloud.

She padded from the light chilly bedroom in the front of the building to the dark chilly kitchen at the side. Caroline and the naval lieutenant had left early that morning. Caroline, she noticed, had washed up their breakfast things, an act of pure generosity on Caroline's part, since, even were she not going away, she herself would not have minded if the dishes lingered until Monday. She had also left a note on the formica surface, weighted down by a salt cellar. 'Honoulable Chinese reftovers in flidgee. Can lecommend shlimp flied lice. Eatee quickee before walkee away. Rove, Calorine. PS Have a super weekend.'

Kate smiled, the more ashamed of her thoughts. Caroline was a nice girl, honestly good-hearted, and she was lucky to have such a flatmate. She only wished that Caroline did not feel so persistently sorry for her, because, quite apart from its being humiliating, there was really no need.

Was there not? she asked herself, standing alone in the kitchen, measuring two teaspoonfuls of tea into the unsociably small pot. The answer, rather surprisingly, was, no, there was not. For all the self-confidence, and all the weekends away with all the naval lieutenants in the world, Kate would not have changed places with Caroline even for an hour. Because she had Friday nights. And even the naval lieutenant did not mean to Caroline what Friday night meant to Kate.

Kate smiled a little, sighed a little, stirred the tea leaves into the boiling water, and set herself to the task of getting through the next six days.

Mrs Herlihy was not a good cook. She was, however, an enthusiastic cook, and one who demanded that those she cooked for partake of her own enthusiasm.

'How is it, Father?' she inquired this morning as always, hovering with anxious anticipation over Bob's first forkful.

'Delicious,' as always he assured her through a mouth crammed with undercooked sausage and overcooked egg. 'Quite delicious.'

Mrs Herlihy nodded in corroboration and left the room.

Across the gleaming table, snowy-haired Father O'Dowd caught his eye and beamed benignly. They had never discussed, and never would, Mrs Herlihy's cooking, and Bob had no idea whether or not the elder priest were even aware of its singular incompetence.

'A busy day for you, Father?' asked Father O'Dowd.

'No more than usual, thanks,' responded Bob.

Saturday tended to be a quiet day at the presbytery, in preparation for Sunday. This morning, he was to say Mass at the convent for Sister Ursula's golden jubilee in the Order, the afternoon and early evening would be taken up, of course, with confessions, and then, after one of Mrs Herlihy's special Saturday suppers, made palatable by a bottle of rather good wine—there were, after all, advantages in having a Soho parish—he would probably look in at the youth club for a quick game of table tennis before an early bed. A day, in essence, much as it had been last Saturday, and would be, please God, on the Saturday to come.

It was a quiet life, a good life. He was serving God in the way he was best able—that he was a good priest the lines outside his confessional this very afternoon would testify—and if that way led him not gallantly to Tyburn nor heroically to a leper colony, well, everyone could not be a martyr or a saint. You followed the path allotted to you. And his allotted path was, apparently, a life of almost embarrassing ease.

He looked at Father O'Dowd, clear of eye and ruddy of cheek, his silver hair haloed in the light that streamed through the french window behind him. A priest made a fine and a healthy old man, and rightly so, God's little thanks to those who gave their young years to Him. The way Father O'Dowd looked was the way he, Bob, would look, doubtless, when his time came.

And nothing in the world was wrong with that. Except that lately, Bob was beginning fully to realise, for the first time, that as the rest of the world aged, so would he, too, age. He had mentioned it to no one, but St Patrick's Day—the day of the group outing to Aylesford —would be his thirtieth birthday.

A priest makes a fine and healthy old man. A priest, however, is never fully a young man: what young man is addressed as Father by adults, can forgive sins, can change bread and wine into God's body and God's blood? When Bob had entered the seminary, he had signed away, as had all the boys who had entered with him, his youth. He had done it gladly: if being a priest meant being older than his years, then older he would cheerfully be. If the priesthood, while elevating him from the everyday worries which seemed to beset his fellow man at every turn, at the same time debarred him from making his own, muddled, mistaken way through life, then that gap in his experience would just have to remain a gap. Twelve years ago, the young manhood he was giving up had seemed, compared with the glory of what he was gaining, so trivial, so simple.

But that was twelve years ago, when he had been very young, and had assumed that, having been young all his life so far, he would be young forever. It was only now, as he began helplessly to hear each tick of the clock speeding his falsely middle-aged youth towards the irrevocable real middle of his life, that he began to wonder precisely what it was that he had done.

Not, of course, that he would change, that he would not do it again tomorrow, today, if asked, and thank God for the privilege. He was a devoted priest, had been so in the past, and could not conceive of not being so in the future, and stuck to his vocation with an effortlessness that, sadly, seemed granted to few of his contemporaries.

The existence of God he could not doubt; nor could he be filled with anything but love for the One who had made him and the world around him. The Catholic Church, similarly, posed no problems to him: it was, he was convinced, the one true Church, and while he, as one lowly member, could not profess fully to understand all its ways, still, he trusted implicitly that they, like the ways of the mysterious God above him, were ultimately for his own well-being and redemption. Of course, these days, and for all he knew always, it was not so much doctrinal difficulties that were causing his fellow priests to leave the Church, as the problem of celibacy. Bob had had his share of offers from women to help him break that particular vow: it would be a repulsive priest who had not, and Bob was far from that. Had he ever been tempted? Of course he had been tempted (briefly, the face of Maureen's friend Alison flickered across his mind—strange how often quite plain girls had such pretty friends); it would have been inhuman, unnatural, if he had not. But nothing he could not deal with, nothing overpowering.

Being naturally conscientious, he sometimes worried about his life's lack of strife. 'If there's no pain,' a visiting American curate who was given to jogging around Soho Square at dawn had been fond of assuring him, 'there's no gain.' Bob sometimes wondered a little uneasily just what pain he could himself lay claim to, and how without it he were ever to advance spiritually. But perhaps his major temptation in life would be to spend it relatively free of major temptations.

'How was it, Father?' Mrs Herlihy was back in the room.

'Absolutely delicious,' he told her.

She nodded, and folded her hands under her apron. 'Well, I hope you've left room for lunch. I hear Sister Martin's been baking her Lancashire hotpot.'

Another strange thing was how often very good women were very bad cooks.

Past Finsbury Park, the Piccadilly Line was almost empty on a Saturday morning. Maureen slumped glumly in her seat, staring at the uninterrupted view of her own ghostly face staring back at her from the carriage window. She was not looking forward to this weekend, had not been looking forward to it since it had been arranged a couple of weeks previously. To feel so about a visit home was not usual with her; on the contrary, she rather enjoyed her parents, and actively liked most of her brothers and sisters. Unfortunately, this weekend would not be spent solely in the company of her family; it was the weekend when she had promised, and could see no way out of her promise, to have tea with Miss Feeney.

Miss Feeney was Maureen's former Spanish teacher, a tall, sad, jovial woman with great greyish horse teeth, and a life, now that she had retired, filled with gallant loneliness, daily Mass, and the occasional visit from a grateful former pupil. The sort of visit that was, God knew, little enough effort on Maureen's part and would,

God and she both knew, irradiate the older woman's entire sad week; the sort of visit that Maureen, frankly, dreaded.

She liked Miss Feeney: it was difficult not to. Miss Feeney had, it was generally acknowledged, a heart of gold, had been a first-class teacher, could even be, when you got to know her, quietly witty. And she had taught Maureen Spanish, and for that Maureen, who loved the language with a love so deep it was almost pain, could not but be grateful.

But she awoke in Maureen a secret terror. Maureen was frightened that when she grew old she would be like Miss Feeney. A laughable prospect, on the face of it: Maureen Callaghan turning into that meek old maid, eternally arranging spiritual bouquets for priests' birthdays and blushing when Reverend Mother spoke to her? Impossible, ludicrously so, anyone would tell you that. But Maureen knew, although she could not say how she knew, that it was far from impossible, that somewhere deep down in those reaches of their souls which defied likelihood, or appearances, or human control, she and Miss Feeney were, nightmarishly, inexplicably, inescapably, two of a kind. She had known it from the first, and the knowledge had haunted her, it seemed, forever, impervious to reason or ridicule. In those very first Spanish classes, it had stood between her and the new liquid golden sounds she was learning; in the Sixth Form, when Miss Feeney had given her special tuition, it had sat with them at each lesson, a third party grotesquely grinning; it would, she knew, be with her after this visit, a chill, dampness on the skin, as if she had inherited the jacket of someone who might or might not have died of a contagious disease.

Once, after a Spanish lesson, Miss Feeney had left behind her handbag. Hating herself but unable to stop herself, Maureen had opened it and looked inside. She had found some loose change, a lipstick, a man's handkerchief, and a packet of cigarettes and a lighter. And a well-thumbed copy of *Playgirl*. Maureen had felt sick, physically sick. 'She confiscated it,' she told herself again and again. 'Found someone reading it and confiscated it.' But she knew it was not so. That night, she had lain awake, trying to pray. 'Please, God,' she had longed to implore. 'Please don't let me be like Miss Feeney. Please.' But the prayer would not come, could not: how could you pray not to be like a good woman? It was soon after that that Maureen had started to question her faith.

One thing, however, to be said for Feeneybats was that she knew exactly when to put away the teapot and get out the sherry bottle. And it was nice sherry, too, nicer than you usually found outside Spain, perfect for the raw evening that had set in so unkindly early. Maureen edged closer to the meagre electric fire and sipped appreciatively.

'Nectar,' she said.

'Life,' Miss Feeney told her, 'has a number of lessons that are painful to learn, but ultimately rewarding. And possibly one of the most painful, but certainly one of the most rewarding, is finding where to find acceptable sherry in London.' She raised her glass. 'Let's pretend we're in Spain.'

It was the sort of thing she said that made Maureen, damn it, like her so much.

'Now tell me,' Miss Feeney continued. 'How is your dear mother?'

Maureen grinned. 'My dear mother,' she replied, 'spent this morning assuring me that I was spiritually dead. I asked her, if that was so, how come I wasn't beating up little old ladies on the streets; and she asked me, *darkly*, if I was so clever, how I knew I was going to make it to the front door without being Struck by the Hand of God.'

Miss Feeney laughed. 'Like mother, like . . .'

'Daughter, yes, I know. She's all right, is my mother. . . . Except it all seems to be suddenly my fault about Bernadette, you know, my youngest sister?'

Miss Feeney nodded, eyes closed. 'I know.'

'You obviously do know.'

'An . . . individualistic girl, I hear.'

'Right little tearaway is what we call her. God knows what the nuns say. Is she really that bad?'

Miss Feeney thought. 'I hear that she's wild. And that she doesn't accept authority easily. But I gather she's no wilder than . . . it often turns out, Maureen, that those who are rebellious in their youth find themselves in later life blessed with a deep, deep spiritual capacity.'

Maureen shuddered; she could not help herself.

'I saw Alison the other day,' she said, quickly, changing the subject. 'Alison Beck, do you remember?'

'Dr Beck's daughter. Yes, a pretty child. How is she?'

'Still pretty.' Maureen, who had never been pretty in her life, grimaced ruefully. 'She's been in Los Angeles for a year, brought me back a book about Mexico. Made me want to hop on a plane tomorrow.'

'It was always my dream to see Mexico,' said Miss Feeney, more wistfully than Maureen could bear. 'I suppose that now I never shall.'

'Alison says it's fabulous.' Hastily, she racked her brain for some light-hearted anecdote. 'She says—oh, you should hear some of her stories! She went to this one town where everybody was talking about a local character who was supposed to have seen an angel. So they went into the bar, and got talking to the barman, and said, where does he live? You know, this character who's a saint and sees visions and everything? And the barman jerked his thumb at this stinking, reeling drunk in the corner, and said, "*acá*." And it was him! Alison says she was surprised an angel was all he saw.'

Miss Feeney did not laugh. 'When you are older, Maureen,' she said, 'you will learn, like Horatio, that there are more things in heaven and earth than are dreamed of in your philosophy.'

'What's the matter, Miss Feeney?' Now that they were no longer teacher and pupil, Maureen was able to tease her very slightly. 'Have you been seeing angels in Trent Park?'

Miss Feeney's daily mile-and-a-half walk in Trent Park was legendary.

Miss Feeney said nothing. Maureen looked at her, and an obscene suspicion too ugly to articulate flitted into her mind. True, the teacher was a good woman. But not that good. Please, God, not that good.

'Miss Feeney?' she queried, waiting now, praying now, for the flash of dull teeth, for the silly brave laugh, for Feeneybats to return to her jolly, lonely, familiar self.

But the older woman did not smile; she stared instead at the cheerless electric fire as if she saw more than was there. 'I did,' she replied at last, slowly, almost dreamily, 'walk in the Park last week. And I . . . did . . .' She stopped.

She stopped.

The moment stretched, reaching into inconceivable dimensions, into infinity. Maureen wanted to stop her ears; she wanted to sin, to rob, to murder, blaspheme, betray, to overturn, to destroy, to do anything to protect herself from this horrid confession of goodness.

'Yes?' she could not stop herself from demanding. 'Yes? What happened?'

The moment hung longer and shattered, as Miss Feeney smiled her grey-white smile. 'I realised,' she said, 'that if you have a lot of time on your hands, and a reasonable amount of imagination, you can believe almost anything. More sherry?'

She turned to the sideboard for the bottle, and Maureen wanted to shout and sing and dance. Batty, she thought, a sniggering adolescent now in her relief. Not that good at all, but quite, quite batty, poor old thing. Poor, batty, lonely old thing, having visions in Trent Park and pretending she doesn't have them, as if anyone cared whether she were batty or not. Poor old thing who now that her mind was going, must surely be losing her power over Maureen, too, because if there was one thing Maureen was most definitely not, it was batty. Poor old, batty old, toothy old Feeneybats, who Maureen knew now would never be able to scare her ever again.

So why was it that when Miss Feeney refilled her glass, and her big scrubbed hand brushed Maureen's, the dampness of a possibly contagious disease seemed to settle on her skin?

Stephen and Anne did not sit together for Sunday Mass, because Anne sang on the altar. In one way, it was a deprivation; but on the other hand, it did mean Stephen could study her openly throughout the Mass, as if she were an actress on a stage. He sat, not in the front row, but half-way down the church on the right of the centre aisle. This was partly because he was shy; partly because he knew she found familiar faces a distraction; and partly as a simple ploy to prolong the unspeakable happiness at communion time of walking through the church to the communion rail while Anne sang. Stephen believed firmly that heaven, when and if he got there, would prove infinitely more enjoyable than anything the world could offer. But sometimes he found it in his heart to wonder precisely how.

Mass over, and pleasantries exchanged with Father Cernis, they strolled back home through the quiet of a Sunday morning on the eastern reaches of the Central Line. Sleepy weekend sounds filtered through the net curtains of the houses they passed, piano scales, a whistling kettle, Beatles music on a scratchy gramophone. Outside the newsagent where they stopped for the Sunday papers, a group of children were playing hopscotch.

'I used to be good at that,' said Anne.

'A likely tale,' he replied. 'Chubbo.'

'I was.' She dug him in the ribs in pretended indignation.

It was eleven o'clock, they had been up for two hours, and the rest of the holy day was their own. When they got in, Anne would put the roast in the oven, and make the strong, milky coffee her French grandmother had taught her, and they would sit for an hour in companionable silence over the papers. Then Anne would disappear into the kitchen, and Stephen would walk to the off-licence for a Guinness for them to share before lunch, and a bottle of wine to go with it. In the afternoon . . . thinking about the afternoon, he took Anne's playful hand in a grasp that was not playful, and she relaxed against him.

'What a strange car,' she said, a moment later.

Parked outside their house, rakish among the roadful of sober sedans, was a gleaming heap of very old, very yellow metal. Stephen looked at it and his picture of the day ahead was shattered. It was his brother Brian's car.

'That's Brian's car,' he said.

'Oh,' she said. 'How nice.'

It was a source of unacknowledged consolation to Stephen that Anne did not like Brian.

'Wonder what he's doing here?' he said. He went and peered through the window. His brother was sitting, his head bent over the steering wheel, in the attitude of one asleep or praying. Stephen rapped. The head jerked up, and Brian's face—Stephen's own face, but so unjustly interesting where Stephen's was merely awkward, humorous where Stephen's was foolish—blinked at him for a startled moment before it regained its customary control. He leaned over and wound down the window. 'Hello,' he said.

'Why are you here?' said Stephen.

'Well, that's welcoming,' said Brian. 'Come to see my li'le bruvver, 'aven't I?'

It was a family joke so well entrenched that its members were barely aware of it, that they frequently addressed each other in bad stage cockney.

'Be'er come in, then, 'adn't you?' said Stephen.

Brian opened the door and unfolded himself from the car. He was just shorter enough and just broader enough than his brother to be tall and slim rather than gangly. Brian was an actor.

'I drove someone home last night,' he said. 'To *Woodford*.' He pronounced the name carefully, as if it were foreign. 'Is that my favourite sister-in-law? Do I get a kiss?'

Anne kissed him politely. They had met on three previous occasions, and each time Brian had been drunk. This time, Stephen was shamefully pleased to note, he was hung over. Stephen led the way up the stone steps of their block of flats, and unlocked the front door that gave straight into the neat-as-a-pin sitting-room.

'Drink?' he could not resist offering.

'God, no.' Brian winced. 'I mean, no thanks. Not yet. 'Ere, you got any coffee?'

'I was just about to make some,' said Anne. Squeezing Stephen's arm as she passed, she went into the kitchen.

Left alone, the two brothers stared at each other across the chasm of shared blood.

'Orl right?' said Brian at last.

'Yer,' said Stephen. 'You orl right?'

'Yer . . . Nice place. This.'

He may have meant it kindly, but Stephen's hackles rose: Brian, when he was not on tour, shared a rambling condemned house in Hampstead with a floating population of variously colourful people. 'We like it,' he said, more defensively than was perhaps necessary.

'So you should. Bit of a way out, though.'

'Not really. There's the Central Line.'

'Oh, yes,' he furrowed his brow as one acknowledging some long-forgotten concept. 'The tube.'

There was another silence.

'How's work?' said Stephen, it being his turn to be polite.

'Got a few weeks off, actually. Got a tour starting in the spring, *Rosencrantz and Guildenstern Are Dead*. I'm Guildenstern. But that's not till April. So I'm on 'oliday, aren't I? How's your work?'

'Oh, fine.' Stephen thought of his daily journey into the office, his daily journey back. 'Fine.'

'I suppose you've been to Mass?' said Brian. 'Like good little Carthlicks.'

'Yes,' snapped Stephen.

In the silence that followed, Anne began to sing. She always sang French songs in the kitchen, because that was where her mother and grandmother had taught her to cook.

'Il était une bergèr-e
Et ron-ron-ron, petit pat-a-pon;
Il était une bergèr-e
Qui gardait ses moutons, ron-ron,
Qui gardait ses moutons.'

'What's that?' said Brian.

'What?' said Stephen.

'That singing. That's not Anne, is it?'

'Well, of course it's bloody Anne.' Did he think they employed a maid, too?

'Really?' There was an unfamiliar tone in Brian's voice, one which Stephen identified after a moment as genuine admiration. 'What an amazing voice. I didn't know she could sing like that.'

'She sang at the wedding.'

'Oh, you know church, everything sounds the same. That's Anne, eh? Well.'

Yes, thought Stephen. That's Anne.

At that moment the singing stopped, and Anne herself appeared carrying a tray full of coffee-cups.

'Brian's just been admiring your voice,' said Stephen.

'Oh?' Anne smiled, blushed, and busied herself with coffee-cups. 'That's nice.'

'It's beautiful,' said Brian. 'Really beautiful. Do you do anything with it?'

She handed him a cup. 'What do you mean?'

'Well, use it. You know.'

'I use it all the time. I sing in church. I sing at school.' She shot at Stephen a quick sidelong glance. 'I sing in the bath . . .'

Stephen coughed hastily. 'He means professionally,' he said.

'Oh. Oh, no, I'm far too lazy.'

'You should,' said Brian.

'Why?'

'*Why?*' Brian thought. 'I don't know,' he confessed. 'But, listen, if ever you do want to, and you want some help, or advice . . . Really. I mean it.' He sipped his coffee. 'God, that's good. That's *good*. Tastes of France.'

'Well, you know Anne's half French, don't you?'

'Are you?' He looked at her, his respect increasing visibly. 'No, I didn't know.'

No, you didn't thought Stephen. You didn't know she could sing, either. Well, she is, and she can, we don't go on about it, but you can just put that in your exciting life and smoke it. He suddenly could not wait for his brother to leave.

But for once in his life, Brian showed no signs of going. He sat back in his chair and stretched out his legs comfortably. 'Well, well. I have a *belle-soeur*. Trust old Stephen to marry a good cook. I suppose you are a good cook, Anne?'

Miracle on miracle; brother Brian was angling for an invitation to lunch with Stephen. An invitation, however, which—flattering though the situation might be—would most certainly not be forthcoming.

'She's a great cook,' he said. 'You must come for a meal sometime. Hey!' He snapped his fingers as at an inspiration. 'You know who's coming to lunch today? Mick—remember my friend Mick with the funny voices? Why don't you stay?'

'You're wicked,' said Anne when, ten minutes later, the front door shut.

'I know,' he agreed, bending to kiss her. 'Listen, we don't have to have lunch at lunch-time, do we?'

'I haven't,' she replied, 'even put the meat in the oven yet.'

'That's my girl,' he said.

Geoffrey sat at his desk, making notes in his small, neat handwriting, wondering why he was finding it more difficult than usual this week to lose himself in his work. There had been nothing by this Wednesday afternoon to mark the week as being in any way different from any other: his work was his work; Francis was Francis; Nigel and Sue were Nigel and Sue—and there, inexplicably, now more than ever before was his distraction. He should, God knew, be used to them by now, their laziness, their silliness, should long have lost its power to annoy him—as, indeed, for the most part, it had. Except that all this week, each flippant remark they had made, each giggling glance they had exchanged, had grated like sandpaper on his nerves. Perhaps he was coming down with something.

He looked up from his notes and across at them, Nigel lolling at his desk like the lord of the universe, and that featherbrained Sue leaning on his shoulder and tittering at his every word, and shook his head. With so much work to be done, they spent their days in foolish frivolity: moreover, appeared happy to do so. It was extraordinary.

At that moment, Sue looked up and caught his eye. 'All right?' she asked loudly, as if speaking to a deaf old man, and giggled.

He met her blank, blue gaze. 'Working hard?' he countered.

Lost for a retort, she giggled again.

Sue was a pretty girl, blonde, and fashionably dressed far beyond the salary of an average research assistant. She looked, now that Geoffrey thought of it, not unlike that girl Maureen had brought to the group last Friday, Alison. Now, *she* had been something special. Geoffrey would not exactly say he—as Nigel would doubtless put it—fancied her: in general, he left the business of fancying girls to twerps like Nigel anyway. But it had been pleasant, for once, to meet another Catholic who was, well, his sort of person.

Self-sufficient as he was, even he felt at times the isolation of the convert's position. Brought up among the English middle class, he had in a profound sense alienated himself from that class when he embraced the Church of Rome. Not that anything had actually been said: neither his mother nor his brother David went in for saying things. But then, neither did Geoffrey, and he could read as if it were a torrent of speech the fractionally raised eyebrow, the glance averted from the austere crucifix in the sitting-room of his flat, the punctilious serving, when he visited for the weekend, of kippers for Friday supper, which, because it would never be commented upon, he would never be able to explain was no longer necessary. Nothing had been said, would ever be said, but a gate, soundless and invisible, had slid shut with himself on the other side; among his own kind, he would now always be to some extent an alien.

And yet he would never, no matter how long he lived, how scrupulously he observed his faith, be one of the cradle Catholics, they with their rich, unquestioned inheritance of traditions and superstitions, of plaster statues crowding kitchen shelves, of the knowledge drawn not from cold study, but imbibed, it seemed, along with their mothers' milk, of which saint to pray to when. They, too, were alien to him, with their strange names, their mongrel ethnic backgrounds, with even their inexplicable social hierarchy: he had once met a navvy who had as a cousin a cardinal; on the other hand the only time Francis ever referred to his own religion was when the party leader—to put it bluntly—bragged about his sister the nun. Geoffrey's lot lay among Catholics, and would for all his life. But he would never be one of them. '

A lonely position indeed; fortunately, Geoffrey was on the whole above loneliness. But he hoped that Alison would return to the group: it would be pleasant to meet her again.

A snort of laughter from the other side of the room startled him, and he looked up sharply.

'Nothing,' said Sue.

'Private joke,' said Nigel.

The power those two had to annoy him today was extraordinary.

The telephone shrilled on Nigel's desk. Indolently, he stretched a long arm to answer.

'Hi. Oh, hi, Francis. Yeah. What, now? Yeah, sure. OK.'

Replacing the receiver, he rolled his eyes at Sue. 'Big Chief wants to see us. No, not you, Geoffrey. Just Sue and me. Shall we?'

He crooked his arm, and Sue, simpering, took it.

Geoffrey was not surprised, Nigel and Sue were regularly called to Francis's office without him, and Geoffrey knew—although obviously no one ever referred to it—that the reason was to discuss the slipshod nature of their work. What Geoffrey could never understand was that both of his colleagues would return from such meetings smiling, joking, and apparently not one whit abashed that they had been caught out cheating their party, their country, and yes, damn it, he would say it, their God. It really was extraordinary.

However, now that they were out of the office, he had the chance, if he so desired, to phone Denis and fix up a drink. Did he so desire? He considered. Denis had not, that evening last week, been as immediately sympathetic to Geoffrey's position as he himself could have wished. On the other hand, towards the end of the evening, he had seemed to gain some picture—insofar as any outsider could gain it—of precisely what Geoffrey was dealing with. And Denis was after all a nice chap. And Denis was a Christian. On balance, Geoffrey thought he would just give him a ring to see what he was up to.

'I don't know why you put up with it,' said Maureen. She frowned into the gloom of the slightly depressing little pub where she and

Denis occasionally met for a lunch-time drink. 'Tell him to get stuffed.'

'Well, you can't, can you?' said Denis.

'Why not?' She shook her head, which all morning in the Malet Street library had been filled with fountains, courtyards, and shadows so sharp they could cut your heart. 'I would.'

'Don't be thick, and no you wouldn't.' Denis sighed into the black, sad depths of his Guinness. 'Poor sod's got no one to talk to.'

'Talk at, you mean. He's a pompous ass.'

'Well, I don't know that it's so much that he's pompous.' He stopped, and absently watched the disintegrating head of his drink. Growing in him lately had been a suspicion that Geoffrey, in some very profound way, saw the world differently from the way most people see it.

'Well, what is he, then?' Maureen demanded. 'Humble and humorous?'

'No, he . . .' He stopped again, and shook his head. 'OK, he's pompous. But God, some people are lonely, aren't they?'

'Not too lonely to dump on suckers.' Maureen had never liked Geoffrey. That he should use Denis, whom she did like, as unpaid community relations councillor was, simply, unacceptable. She herself had spent the previous evening with Jonathan. 'Tell you what. You can buy this round, and I promise not to talk about Geoffrey any more.'

'All heart, aren't you?'

But he smiled at her as he collected the glasses, and she stuck out her tongue at him in a rare display of affection.

She waited while he stood at the bar, drumming her fingers impatiently on the table. She had made it her business that week to keep mind and body as fully occupied as humanly possible, in an effort to shut out the thing she had glimpsed on Saturday; but even so, it drifted constantly around the edges of her mind, unstoppable, like a chill draft through a badly fitting window. It seemed a disproportionately long time now until Denis returned.

Finally, he was there. 'Talking of not talking about Geoffrey,' he said, 'I like that friend of yours.'

'Alison? She's nice, isn't she?'

'Seemed it.' His tone had turned uncharacteristically curt, and he avoided Maureen's eye.

This was a new departure: Denis had never—bizarrely, but that was bloody Irishmen for you—to Maureen's knowledge expressed an interest in a girl before. Denis and Alison. Well, why not?

'She liked you, too,' she said encouragingly. And it was true: at any rate, Maureen had said, wheeling her bicycle while she walked with Alison to the tube station the previous Friday, 'Of course, Denis is my special mate,' and Alison had replied, 'Yes, he seemed nice.' So there you were.

'Of course she did.' Denis had returned to his normal tone. 'I'm universally irresistible.'

'Well.' Knowing—although it did not always prevent her—the futility of trying to draw Denis into serious conversation when he did not want to be drawn, Maureen decided not to press the point. Not yet, anyway. 'I'm seeing her tonight, so I'll ask her to come again. To worship at your shrine.' Suddenly, she frowned. It was her third glass of wine, and she had had neither breakfast nor lunch. Slowly, uncontrollably, she could feel her mood sinking, the way it all too often did. 'It doesn't seem fair, though. Does it?'

'What?'

'Oh, you know. Everyone likes Alison. Well, so they should, because she's nice. But she didn't make herself nice, she was born nice. And no one likes Geoffrey because he was born Geoffrey.'

'Thought we weren't talking about Geoffrey.'

'Oh, well.' A black bad mood was upon her now, enveloping her, like a mist creeping from some harsh mountain-side of her ancestral landscape. Fighting Irish, as Jonathan would so infuriatingly call her. But that was Jonathan's lucky limitation, because he could never see with the merciless clarity with which she herself saw now, what a bleak, barren hole was this world, with Geoffrey laying upon Denis the burden of his unrecognised intolerable sadness, with kind Denis who could not bring himself to ask for kindness from others, with—as suddenly, as she had known that sooner or later it would, the badly fitting window flung itself open and the full icy blast rushed in—lonely, loopy, good Miss Feeney driven to find consolation for her goodness in visions of angels, and fountainhead of all this misery the cruel, arrogant Church, whose members were its members not, it seemed, by choice, nor even—witness Geoffrey—accident of birth, but by some unkinder accident, as unjustifiable as it was inexplicable.

She looked at Denis, a victim like herself who might just understand what Jonathan could not.

'Do you find it difficult?' she asked abruptly. 'Being Catholic?'

Denis smirked. 'Not as difficult as some.'

'No, I don't mean faith. I mean, you know. *Being*. Like, I am. I hate it—I can't tell you how I hate it—but I am. And Alison, she was baptised and the whole bit, but she *isn't*. And Jonathan, my friend, Jonathan, he isn't either. And they're . . . different. Not like us. Proper people, you know?'

'If ye're Oirish,' carolled Denis, 'come into the parlour; There's a wel-come there for you . . .'

'Not Irish, either. Look at Anne. Well, look at Geoffrey. It's something else. We're not like other people. We're not . . . we're just not. Did you ever hear that story about St Teresa of Avila? About how she had this awful life, and one day she was old and sick and riding a horse through Castile, and the horse threw her? And she lay on the ground and said to God . . .'

'"If this is how yeh trate yer friends, 'tis no wonder ye've so few."'

'Well, she didn't say it in a cod Irish accent.'

'No, but the nun who taught me kindergarten did.'

Maureen frowned, disliking him. 'Catholics,' she repeated stonily, 'are not like other people.'

'I,' announced Denis, twitching and beating the air, 'am a paragon of normality. I am a monument to sanity. I . . .'

'Oh, cut it out.' Maureen's irritation increased. 'Seriously, Denis. Don't you—stop it!—don't you, honestly, find a . . . a worrying proportion of practising Catholics to be . . . personally inadequate? To say the very least?'

Denis stopped twitching, and his eyes met hers.

'Seriously?'

'Seriously.'

'You want to know what I really think?'

'*Yes.*'

He thought.

'I think it's your round.'

And that, thought Maureen, trudging grimly up Gower Street under the gathering rainclouds of the afternoon, a liver sausage and tomato sandwich under her arm, was the root of the whole problem. The

49

closed mind. Disguised, often, under jokiness such as Denis's, or an appearance of informality such as Father Bob's, but closed, nevertheless, as firmly and irrevocably as the gates of heaven against those who had died in a state of mortal sin. And that was why the Church could never change: people outside it could never see—well, how could they possibly?—the terrible, the tragic things it did to its members; those inside it, would not. Which left it, unchangeable and unchanging, a nightmare institution, a staircase leading nowhere, a shuffling mad circle of guilt and loneliness and despair, with only Maureen shuffling her own circle in a different direction, crying, 'This is wrong; this should not be.' But recognition of a wrong was not its cure: she was a Catholic as intrinsically as she was Maureen, and the times she broke clean from that circle were, she knew, the times of the worst horror of all.

Rounding the corner into Torrington Place, she found herself wanting to see Jonathan. Jonathan who was so unimaginably free from all thoughts of religion, whose heart was always light and whose conscience clear, Jonathan who everyone agreed was so good for her, whose never-failing joyous mundaneness was so many miles, so many light years from the terrors of Mother Church. Oh, yes, she wanted to see Jonathan very much, and she wanted to see him now.

Instead of turning right towards the library, she turned left into University College, pushing her way unseeing through the groups of students who lounged in the courtyard, talking, in that undergraduate fashion she had found annoying even when an undergraduate herself, with utter frivolity of serious things, and with intense seriousness of trivia.

'Hi, Maureen.'

Someone had detached herself from one of the groups and was speaking to her. It was Jenny, a girl from the first-year tutorial group she took once a week. Bright, Maureen registered, but on the lazy side. In fact, now she came to think on it, she had an essay which was at least two weeks late.

'Where's your essay?' Maureen snapped.

'I'm sorry.' Jenny smiled apologetically; she had a rather sweet smile. 'I'll try to get it to you by the end of the week.'

'Look.' Jenny had smiled that smile once too often at Maureen. 'If you don't want a degree, that's your business. But in that case you might consider giving up your university place to someone who could make better use of it.'

She did not see the expression on the younger girl's face, nor did she ever realise that after that, Jenny only addressed her when Maureen had spoken first. She crossed the courtyard to the Chemistry Department, and walked down the echoing corridor to Jonathan's office. His door was ajar, and for a moment she paused, watching him deep in his notes. Dear Jonathan, she thought. Dear, sensible, funny Jonathan, to whom it mattered not one whit whether she was Catholic or not Catholic, or in or out of a state of grace, who loved her anyway. She pushed the door open and went in.

'Hello.'

'Passion flower.' He got up and folded her in his arms, and she buried her face in his sweater, awkwardly, waiting for him to drive her demons away.

Feeling her awkwardness, he held her away, and looked at her.

'Uh, oh,' he said. 'Fighting Irish.'

It was, of course, the worst thing he could possibly have said. In a split second, her feelings somersaulted, turned themselves inside out, and she froze.

'Don't call me that.'

He kissed her forehead. 'Sorry, my sweetness and my light.'

She aimed a not-entirely-joking karate chop at his stomach. 'And don't jolly me along.'

'Oh dear, oh dear.' Still holding her, he peered into her eyes. She glared back, furious, with him, with herself. It was not supposed to be like this. His good humour was supposed to alleviate her bad, not aggravate it, and she lacked the words to ask for the childlike comfort she craved.

'What are you looking at?' she snarled.

'You, my poppet. There, there, little girl.' He kissed her again, and led her to a chair. 'You have a nice sit down, and . . .'

'Don't be funny.'

'. . . eat your sandwich, what's this, liver sausage? Yum, *yum* . . .'

'I said, don't . . .'

'OK, I won't. Eat your sandwich, and,' he picked up his notes and headed for the door, 'I shall see you later. Angel.'

He was leaving. She stared at him incredulously.

'Where the hell are you going?' she said.

'To cower in the library, my sweet. I'll see you later.'

He was actually leaving. She could hardly believe his perfidy. She did not want him to go; she needed him not to go. She needed him to stay, to be calm, to be carefree, until she herself changed, calmed, became like him. He was her only hope for sanity she realised frantically; she needed him to stay.

'You shit,' she said. 'Who needs you?'

He blew her a kiss from the door, and was gone.

Left utterly alone, Maureen bit into her sandwich, wondered how he stood her, and wished she were Alison. It started to rain.

Already, it seemed to Alison almost as if she had never been away. She had enjoyed America, certainly, had learned a lot there beyond a doubt; but a year spent 6,000 miles away had impinged upon her enjoyment of her London life not a jot more than if it had been a 52-week long film, which she had been delighted to sit through, but upon which the final credits had now rolled, returning her to her everyday world with no more complicated emotions than a happy memory of a pleasurable time.

And now here she was, back in her fashionably pastel, plant-overrun office, with the rain tipping down over Beauchamp Place outside, and her colleague Sally sprawled at the desk opposite exactly as she had been a year ago, and nothing but her rather pleasingly unseasonable tan, and several pairs of the sort of designer jeans you could get only in America, to show that she had ever been further afield than the wine bar at the corner of the road. Even the typewriter had not changed: it still stuck on the letter 'p'. Which, since Alison was currently engaged in the task, not at any time inspiring, of writing a press release for a plastics firm, was even more frustrating than usual.

'How,' she inquired of Sally at last in exasperation, 'do you jazz up a story on Pilkington's Paramount Plastics?'

Sally shrugged, and tossed a paper plane onto Alison's desk. 'Don't ask me, ducks.' Sally affected the speech of an elderly theatrical, which Alison found alternately amusing and irritating. 'I only works here.'

'Do you?' Alison tossed the plane back. 'When's that?' Sally's laziness was legendary.

'Oh, she was a witty one, was Miss Beck. Laugh!' Sally yawned.

'Actually, talking of working, you'd better at least look as if you're doing some. I happen to know that Barry's been out to lunch with none other than Mr Pilkington himself. And you know what that means.'

'Oh, no.' Alison pulled a face.

'Oh, yes. Guess who will be bringing guess who back to the office to meet, well, guess who.'

'Guess whom.' As a retort, it was well on the lame side, and, worse, it provided immediate ammunition.

'Oh, Miss Beck was an educated lady. Never heard a word fall from her lips that wasn't used proper, not like some of them you see these days. Never . . . oh, hello, Barry.'

Their immediate superior was looming at the door, spangles of rain glittering in his expensively cut hair, the *bonhomie* of one who had lunched well shining across his plump face.

'Alison.' Ignoring Sally, he beamed across the office. 'My dear and only Alison, returned to me from the California sun, my Alison who is about to send the sales to Pilkington's Plastics soaring above the very firmament.'

'Hi, Barry,' she said.

'Alison, I want you to meet our newest client, Adam Pilkington. Adam, Alison Beck.'

He didn't look like a Pilkington. Pilkingtons were short and fat. They had fluffy grey hair around a bald spot, and wore greying, fraying, easy-care shirts. Sometimes they had egg stains on their ties. He did not look like a Pilkington at all. Alison hastily adjusted her expression from the sort of smile you gave most Pilkingtons to the sort of smile you gave this Pilkington, and held out her hand.

'Mr Pilkington,' she said.

'Adam,' he corrected with a smile of his own.

It was not the smile of a Pilkington.

'Funny,' she blurted, 'you don't look plastic.'

'And you,' he countered, not dropping her hand, 'don't look like any of my public relations.'

'Well, well.' Barry rubbed his own hands, and beamed again. 'I'll just leave you to get acquainted, shall I?' Turning with ponderous subtlety to hide from Adam Pilkington the enormous wink he bestowed on Sally, he negotiated his way out of the room.

There was a silence.

'Soaring,' he eventually inquired, one eyebrow raised above a dark, deep-set eye, 'above the very firmament?'

She smiled slightly, conspiratorial, but stopping short of disloyalty, and stretched her arms to the side, giving a brief impression of an aeroplane in flight. Barely noticeably, his eyes shifted from her face to her breasts and back again.

'I suppose we should fix a meeting,' he said. 'To, er, discuss the account.'

She smiled again, feeling an unmistakable tingle of anticipation. 'I suppose we should.'

Again his eyes moved from face to breasts to legs, and back to face. 'How about dinner? Tonight?'

'Tonight?' This, she realised, and the tingle grew with the realisation, was one swift operator. 'Sorry, I can't.' Alison had never stood up a girlfriend for a man, no matter how promising: she had never needed to.

'Can't?' He frowned.

There was no point, however, in giving the wrong impression. 'I'm seeing a school-friend: I've promised to introduce her to the wonderful world of tacos. Mexican food, you know? Look.' She turned and bent to rummage in the Harrods bag that lay on the floor, allowing herself as she did so a secret grin: there were, after all, not many women who could afford voluntarily to exhibit their tight jeaned back view to a strange, attractive man. She stood up, exhibiting a small jar of sauce. 'Salsa. Marvellous stuff. Blows your mouth off.'

'Marvellous. How about a drink before the tacos?'

Good: he was persistent, too. So many attractive men weren't. 'A happy hour?' She pretended to consider it. 'Why not?'

'Why indeed? There's a perfectly decent wine bar on the corner. Shall we say six?'

'Fine.'

'Six it is, Ms Beck from California.' The eyebrow lifted again. 'Oh, and don't forget to bring the, er, salsa.'

'Now that,' said Sally as the door closed, 'is what I call not fair. If you had the slightest idea of the lengths I went to just three weeks ago to unload this very account onto your desk . . .'

'You did *what?*'

'And then what happens? Mr Pilkington happens.'

'Serves you bloody well right, then.'

'As in hello, Mr Pilkington, my name is Sally, and I'm the one you stared glassily through and beyond while you bent yourself over backwards trying to fix up a date with Miss Repartee here. "Funny, you don't look plastic," forsooth!'

'He probably,' said Alison, comfortingly, 'just felt sorry for me.'

'That,' said Denis flatly, 'is a lie. It's a good story, mind, and I like it. But it's a lie.'

'I swear to you.' Philip shifted his glass to his left hand, and laid his right hand on his heart. 'I most solemnly swear that that is what he said. "You can cover the story if you like, but I'm not sending you, so don't try to put your cab fare on expenses." And you do realise, don't you, that we're talking about something that's happening, oh, all of half a mile away?'

Denis laughed. He had a loud, barking laugh, and even across the din, heads turned. It was the end of the working day, and he and Philip were engaged in the traditional journalistic pursuit of standing in the pub and complaining about the editor. It was a journalists' pub, and on his way to the bar to buy his round, Denis had overheard snippets of a full half-dozen more or less similar conversations from the staff of a full half-dozen more or less different publications. Which went to prove, if nothing else, that both he and Philip were at least normal.

Rather, Philip was. He himself, of course, would never be quite like others, but that was the hand he had been dealt, and there was no benefit in repining what could not be repaired. It had not, however, made it any the easier that lunch-time when bloody Maureen had started her harangue about Catholics and other people. She had been, as usual, talking through her oversized hat: granted that he himself was not, and never would be, whole, there were plenty of other Catholics leading perfectly full and rounded lives, all over London, and probably in this very pub, too. Rapidly, his eyes darted around the room. There was Mike behind the bar, of course; a woman in the far corner whom he saw frequently at Ely Place; a man on his left with a flat face and curly black hair drinking Guinness; and actually walking through the door was a columnist who was a known agitator for a return to the Tridentine Mass. All of them carrying on perfectly normal conversations, laughing perfectly normal laughs, behaving, in general, for all the world as if they were exactly like everyone else. Whatever everyone else was like.

'Did you hear about the prostitute who married the editor?' he asked.

'No, tell me about the prostitute who married the editor.'

'Very sad. He dragged her down to his level.'

'Are you two talking shop again?' Ruth's voice was on them, startling them.

'Ruth!' Denis clenched his teeth in an angry grimace. 'I told you never to meet me here . . . he'll start to suspect.'

'Hello, Denis, Phil.' She kissed Denis, and poked Philip in the ribs. 'This is Charlotte.' There was another girl with her, dark, rather small, and rather pretty. 'We used to share a flat. You were talking about your editor, weren't you? You have got to learn to talk about something else.'

'That's all very well,' said Denis, 'but you don't have to live with him.'

'Oh, don't I? Anyway, when are you going to come over to fix our shelves? Because we'll be living out of a suitcase forever if Ten Thumbs here has his way.' She leaned affectionately against Philip.

'I keep telling you,' said Denis. 'You moved in with the wrong bloke. Look, pack your bags tonight, and . . .' He turned to Charlotte. 'What's she like to live with?'

'Terrible,' said Charlotte instantly. 'Don't do it.'

'Really?'

'Really.'

'Bossy?'

'Bossy. Terribly tidy. Chatty in the mornings. I don't know how Philip stands it.'

'Ah, he's a man of iron, is Philip.'

Together, they looked admiringly at Philip, and out of the corner of his eye, Denis caught a rather different glance from Ruth.

'Listen,' she said, casually, 'we were thinking of going out for a meal later, the three of us. Why don't you come too? If you're not doing anything else, that is.'

And that, of course, was the end of that.

'Oh, damn,' he said. 'That would have been good. But I'm booked. Dinner. With friends.'

Her eyes narrowed. 'Who did you have lunch with?'

'Ruth!' said Philip.

'Men!' said Ruth. She turned to Charlotte. 'I phoned Phil at lunch-time, and he said Denis had already gone to meet someone for lunch, and I asked him who, and he didn't know! And look at them—he still doesn't know!'

'Aargh!' Denis clutched his chest. 'I'm having a heart attack!'

'Who *were* you with?' said Ruth.

Denis was genuinely fond of Ruth; but even so, there were times when . . . .

'My mother,' he said. 'Now there's a juicy titbit for you. Anyway, I've got to go.' He kissed Ruth, and nodded at Charlotte. 'Maybe I'll see you again some time.'

He left the pub, and wandered into the damp night, wondering, with some annoyance what he was going to do now. He had intended to stay in the pub all evening: Philip and Ruth were usually good for an hour at least, and he had already spotted an acquaintance from another paper in the middle of a different group which looked set fair to stay until closing time. After which, a brisk walk to Charing Cross would clear his head, and the last train to Clapham would have him home and in bed, and the evening disposed of, with no more trouble than the mildest of hangovers the next morning. But that was before Ruth's little suggestion, after which he had had really no choice but to leave.

Charlotte had seemed a perfectly nice girl. But what Ruth seemed so exasperatingly incapable of understanding was that the sort of potentially romantic encounters which were fine for other people, were not, and never would be, for him. It was commonly agreed among the wide circle of Denis's acquaintance that he would give you the coat off his back, as, indeed, he would. He was, in fact, an almost compulsive giver, lavishing not only such material goods as he had, but his time, his attention, his affection, on anyone whom he saw to be in need of it, from Geoffrey, to the party of handicapped children he helped take to Lourdes every Easter, to old Mrs Jennings down the road, who was too ill to get to the shops on a Saturday morning. There was, it was said in tones ranging from admiration to suspicion to incredulity, nothing he would not do, at any time, for anyone: except, Denis himself knew, for one thing. He would not, must not, under any circumstances, allow himself to grow too close to anyone. Loving his neighbour when the neighbour was not immediately lovable was easy for him, the less lovable, on the whole, the easier. But anything more complicated, anything which might at some stage involve a taking as well as a giving, became immediately fraught with difficulties, even with dangers. Friendship, therefore, was suspect; and the final taboo was falling in love.

It had been so for him ever since he could remember; with things as they were, it could hardly be otherwise. Popularity had never been a problem, if you counted the number of those who liked and sought his company; but from his school-days on, he had kept himself deliberately slightly apart, a man without ties to any one friend or group of friends, who wished well to the world but must not let himself draw too close to it. There were enough people, and more, around London who knew him as a good chap. There were few, men or women, who knew him better, and that was how he planned to keep it—for men and, particularly, for women. Love might be —apparently was—what others expected, hoped for, took for granted they would one day achieve. For him, it was, and must remain, a forbidden fruit.

Of course, being an imperfect human being, he slipped occasionally. For instance, he would have to watch his reaction to Maureen's friend Alison, if he ever saw her again. Already he had caught himself at odd moments, thinking about her, wondering . . . And this very lunch-time, he had let himself slide so far as to bring her name, unprompted, into the conversation, although, thank God, Maureen would have no way of knowing it was not just that, casual conversation, and good God, there was no particular reason why he should *not* mention her, was there?

He shook his head into the damp wind. Of course there was a reason, there was every reason. She was as forbidden to him, as firmly, unalterably closed to him, as if she were the lady of the manor and he the leper at the gate. It was the way it must be. The only way it viably could be.

He had arrived at Charing Cross, but there seemed little reason to go home just yet. Mildly cursing Ruth, he crossed the Strand, and threaded his way through the back streets towards Leicester Square, where there would probably be a film starting soon. Something action-packed, he thought.

On the whole, he decided, it would probably be better if he did not see Alison again.

* * *

58

It was indeed a decent wine bar, and it was more than decent wine that he had ordered for them. In the twenty or so minutes that they had been discussing the account, Alison had learned a considerable amount about Adam Pilkington. She had learned that he was left-handed; that he loved France; that he had wanted to be a painter until family pressure had forced him to take over the firm; that he had a mole over his left cheekbone which gave him a faintly decadent, eighteenth-century appearance; and that he was married.

This last should not have surprised her. He must, after all, have been around his early thirties, so that, given that he was not homosexual, it would have been surprising had he been single. There was really no excuse for the disappointment that struck so dull to her heart when he had so casually mentioned his wife. But there it was. He was married.

'So,' he said now, pouring with careful equality the last two glasses of wine, 'did you learn a lot in the States?'

'Oh, yes.' She smiled at him; married or not, he still appeared to be rather charmingly fascinated by herself. 'It's a different country, you know, like the old cliché, separated by the same language.'

'Mm-hmm.' He raised his glass, and looked into her eyes with a meaning that, married or not, was unmistakable. 'And did you leave your heart in San Francisco?'

'I was tempted.' She smiled again, blandly, teasingly misunderstanding him. 'It's a lovely part of the world.'

'I know. My wife's from round there.'

His wife again. But at least he was open about her—and two could play at the corny songs game. 'You wish they all could be California girls, right?'

'God, no!' Rather gratifyingly, he sputtered into his drink. 'Sorry. No, she's . . . she's not like that. She's one of those ultra-European Americans, you know? . . . There's just one thing that we do have, and that's a very California-style marriage.'

Oh, yes? For the first time, Alison's danger antennae twitched. 'The mind boggles,' was, however, all she said.

'As well it might, my English rose. Fortunately, or unfortunately, to misquote another old cliché, my wife understands me rather well. . . . so how about that dinner?'

'Dinner?'

'What, for instance, are you doing tomorrow night?'

Now, this was not on. For him to flirt with her was one thing; but to assume that she, Alison Beck, would rearrange her entire social life at the bidding of a married man . . . As a matter of fact, she had had nothing planned for the following night. But this was a man who, it was becoming apparent, was altogether too sure of himself, and it would, she decided, be pleasing to see him disconcerted. She had an unexpected inspiration.

'Tomorrow night,' she told him, lying with impeccable non-chalance, 'I'm going to a religious discussion group.'

The effect was all she could have wished: he said absolutely nothing.

'At Our Lady of Sorrows,' she added with relish, remembering the baroque, messily emotional name of Father Bob's church.

He took it, she had to hand it to him, rather well. 'Funny. You don't look Catholic.'

'Baptised, confirmed, and the nuns' first choice for crowning the May Queen.'

Damn: the mention of the nuns had been a mistake. Most men thought they knew about girls from convents. Slightly, almost furtively, his eyes lit up.

'You're a good convent girl, then?'

A common enough question, and one to which she had over the years developed a store of answers ranging from the mildly humorous to the downright ribald. This time, she played it straight, hoping to regain the lost advantage. 'It's a jolly good education, actually. And my nuns were *nice*. Gutsy, independent, *classy* ladies, you know?'

Which, of course, did not regain the advantage at all, but blew it sky-high as he looked at her and she felt herself blushing.

'I know,' he said. 'Dinner? Next week, whenever you're free? To discuss the account? Please?'

'To discuss the account.'

'To discuss the account.'

Well, why on earth should she refuse?

Sitting in the taxi which he had insisted on paying for, Alison wondered what in the world could have put into her head that rather strange evening she had spent with Maureen the previous week. Strange had been the word she had mentally used for it at the time, and now, a perfectly unremarkable six days later, strange was the word she would use still. Not unpleasant, not dull; just, well, strange.

Much of its strangeness, oddly, had consisted of the sheer ordinariness of the people she had met. It was true that they had talked about religion a lot, and in a way that Alison had not talked to anyone but intimates since St Joseph's; true that they had, indeed, inconceivably, gathered there, on a Friday night of all nights, for the express purpose of doing so. Which was certainly something that, in normal circumstances, it would never have crossed Alison's mind to do. But apart from that, they had seemed for all the world the sort of people you might meet at any party, or work with in any office. But then again, that was probably how Maureen seemed to those who did not know her. Most people, she found, behaved in pretty much the same way, until you got to know them. Who knew, for instance, what, beneath the smooth surface, Adam Pilkington was like? Alison shivered, slightly, pleasurably. She had a feeling that, in one capacity or another, she was going to find out.

As the taxi drew down the narrow Kensington street where she was living, it passed Maureen, sailing through puddles on her battered bicycle, a large bottle in the basket in front of her, the bright red cape she wore to defy the winter dark billowing behind. The two reached Alison's front door together.

'Hello,' said Alison.

'Oh,' said Maureen with elaborate sarcasm, 'but you shouldn't have rushed. You almost got here before me.'

It was a typically Maureen comment, but there was an edge to her voice which Alison knew only too well. 'Have you ever had an American-style dry martini?' she asked. 'With lots of gin, and just a couple of drops of vermouth?'

Maureen's face brightened. 'I have not,' she admitted.

'Well, then.' Alison sighed with mock impatience. 'What are we waiting for?'

She led the way upstairs to the flat she was renting from another member of the firm. Maureen looked around. It was an extremely nice flat. 'Not bad,' she remarked appreciatively.

'Yes, I fell on my feet, didn't I? I really should buy somewhere, though. D'you want the grand tour?' She led the way, talking. 'This is the living-room, nice, isn't it? Light during the day, too. . . . The bedroom, and don't ask me what use he put the Great Bed of Ware to, because you can go blind thinking about it. . . . The loo, in case you're interested. . . . And, most important of all, the kitchen, with, more important than anything, the booze. Look. Do sit down. Decent gin, the imported stuff. Chilled shaker, chilled glasses. Just a whisper of vermouth—so—shake it up, add an olive, and there you go. As J.J. used to say, enjoy.'

Maureen drank. '*Not* bad,' she repeated.

'Yes, I thought you'd like it. Sorry I'm late, I was with a client. But this won't take long, and you can entertain me while I chop the onions.'

Sipping her drink, Maureen felt, almost physically, her spirits begin to thaw. There were after all, it occurred to her, few sensations more comforting than that of sitting in a bright kitchen on a cold, wet evening, having alcohol poured down your throat and watching someone else cook for you.

'I was rotten to Jonathan today,' she announced. 'Really rotten. I went stamping into his office with steam coming out of my ears, and he said, "Why are you in such a bad mood?" and I said, "Jesus Christ, I am *not* in a bloody bad mood, damn you!" Which was sort of the end of the conversation, really.'

Alison laughed. 'Poor guy. Does he, uh, mind?'

'When I'm like that? No, he's very nice about it. He's very nice about everything.' Absently, she reached over the table for a piece of raw onion. 'That's the trouble.'

'Yes, I can see that it would be. Niceness.'

'Well . . .' Maureen stopped, munching and thinking. 'It sort of implies, if he's nice *all* the time, that he doesn't, you know, care. Oh, not about "Us", I mean that's not an issue, but about . . . oh . . . himself . . . and things . . .' she trailed off.

'Maureen, if you got together with someone who *cared* the way you do . . .'

'I know, that's what everyone says.' She took another piece of onion. 'Do you remember Sean? An Irishman I was seeing last year? I mean, fireworks.' She whistled softly, shaking her hand in the air like a Spaniard. 'Even I noticed. But there must be a medium, mustn't there? Something in between that's . . . right . . .'

'Will you leave that bloody onion alone! Why were you in a bad mood anyway?'

'This afternoon? Dunno. I suppose there must have been a

reason.' She put her feet up on a chair, casting her mind back over the day, over the memory of Miss Feeney, and her fury with Denis. Suddenly, she remembered something else about Denis. 'Anyway. You made a big hit last Friday night.'

'Did I?'

'Did I?' she mimicked, opening her eyes very wide, and pushing her teeth out in exaggerated simplicity. 'You know damn well you did. Can I help, by the way?'

'All under control, thanks. It's easy-peasy, actually. The only problem is finding the ingredients.' Her voice rose to a Home Counties screech, in imitation of an aunt who had hilarified the childhood of both. 'Thank *Gawd* for Harrods.'

She had, Maureen noticed, bought the minced meat at Harrods, too. She realised for the first time that Alison was richer than she: not merely that she came from a richer background—that had been written into their relationship since before either had known fifty pounds from fifty pence—but that Alison herself had over the past year or so grown from the fashionably penniless student, and the genuinely struggling working girl of Maureen's recollection, into the sort of young woman who talked of buying a flat, and could afford occasionally to shop for minced meat at Harrods. Maureen should not have been surprised at this, since it was hardly a state secret that public relations people tended to be paid more money than academics; but she was surprised nevertheless. Envious? Not exactly. But she was made suddenly and vividly aware, sitting at the scrubbed pine table, watching Alison mix the second batch of martinis, that material goods were a facet of their relationship in which her friend would always have the upper hand, and that that was something she herself would just have to get used to.

'I went to see Miss Feeney last week,' she said.

'Feeneybats? From St Joseph's? That was nice of you.'

'Oh, well. She did teach me Spanish, you know. You were spoken of. 'A pretty child.' Pity about the brain, I said. . . . It's rather sad, really, she's quite lonely, you know.'

'Poor old thing.' Alison emptied a tin of refried beans into a saucepan.

'Yes.' Maureen paused. She had not intended ever to confide to another human soul the terrible thing that had so nearly been told her; but then, the gin was warming her stomach, and it was so

63

miserable a night outside. She decided to put a toe in the water. 'I think it might be getting to her a bit.'

'What might?'

'Well, loneliness. Not using the brain, you know. I think she might be going a bit . . .' She made another Spanish gesture.

'Batty?' Alison laughed at some memory of her own. 'But she always was, wasn't she?'

'Well, yes, but. . .'

'Wasn't that why we called her Feeneybats?'

'Was it?' Maureen's voice flattened, went dead. She would never tell Alison now. 'So it was.'

'Why do you think so, anyway?'

'I don't know. Just a feeling.' She changed the subject: Alison did not deserve to hear more about this. 'Remember Denis? From last Friday?'

'Denis?' Alison, watching the heating oil, did not notice the change in tone. 'Of course. Why?'

'I saw him for lunch. He'd kill me if he knew I told you, but he wasn't half keen to know if you were coming to the meeting tomorrow.'

'Was he?' She turned from the oil, pleased. He was no Adam Pilkington, but it was gratifying all the same.

'He was.' Maureen's eyes, orange-brown Irish eyes which could in an instant soften to treacle or harden to wood, were fixed on her. 'Well. Are you coming?'

Something was wrong, Alison realised with irritation. Maureen had always been like this; you could be carrying on a perfectly ordinary pleasant conversation with her, and suddenly, with no warning in the world, for no reason in the world, she would start to disapprove of you, even to dislike you. It was infuriating. And the most infuriating part was how very much Alison minded about it.

'I don't know,' she replied. 'I hadn't thought.'

'OK. Just an idea.' Maureen returned to her martini.

It was clearly very far from OK. Alison turned back to drop the taco shells into the now bubbling oil, wondering as she so maddeningly could never stop herself from wondering, just what she could have done this time to offend. Obviously, not to have decided to go to the group was the wrong answer, but Alison knew from experience that was not the issue here. No, she had clearly, at some time during the last few minutes, failed some test which she had not known was being set, which God damn it, had no right whatsoever to *be* set. However, agreeing to go would, it seemed, somehow redeem her in Maureen's eyes—and she did, God damn and blast it to hell, want so very much to be redeemed.

She turned from the oven. 'I suppose I could,' she said. 'I mean, if you don't mind being seen out with me, of course.'

Maureen shrugged. 'Whatever,' she mumbled through a mouthful of olive. And tried not to look too pleased, which fooled neither of them in the slightest.

The days were drawing out, Anne noticed as, virtuously Friday-afternoon weary, she climbed the steps to the flat. It was four o'clock, and there was still no hint yet of dusk in the sky; and on the way home, she had seen the first crocus pushing its golden head through the sodden earth of someone's front garden. Spring was on its way.

She went straight to the kitchen, put the kettle on for her pot of tea, and hummed to herself while she waited for the water to boil, and debated luxuriously whether to have a bath now, quickly, while the tea was standing, or to wait until just before she left to meet Stephen at the group. On the whole, she thought she would wait. A bath now might just wake her up, and this late-afternoon languor was simply too delicious not to take advantage of. She made the tea, set out the plate of ginger biscuits—Stephen's favourites; she was officially on a diet—and took the trayful into the living-room. She turned on the gas fire and dropped gratefully onto the sofa, bought long for Stephen's legs, ridiculously too long for her own.

She was, she realised, very, very tired. Light as it was, she turned on the reading lamp, because if she were to drop off nothing would be more depressing than to wake to a dark room, and opened the magazine which was her Friday afternoon treat. Photographs of greyhound-slender women, opposite recipes for chocolate cake which she really could not allow herself to read. A quiz, How Well Do You Know Your Partner, which she put aside to do later with Stephen: brotherless herself, she had been amazed to learn, among so many other new things, that men, too, like to do foolish quizzes. A story about a girl who worked in an office, a sad, lonely girl, as she had been before Stephen, sure that no one would ever love her, although of course, by the end of the story, someone would. Blissfully, she felt her mind already start to wander. In a moment, she would lower and then drop the magazine, would take her glasses off, would slide down the sofa until, the red rays of the gas fire licked not only her legs, but her face and neck and hair, and slowly, very slowly, would drift towards the drowsy suburbs of sleep.

And then the doorbell rang.

It was an unpleasant bell, loud, strident, and very new. It was also a bell that demanded to be answered. Anne dragged leaden limbs from the sofa, stepped into her shoes, ran an automatic hand through her hair, and opened the door. It was Brian.

'Oh,' she said in surprise. 'Hallo.'

'Bonsoir, belle-soeur.' His French accent was, predictably, better than Stephen's. 'I've been to Woodford. Again.'

'Well, come in.'

He came in, loping with the easy grace which had so thoroughly passed his brother by, and peered around the room.

'No Stephen then?'

'He's at work.' Where else did he think he was?

'Oh, yes. Work.' He looked at his watch, and looking up, caught sight of the teapot. 'Oh, I say. Afternoon tea.'

Anne sighed, surreptitiously. 'I'll get you a cup.'

When she returned from the kitchen, he was well ensconced in the armchair by the fire.

'Well, this is rather cosy, isn't it?' he said. 'It must be nice to be a teacher. Come home to afternoon tea.'

She handed him his cup. 'You don't exactly go down t'pit every day yourself.'

'Oh, but afternoon tea. You can't really have it properly unless you've been up and doing all morning, and I usually haven't.' He shook his head over the teacup. 'I'm a lazy sod, you know. You married the right brother.'

He was joking of course, but she sensed that in a curious way, he meant it, too. For the first time in their acquaintance, he was neither drunk nor hung over, and for the first time, she felt a stirring of warmth towards him.

'But you must work hard in your job,' she said.

'Oh.' He shrugged. 'That.'

She looked at him, wondering, for the first time, what he

thought about, how he felt. 'Why did you want to be an actor, anyway?'

'Truth?' he asked.

'Mm.'

'Because I'm a terrible show-off.'

She laughed.

'Really. Stephen was always *deeply* ashamed of me when we were kids.'

'Was he?' He had stumbled onto one of her favourite topics of conversation. 'Was he really?'

'Oh, *yes*. We used to go around the neighbourhood cutting hedges for fifty pence, and at one house, this little old lady liked us so much that she gave us seventy-five pence, and I refused, because it wasn't in the bargain.'

'You little creep.'

'Absolutely. And after that, he just wouldn't be seen out with me. We used to take different buses to school.'

'I don't blame him a bit.' His tone held genuine affection and she was surprised how much she was liking him. And then, of course, he had known Stephen as a child. 'What was he like, anyway?'

'Old Stephen? Funny little kid. Terribly respectable, never, ever got into trouble—I used to live in it—but very much his own man, you know? He always wore his school cap just—*so*. . . . And now here he is, my little brother, all grown up and married and working in the City, while the ne'er do weel eldest spends his days racketing around the suburbs trying to knock some sense into a crazy redhead.'

'Is she crazy?'

'Nuttier than a fruitcake. Anyway. Let's talk about you: what do *you* think of me?'

She laughed again. 'You really are a show-off, aren't you?'

'Oh, you ain't seen nuthin' yet. It's the stage, you know, it's terribly bad for you. I mean, not many people actually get clapped for going to work. . . .' His tone changed. 'But you must have had some experience of all that, with your voice, I mean.'

'No.'

'But you must have done something with it, surely. Didn't anyone ever suggest you, I don't know, had it trained? Or something?'

'Well, teachers at school were always saying things like that. But I never did.'

'Why not?'

Anne was silent. It had indeed been suggested to her throughout her life that she, as Brian put it, 'do something' with her remarkable voice, but always she had refused. The reasons why were complex. It would be easy to say that she was shy, easy to say that she was lazy, and to an extent, both were true. But her reluctance went deeper than that, deep into regions that she could neither explain nor attempt to justify. Born in her, it seemed, along with her voice, was a profound conviction that that voice was a gift of God, and that as such it was sacred, to be shared, not with strangers for her own personal glory, but simply, modestly, with those she loved, with Stephen, and the children at school, and the sparse congregation at the ten o'clock Mass, and God himself. It was an attitude few people understood, and she expected no understanding. Stephen had understood from the first, even in those unimaginable days before he had loved her, and even then had loved it in her. But Stephen's brother the actor would never understand.

'I just didn't,' she said now.

'Well, I think that's a waste,' he said. 'I mean, I can say things like this, can't I? I mean, we are family. Listen, if you had that voice trained, think of the people you could reach.'

'I reach enough people,' she said. 'More tea?'

'No, and don't change the subject. Do you want a confession?'

How unpredictably close they had drawn over a cup of tea on a damp afternoon.

'Do I get a choice?'

'Absolutely none. Do you want to know why I dropped in today?'

'You wanted to see if my tea was up to my coffee.'

'No! Well, in a way, yes. I was hoping you'd offer me some tea, and I was hoping you'd go into the kitchen to make it, so that I could hear you sing again.'

She laughed at him: she could not help it. 'Well, all I can say is, I'm going to start taking different buses from you, too. Anyway, I've got to throw you out now, because I have to take a bath, and then go and meet Stephen in town.'

'Really? I'll give you a lift.'

'In this traffic? I have to be there by seven.'

'I know a short cut.'

'From the crazy redhead?'

'No, I've known it for years. Ask Stephen, I'm good on short cuts. You go and have your bath, and I'll sit and look at myself in your mirror. Go on.'

She hesitated, and then shrugged. 'OK. Thank you.'

She went into the bathroom, ran the hot water, and stepped out of her clothes, realising, slightly to her surprise, that she was smiling. He was, she decided, lowering herself into the welcoming water, really rather nice. And it was not, after all, his fault that he had been given so many gifts that her Stephen had not.

'Anne,' came his voice from outside the door.

She jumped, suddenly aware of her nakedness. 'What?'

'If you ever do change your mind, about your voice, I mean. . .'

'What?'

'I just want you to promise you'll tell me, because I've got contacts, you know, and I could really help you.'

She shook her head, in the beginnings of familiar exasperation.

'You'll be the first to know.'

'Promise?'

'Promise.'

'Good.'

Still shaking her head, she slid into the bath, thinking vaguely of Stephen, who had never reproached her with waste. She began to soap herself. Out of long habit she opened her mouth to sing, and then shut it, remembering that Brian would be listening. But then, not to sing in the bath was to her as unnatural as not to breathe; and he was, as he himself had pointed out, family. She opened her mouth again, and her song filled the small flat.

At last the final customer had been ushered through the bookshop door into the dark evening, and in the office, the old-fashioned wall clock said six. Kate patted her freshly washed hair, smoothed down her crisply pleated navy skirt, and began to tidy her already tidy desk, wondering, as she always did at this time, how she was to fill the interminable hour and a half that stretched between now and the beginning of the meeting. She had a number of ways of doing this. Sometimes she walked down Oxford Street, looking at the clothes in the shops; occasionally, she ate an omelette, quickly, before fasting time, in an anonymous coffee shop behind Leicester Square; when it was very cold, she went and sat in Margaret Street library trying unsuccessfully to concentrate on a book; most often, she simply wandered around, up and down and through a darkened Soho, gazing sightlessly in the windows of the closed food shops in the blank streets, oblivious to the whistles and suggestions from men in brightly lit doorways, going up one street and down another, and glancing every five minutes at her watch, just in case half an hour had passed without her noticing. It was what she would probably do tonight.

Tonight. At the thought of where she would be in two hours' time, her heart under the navy jumper and spotless white blouse leaped. She wondered, hugging herself in her excitement, what would happen. Would Maureen's friend, that glamorous girl, be there again, too? Would Maureen and Father Bob have one of their famous rows, or would Denis manage to steer them clear of it? And Denis—would he look at her as, she surely could not have been imagining it, he had looked at her last week? Her heart jumped and somersaulted under her prim office clothes.

'You coming to the pub, Liz?' Elaine, the office secretary, pushed her plump, good-natured face around the door, and addressed Kate's work-mate. Liz and Elaine were office inseparables. They lunched together, shopped for clothes together, discussed television and boyfriends in front of Kate, and behind Kate's back, Kate knew, in tones of utter puzzlement, Kate herself.

Liz at her desk stretched long, slender arms, and silver bangles jangled. 'Have I ever let you down? Who else is coming?'

'The usual gang. Judy, Richard . . .' she grinned slyly, 'John . . .'

'Oh, God.'

John was the newest sales assistant, an untidy youth who followed Liz's every movement with eyes which, when Kate was losing her battle for charity, reminded her of nothing as much as those of a St Bernard dog searching for its master in the snow.

'Well, maybe tonight he'll meet someone else.'

Liz snorted. 'Maybe the Pope's Jewish. Whoops. Sorry, Kate,' She rolled her eyes drolly at Elaine.

'Hey, Kate,' said Elaine. 'Why don't you come to the pub, too? Go on. We have a good time.'

Elaine felt sorry for Kate. Kate sometimes wondered, if all the people who felt sorry for her were laid end to end, just how far the line would reach. But it was a kind offer, although obviously she could not accept. There was fasting time to think of, and besides it really would not do to turn up for Mass smelling of alcohol.

'I can't,' she said. 'I have to meet some friends.'

It was a classic situation of Catholic folklore; except that, according to the folklore, she had not said what she should have. According to her mother, her headmistress, and doubtless, although they had never actually discussed it, her aunt the Carmelite, what she should have said was, 'I'm sorry, I'm going to Mass, and then to a discussion on the mystery of the Holy Trinity.' And they, according to the folklore, would have laughed and pointed a scornful finger, and gone on their way; and then, at some point between now and when they died, they would have remembered that Kate Waters had gone to Mass when she did not have to, and possibly, if she herself had set an inspirational enough example in her daily life, might even have been moved further to investigate the Church. So much for the folklore. Kate, however, that evening felt she really could not face the eternal responsibility for a couple of souls; and besides, it gave her a distinct frisson to hear herself refer to the group, so casually, as her friends.

'Come on,' said Liz. 'Do you good. And you never know—John might even buy you a drink. Now there's a prospect.'

'I'm afraid I really can't,' said Kate. And just for the hell of it, she said it again. 'I have to meet these friends, you see.'

Anne was dead. She had stepped out from behind a car, carelessly, because she would keep putting off getting new glasses, and now her small, mangled body was lying by the roadside, its face covered by a blanket, waiting for the useless ambulance that would carry it away. She was dead. And no one would ever know whether, in her last few seconds of life, she had thought of God, or of her mother, or of Stephen, who, having overslept, had barely spoken to her on that, their last morning, or whether the pain that had rammed into her had simply overtaken everything, blotting it out, darkening her mind and soul before she went to join the greater darkness ahead. Anne was dead.

Anne was twenty minutes late for the meeting. She must clearly be dead, because she was never late, knowing that the Mass could not start without her to sing the opening hymn. Maureen was scowling and Denis cracking jokes about runaway wives while Bob was looking at his watch, and murmuring that with or without her, they

71

really should get started soon, and no one but Stephen knew the terrible thing that had happened and that could not be undone. He left them in their ignorance; they would know soon enough.

And then the door opened and there she was, pink-cheeked and hurried, and he loved her more than even he had ever loved even her.

'Where the hell have you been?' he said.

'Where have I been?' She plumped herself down on a chair and stared at him in that half-stern, half-joking way she had. 'I've been in your blasted brother Brian's car. He said he knew a short cut in from home, and we ended up half-way to Cambridge, that's where I've been.'

'You didn't take a lift from Brian, did you? Everybody knows his short cuts.'

'Well, so do I, now. He's quite mad, you do realise that?'

'Everybody knows that, too.'

'Well. Sorry, everyone.'

'That's all right,' said Bob. 'It wasn't your fault.'

'Yes, it was. I married into a mad family, and I should have known better. Shall we start?'

'When you're ready.'

In half a minute, she was ready. She lifted up her heart and voice to God, and sang.

'But I don't like God,' said Maureen. 'I'm sorry, but I don't. He does terrible, awful things to people. Look at Job.'

'Maureen.' Praying for patience, Bob shook his head. 'You're missing the point.'

'You're always telling me that. And you carefully never say what the point is.'

'The point is that the Church's teachings . . .'

'The Church, the Church. We're talking about God.'

'The Church is God.'

'The Church is God, what rubbish. Look . . .'

'Ah, she's a darlin' girl,' said Denis. 'Sweet, she is.'

'Look, the Church was OK when it started.'

'Chalk one up for the Church, Bob,' said Stephen.

'But it's populated by, by people who haven't thought about a damn thing since the dawn of history. Well, look at *her*.' She pointed at Alison. 'Her parents joined the Church before she was born, and it was because they'd thought about it, they had reasons, they'd made a rational decision, for God's sake. But how many of them are there? Mine . . . my God, nobody had rationalised in my family since 432. You *shall* keep the faith, as the Church tells you, you shall do as you're told, believe what you're told, because . . . well, there was no because. Because St Patrick drove the snakes out. Because.'

'Come off it,' said Alison. 'Your parents weren't exactly fresh off the potato boat.'

It was true. Maureen's grandparents had left Ireland young and done well in England, and her parents had done even better. In practical terms, she had less conception of life in Ireland than she had of life in Spain. Yet she would never be properly English, either.

'That's not the point,' she said. 'The point is that as far as religion goes, theirs was—*is*—is, out of the *bogs*. And so is most Catholics', as far as I can see. And that's a completely separate issue from what you think or don't think about God.'

'Do you,' Bob asked Alison, 'as a matter of interest, think of yourself as a Catholic?'

'Do I . . . oh, golly.' She grimaced apologetically. 'Um, I'm not quite *not* a Catholic, but I suppose . . . technically, no, not really. Does this mean instant eviction?'

'I think we'll let you stay,' he told her.

'Phew.' She rolled her eyes at Geoffrey in mock relief, and he smiled.

'I maintain . . .' said Maureen.

'Oh, God,' said Denis. 'She's maintaining.'

'I maintain,' continued Maureen, 'that, Church or no Church, God, if there is a God, does unpardonable things. Look around you. Look at what's happening in the world. Look at . . . I bet you all know someone who's having a really rotten time for no reason at all, and that's God's doing. Don't tell me it isn't.'

'God does good things, too,' said Stephen.

'Well, like what, for instance? I mean, it seems to me that, for every good thing that happens, there's a price to be paid somewhere, but quite often lousy things happen and there's no compensation at all, and that doesn't seem to me fair.'

'What a ray of sunshine you are,' said Alison.

'Well, let's examine this,' said Bob. 'There's an obvious example of someone in this room who has been given a rather wonderful gift. Anne's voice.'

'Bob!' Anne blushed, and frowned.

'She didn't ask for it, she did nothing to earn it, to deserve it, if you want to put it that way. And yet when she was born, God said, "I will give this child—that."'

'Bob, I really don't think . . .'

'But that's what I'm saying.' Maureen pushed her hair from her eyes, and glared at Bob. 'You say, what a good God he is to give her that gift. I say that I bet you it's caused her all sorts of problems, and questions, and conflicts, and how do you know she *wanted* to have a good voice anyway?'

'I find this conversation,' said Anne, 'highly embarrassing.'

'Oh, don't be so wet,' said Maureen. 'Listen . . .'

'No, you listen,' said Stephen. 'Don't tell Anne not to be wet. Let me tell you about her.'

Anne groaned and covered her face.

'Last week,' Stephen began, glaring at Maureen, 'last week, my brother Brian, who is an *actor* and *knows* about these things, actually *asked* her to become a professional singer. Do you know what she said?' Abruptly, he forgot Maureen, and turned to beam on his wife, pride naked in his face. 'She said no.' He paused, and actually blushed himself. 'Do you understand? She said *no*. She said . . . she said she was quite happy with her life the way it was. She said . . .'

'Is your brother Brian Collins?' said Denis.

Stephen's eyes flattened. 'Yes.'

'Is he? I've seen him: I saw him at that thing at the Bush. He's good. You've kept pretty quiet about it, I must say.'

'Well, he is,' snapped Stephen. 'And he was practically begging her to do something with her voice, and she said . . .'

'I said no,' said Anne. She had uncovered her face, and was eyeing Stephen curiously.

Stephen nodded in triumph. 'She said no.'

'Well, there you are,' said Maureen, 'that's just one conflict this last week. I bet you there's been a million others, every week, and all because of what you call this wonderful, generous gift. He's a bugger, God.'

'And there *you* are,' said Denis. 'Slagging off God again. Face it, girl, you're a heathen.' He stared hard at Alison. 'You obviously spent your childhood surrounded by pagan influences.'

'It's no life, is it?' said Alison to Geoffrey. 'Being English among barbarians.'

Denis immediately put his arm around Kate, who happened to be sitting next to him. 'A nation once again,' he sang. 'A nation once again . . . And Ireland, long a province, be . . .'

'Denis!'

'Sorry, Anne.' He leaned further towards Kate, and spoke out of the side of his mouth. 'She pretends she's got sensitive ears, but really she's just cheesed off not to be Irish.'

'I must say,' said Bob, 'I'm really quite pleased to have a couple of English—real English—Catholics here. We are in England after all.'

'There aren't many of us around,' agreed Geoffrey.

'My headmaster was English,' said Bob. 'Father Carrington. I shall never forget him during the England–Ireland match on St Patrick's day. "Good shot, Martinelli. Play up, Szymanski! Come along, England!"'

It was a memory which touched a chord with most of them there. 'I never met any English people,' said Maureen. 'Not until I was eighteen. Apart from Alison, of course. I used to think she was really weird. Then I went to college, and discovered I was the weird one.'

'It took you eighteen years to work that one out?' said Denis.

'On which charitable note,' said Bob, 'I think we should close the discussion. So, if you'd like to haul yourselves up for the blessing?'

They shuffled to their feet, and bowed their heads while for a few seconds he shuffled off Bob Power, and became a priest, anonymous vessel of an ancient divinity. Then Denis opened the bar.

Most of the group did not stay late, Anne and Stephen leaving early for the long ride home, Bob, Maureen, and Alison claiming fatigue, and quiet Kate, as always, melting in with the general departure. In half an hour, it was only Denis and Geoffrey left at the bar.

'Load of sissies,' said Denis, draining his Guinness. 'I suppose the real men had better have another drink.'

Half of him hoped that Geoffrey would refuse, and go on his way, too. But he nodded readily enough, and Denis had, after all, no other plans for the rest of the evening.

'How's work?' said Denis.

'The same,' said Geoffrey, shortly.

'Well, here's to the weekend then. Hey, I didn't know Stephen's brother was Brian Collins.'

'Don't know him.'

'Oh, he's good. I mean, he's not Olivier, but I've seen him a couple of times, and he's good.'

Geoffrey did not respond. His knowledge of his party's history and policies was exhaustive as, indeed, was his knowledge of the Church, but on many other subjects his lack of information and interest alike was vast.

'I always like him when he tries to shut Maureen up. Stephen, I mean. She just ploughs straight through him.'

'Maureen.' Under his blond beard, Geoffrey pursed his lips. 'That woman,' he said, 'is rude.'

'Oh, she's not so bad. Once you get to know her. Anyway, her friend seems nice, doesn't she?'

Once again, Geoffrey looked blank. He probably, thought Denis in sudden exasperation, had not even noticed her. Which on the other hand was just as well. Because that made twice, once with Maureen and once now here, that Denis had brought her un-prompted into the conversation, and to think of her was so easy, so sweet, and so deadly dangerous. He would talk of something else entirely.

'What are you doing at the weekend?'

'This and that.' Geoffrey shrugged, his head held high. But the waves of loneliness that rolled from him were almost visible, almost audible.

Denis cursed to himself, mentally previewing his own weekend. A party on Saturday evening, barely a party even, a get-together with college friends, rife with reminiscences and in-jokes as inexplicable as they were inevitable. He surely could not be expected to take Geoffrey, to take any outsider, to that? Sunday, however, was an all-day Marx Brothers festival at the National Film Theatre. Denis was an ardent fan and the thought of Geoffrey sitting upright and unsmiling beside him depressed him utterly.

'There's a Marx Brothers thing at the NFT,' he said. 'All day Sunday. Feel like coming?'

Geoffrey pretended to consider it. 'I might, actually,' he said at last. 'I'll let you know.'

Denis's heart sank at the sure and certain knowledge that, some time on Saturday afternoon, or possibly on Sunday morning before he left for early Mass, Geoffrey would indeed let him know.

'How is it, Father?' asked Mrs Herlihy.

Bob, swallowing his first mouthful, pantomimed appreciative nods. 'Delicious,' he told her, as soon as he could speak. 'Quite delicious.'

Mrs Herlihy nodded herself, and left the room.

Father O'Dowd, a silver-haired silhouette against the lush February grass of the presbytery garden outside, smiled at him. 'And how are you this morning, Father?' he inquired.

'Very well, thank you, Father,' said Bob. 'And you?'

'Oh, I am in excellent health, thank God. Thank you, Father.'

He looked, in fact, physically in rather better condition than Bob himself felt that morning. Bob had not slept well, having quite unexpectedly found himself fighting off a positive barrage of impure thoughts, many of them centring on that extremely attractive girl Alison, who had been at the group the night before. The consequence this morning—since he could no longer shrug off a sleepless night as he had been able to five years before—was a distinct sensation of sandpaper behind the eyeballs. He was not concerned by this: on the contrary, he felt, spiritually, refreshed, even reinvigorated. It would do him good, he knew, to have a bit of temptation in his life; it would flex the spiritual muscles, and help to drive away those other temptations which lurked so subtly where no temptations were obvious, those of self-righteousness, of spiritual pride.

'Thanks, Boss,' he said to his creator through rubbery scrambled egg, addressing him, silently, as he often did. 'I'm sure I need this. So thanks. Oh, and help me to fight it, OK?'

'A busy day for you, Father?' asked Father O'Dowd. 'I notice that this morning, you've broken far enough with tradition to be dressed as a priest.'

'Slightly.' Bob adjusted his dog collar. 'I'm back at the convent. The Upper School retreat, you remember?'

'Ah, yes.' He smiled again, impassively, as he scraped the black burn from his toast and spread it lavishly with butter. 'I suppose, for an occasion like that, Sister Martin will have spared no culinary effort. What luck.'

Bob finished his breakfast, went into the hall, and climbed into his heavy black overcoat. At the mirror by the old-fashioned coat stand, he paused, as he seemed to be doing rather often lately, and checked his reflection. It was not an unattractive face which looked back at him, heavy and hispanic, the features of the Celt framing the dark eyes that are the living legacy of the wreck of the Armada: it was not for nothing that his nickname in the seminary had been Tyrone. But it was a face that was changing, a face whose eyes were starting to crinkle in smiling, whose neck above the so-seldom-worn collar was beginning just perceptibly to thicken, whose heavy black hair threw into relief the first flecks of silver at the temples and above the ears. Again, it was not changing unattractively: the Powers had always aged well. But it was changing.

He looked at himself for a moment, and then stepped out into Saturday morning Soho, cutting expertly through the maze of deserted side streets around the jungle that was Oxford Street. It was a cold morning that promised yet more rain, and he turned his coat collar up, wishing he had brought his umbrella, and thinking with a pang of envy of the American priest who, when he left, had been on his way to a parish in Hawaii.

'Got a light, gorgeous?' said a voice.

Bob turned around. It was a prostitute, a thickset woman of maybe forty, with dull red hair and a square Irish faceful of freckles. Take the make-up off her, flashed across Bob's mind, dress her in old slacks and an Aran sweater and she'd be the image of his cousin Maeve in West Cork.

'I beg your pardon?' he said pleasantly.

'I said . . . oh.' She caught sight of his full front view, and her face turned the colour of her hair. 'Sorry, Father.'

'That's all right,' Bob smiled at her. 'My name's Bob. What's yours?'

'Oh, God. I mean, Mary. *Sorry*, Father.'

'Well, Mary, it's nice to meet you. It's a cold old day, isn't it? Do you live around here?'

'Listen.' She turned from him to fumble in her flashy, shabby handbag, brought out a couple of notes, and pressed them into his hand. 'Say a prayer for me, will you, Father?'

'I most certainly will, Mary.' She was older than he had at first thought: the hand that had held the money was already spotted. 'I'm at Our Lady of Sorrows, do you know it? Well, come in and see me if you're passing, won't you? Good-day, now.'

'Good-day to you, Father. Sorry. Good-day.'

Bob passed on his way, smiling. It was by no means an uncommon encounter for a priest whose parish was in Soho, and it was one that rarely failed to leave him, somehow, satisfied, even joyful. Christ, after all, had walked among the publicans and sinners, had pardoned the woman taken in adultery, had loved weak Peter, who had betrayed him. The sins of the flesh were the sins of the flesh, were part of Mother Church's view, were her expectation, indeed, of poor, struggling mankind; they were not to be condoned, certainly (had not Christ said to the woman, 'Go now, and sin no more?'), but were, when it came to it, so trivial, a child's scratches, to be cured by the mother's kiss of faith, and the ointment of repentance. No, the true danger was lack of faith, was straying outside the Church's protective arm to the who knew what that lay outside. That, not sin itself, was the road to ruin. 'Do you really mean,' that blasted Maureen had asked in her infuriating way a couple of weeks previously, 'that if I commit murder on Monday, Wednesday, and Friday, and go to Mass on Sunday, then I'm a better Catholic than if I don't commit murder, and don't go to Mass?' Which was unanswerable, because, as Maureen knew full well, the answer was yes. To break one of God's commandments was not irrevocably important: that was why there was the sacrament of confession. To construct a life which did not hold each and all of them—from thou shalt not kill, to remember that thou keep holy the Sabbath Day—as its very axis and foundation, that was important, that was where the danger lay. The chances were good that that woman he had spoken to, sinning daily as she did, had at heart a purer faith than Maureen's.

Thinking of Maureen brought him back, as a corner of him had known it would, to thoughts of Alison. She, now, was in his experience an unusual girl. In no sense to be classed with what he mentally termed the brassy numbers, younger sisters, in attitude if not in act, of Mary there. Yet aware of her sexuality in a way that Anne, for all her husband, Maureen for all her talk, and certainly poor little Kate, just were not. Decent Catholic girls, usually, weren't. But she . . .

'OK, Boss,' he said. 'Bringing on the heavy guns, huh? Well, I can take it. You'll see I can take it.'

A smothered giggle, and a whisk of scarlet around a corner, told him he was approaching the convent. He turned his head, and saw the quivering, school-uniform-clad fourteen-year-old bodies of Bridget Fahey and Marie Therese O'Donnell crammed improbably into the entrance of a closed men's underwear store.

'Good morning,' he said.

They exchanged glances of agonised hilarity, and Bridget Fahey, who was universally acknowledged to be in love with him, turned plum coloured.

'G'morning,' she mumbled.

'Good morning, Bob,' said Marie Therese, who was bolder.

'We're all wearing our uniforms, then,' said Bob.

'Yes,' said Marie Therese. 'Gussie told us to.' She stopped, clapped one dramatic hand over her mouth, and clutched Bridget's arm with the other.

'Well,' said Bob, 'if *Gussie* told us to, Gussie probably had a reason, didn't Gussie? Don't you think you'd better run on ahead, and let Gussie know you've arrived?'

'Yes, Bob.'

They ran off, clawing at their throats with the agony and the ecstasy of the incident. They were turning into women, he noted, their waists were indenting, and Bridget had already the promise of a good pair of legs. He looked after them, smiling, until they disappeared around the convent gate, and continued to smile until he reached the gate himself, and Sister Augustine, all aflutter and her face possibly two shades lighter than Bridget's, came out to greet him. Sister Martin's cooking notwithstanding, Bob usually found he enjoyed his visits to the convent.

Anne and Stephen went shopping on Saturday mornings, going as early as possible to avoid the crowds, and coming home with as much of the week's load of groceries as their straining arms could carry.

'We have got,' said Stephen, pausing in unloading his basket to rub a shoulder, 'to buy a car.'

By the food cupboard, where she was stacking tins on shelves, Anne snorted. 'Not if you drive like your brother, we haven't.'

He was hurt. 'I don't drive anything like Brian. Haven't you ever driven with me?'

'No.'

'Well, I'm good. What was he doing here, anyway?'

'Brian?' She closed the cupboard door, and bent to inspect the refrigerator, unconsciously smiling to herself. 'I think he's got some girlfriend who lives out here. He obviously thought he was quite out in the wilds. I mean, he was almost wearing a safari suit.'

Stephen did not laugh. 'Well, I hope he's not going to start barging in here, bothering you.'

'Oh, he doesn't bother me. And he's family, after all. He's funny, isn't he?'

'Rib-tickling.'

'No, he is.' Reaching up for tomorrow's leg of lamb, she shot her husband a sidelong glance. 'He was asking me about my voice again.'

'I hope you told him where to go.'

'I think he meant it quite nicely, really. I think he was trying to help. I mean, he is a professional and everything.'

'Listen, Anne,' Stephen took a cauliflower and carrots from the bottom of the basket and handed them to her. 'Don't get involved with Brian.'

'I'm not getting involved with him.'

'I know he's my brother, and he's charming and he's fun, but don't.'

'Why? What does he do that's so terrible?'

Stephen was silent.

'Apart from showing off all over the place, and driving like a lunatic, and drinking too much?'

He was still silent.

'Well?'

'He's . . .' He searched for the word. 'He's . . . an actor.'

'Lord.' She turned from the refrigerator, laughing at him. 'Not—an *actor*!'

'Listen, you don't understand about actors. Show-business people. They're nutty people, you know. Nutty. They spend their whole lives showing their private, *intimate* bits to rooms full of people, strangers, God knows who, and then when you try to find where *they* are, really, there's nothing there. Nothing. It's all gone. Been used up for those strangers.'

She was still squatting on her haunches, looking up at him, no longer laughing. 'I didn't know you felt so strongly about it.'

'Everyone thinks it's sour grapes between Brian and me, but . . . Do you know that last year he forgot my mother's birthday? I mean, all the year round, he's great, much better than I am, at taking her flowers and, oh, waltzing her round the living-room, and she thinks he's wonderful, well, she thinks we're all wonderful, but she *really* thinks he's wonderful. Anyway, all this, and come the day, the one day, and there's nothing. No card. No phone call. And I phoned her from work, and she said she'd heard from all the kids but him, so I phoned him, and of course, he felt terrible—too bloody right he should have felt terrible—and he poured, apparently, half a florist's shop and half an off-licence into the back seat of his car, and zoomed all the way down to Basingstoke in time for tea, and of course she's been talking about it ever since. But he'd forgotten. Mum's *birthday* . . . And then I met someone who has something really very . . . *showy* to show off with, and she doesn't want to show off with it at all. She saves it, all of it, for herself. And for me.'

'Did you, now?' Anne stood up, and closed the refrigerator door. 'You were lucky then, weren't you?'

'Yes,' said Stephen. 'I was.'

'Bob can be OK, can't he?' said Maureen, as she and Denis huddled in the pub one bleak lunch-time early in the week.

'Careful,' said Denis.

'I mean, usually he's the pits, but when he's not being a priest pretending not to be a priest, he's really quite all right. He was last week, anyway.'

'Can we have that in writing?' said Denis.

'Of course,' she continued, with a sideways glance at him, 'last week, he was showing off like mad in front of Alison.'

Denis's colour changed, and he was suddenly fascinated by his drink. 'Was he?' he asked, after a pause.

Maureen grinned, unrelenting. 'Didn't you notice?'

'No. Hey, listen.' He jerked his head to signal a change in the conversation. 'I was wanting to talk to you. About Bob.'

'Of course you were.'

'I bumped into Father O'Dowd the other day, you know, the PP at Our Lady of Sorrows? Well, I was thanking him for letting Bob off on St Patrick's day . . .'

'You smarmy bugger.'

'And he told me St Patrick's day was Bob's birthday. His thirtieth.'

'Really? I thought he was older.'

'*Bob?*'

'*Yes.*'

'Well, you were mad then, weren't you? Anyway, I thought we could do something. Buy him a present. Take up a collection, you know.'

'Yeah.' She shrugged. 'Why not? A bath chair perhaps? Or . . .'

'Shut up. I thought a crucifix. Well, I'll ring around the others, and we'll all stay behind after the meeting to talk about it. Do you know Kate's number?'

'She works at some bookshop. Milton and Something. Near here. Hey.' No, he was not to get off the Alison hook so easily. 'I could ask Alison, too. Maybe she'd like to come to Aylesford.'

'Do you think she would?' Denis's face lit up; then he doused the light. 'Well, if you're talking to her. Well, there can't be too many Milton and Somethings in the Yellow Pages. Good.' He drummed nervous fingers on the table.

'I can give you Alison's number if you want,' offered Maureen.

'No, that's OK. You talk to her. No.' He was, she noted, twitching almost visibly. He drained his Guinness, and glanced at the clock. 'God, is that the time? I've got to go. Sorry. See you on Friday, OK?'

As he left, he bumped into two separate people and the doorway. The image that sprang irresistibly to Maureen's mind was a cat on hot bricks. Although why he should be quite so embarrassed, she had no idea: it was no disgrace, surely to be attracted to a girl like Alison, and there was certainly no other girl that she knew of to complicate things. So why not come out and admit it?

But that was Denis again. All the jokes, all the clowning, and yet when it came to it, he never really told you anything about himself, nothing personal. And, Irishman or not, for him to remain so exclusively unattached was nothing short of unnatural. He was, so far as she could see, peering beyond the familiar myopia of friendship, physically perfectly presentable; and he was kind, and reliable, even, in his infuriating sort of way, good company. And yet, in the year that

Maureen had known him, there had been no more sign of a girl in his life than there had been in, well, Father Bob's. It was a mystery.

So many things were mysteries. Denis. Teresa, crying to her God, prone on the plain of ugly Castile. Poor, smiling Miss Feeney giving her life to God's love, and receiving, as a reward, an old age of mad, sad hallucinations. . . . Jonathan, now, he was no mystery at all. He was solid, was real, was rooted in the here and now. The only mystery about Jonathan was why he put up with her as he did. She had seen him last night, and he had been sweet and so had she; and this morning he had kissed her and called her his wild Irish rose, which always pleased her, putting, as it did, her differences from him at a distance, shrinking them to a part of a sugar-coated music-hall song; and for those hours she had felt utterly safe, protected from the creeping terrors of the visions of goodness in Trent Park. Dismissing Denis from her mind, Maureen allowed herself a small smirk as she finished the remainder of her wine.

Denis trudged down the bleak wastes of Queensway towards his office, fighting himself every inch of the way. The joy which had bubbled in his heart at the idea of a whole day with Alison was so warm, so sweet, so not to be entertained. No good could come of thoughts of her; it was written into the situation, had been from the start. Not to admit this was folly, was worse than folly, was a clear, sheer path, leading nowhere but downwards. He must not allow himself the luxury of these feelings, he knew that: he must conquer himself, he must be stronger than himself. It was the only way.

Unless . . . unless a miracle really did happen, unless somehow, who knew how, Alison, by the strength of being Alison, were able to surmount the insurmountable, to alter the past, the present and the future, to make him, fantastically, worthy of what he was not, capable of what he could not.

For a few glorious moments, as he rounded the circle of the Aldwych into Fleet Street, he allowed himself to indulge the fantasy. To believe that Alison was different from everyone else, was more than merely special. That the chemistry that he swore had been between them when her steady blue eyes had met his darting grey, and her low chuckle had mingled with his barking laugh, could magically make it for him all normal, all all right, all as it was for everyone else.

It was a golden fantasy indeed, one which lasted him clear past the fairy-tale turrets of the Law Courts and to the dingy grey door of his newspaper's office; where, with a painfulness cruelly sharpened by contrast, the reality of the situation rushed in upon him, surrounding him, seeping to the very marrow of his bones. He would never be like others: not even Alison could change that. Never. Never. He stalked up the narrow stairs and into the cramped little features department where, reaching his desk, he dealt it a savage kick.

'Ah, O'Leary,' benignly greeted his editor, 'Drunk again, I see.'

'As a matter of fact,' replied Denis with dignity, 'I am stone cold sober.'

'Sober? At three in the afternoon?' Sighing, the editor shook his head. 'Not natural, lad, not natural.'

If he only knew the half, thought Denis with an inward smile: joking with himself had always been a reliable way out of the pit of despair into which, try desperately as he might to avoid it, he still occasionally fell. Another way was to keep busy. He sat down at his desk and reached for the telephone directory; and as he looked for the number of Milton and Something, he tried, and failed, not to wonder whether Alison would really join them.

'Are you eating *again*?' demanded Elaine's voice, somewhere on the edge of Kate's consciousness.

'Got to,' replied Liz's, even more indistinctly through a mouth crammed with chocolate. 'Blood sugar level drops at 11.00, 3.15, and 5.30.'

Even on the edge, Elaine's silence was eloquent.

Kate smiled to herself, quietly, over her filing. She always filed on Tuesday afternoon, and did not find the job nearly so detestable as did most people. Partly, this was from the mere fact of its being Tuesday afternoon, and therefore, just over half-way to Friday evening; and besides, there was, to her, a certain joy in losing herself completely in the mindless routine, in putting the 'A' files under 'A', the 'B' files under 'B', and so on and on until time lost its meaning, and before you knew it or an aeon later, the cabinet was in order again, and the afternoon was over. So engrossed was she in her task that she barely heard the telephone ring, and certainly did not stop, as she all too often did, heart pounding with the foolish, one in a hundred thousand million hope, that it might just be someone from the group, for her.

'Kate!' Liz's voice again, chocolate-free now. 'Hey, Kate! Wakey-wakey!'

'What?' She emerged, blinking, from the files.

Liz held out the receiver, and spoke clearly, as to an idiot.

'Tel-e-phone.'

'Oh?' She was not expecting a call. 'Who is it?'

'Personal.' She winked at Elaine. 'Sounds *rather* nice. Name's Denis.'

It could not be true. Denis was not calling her. It would be a different Denis, a cousin, or someone cruel who had read her heart, had eavesdropped on her dreams, and was playing on her the most heartless of practical jokes. She took the receiver, holding it gingerly, as if it were something very fragile.

'Hello?' she said carefully.

'Katy, old war-horse. How goes it?'

It was true! Denis was calling her!

'I'm fine,' she said. 'How are you?'

'Me? Oh, blooming, blooming. Listen.' His voice dropped, became conspiratorial, so that she thought her heart would burst its ribcage. 'You know our little Aylesford trip? On St Patrick's day?'

'Yes?' For all the world as if, over the last couple of weeks, she had thought with much concentration of much else.

'Well, it turns out it's old Bob's birthday.'

He was confiding in her!

'So we thought we'd all stay behind after the meeting, talk about buying him a present. What d'you think about a crucifix?'

He was asking her opinion!

'So don't rush off, OK? A word to the wise, you know.'

He was calling her the wise!

'You will be there on Friday, won't you?'

'Oh, yes.' She had never missed yet, and could not now imagine that she ever would.

'Fine. Well, I'll see you then. Look I've got to run. Don't take any wooden nickels, pardner, OK?'

'OK.' That was the thing about Denis: he joked so much you could not help joking back. 'Goodbye.'

She put the receiver down, hoping that her expression did not appear quite as it felt, and looked up to meet two pairs of eyes agleam with curiosity.

'So who's Denis?' said Elaine.

Kate had not thought that her heart could pound louder, but it did. 'Just a friend,' she replied.

'Just a friend!' scoffed Liz. 'You could fry an egg on your face right now.'

'Fried eggs,' moaned Elaine, who was on a diet.

'Nice bit of bubble and squeak.'

'Sadist.'

'And a sausage.'

'I hate you.'

'Who is he, anyway, Kate?'

But Kate had gone. She had locked herself in the lavatory, and was sitting on the covered seat, hugging herself, and shedding tears of pure joy.

Geoffrey was delighted to hear from Denis. They discussed the weather—Geoffrey thought he felt spring in the air, and Denis thought Geoffrey was mad. They discussed the Marx Brothers festival—Denis had thought that Geoffrey had maybe been bored, and Geoffrey assured Denis that he had had a fascinating time. They discussed Father Bob's birthday present, and both agreed that a crucifix was the obvious choice. Then Geoffrey hung up, linked his hands behind his head, and contentedly surveyed the empty office.

'"In the spring,"' he murmured, and it *was* spring, damn it and damn Denis, '"In the spring a young man's fancy lightly turns to thoughts of love."' And he immediately returned his own thoughts to the joys of being in love with Alison Beck.

Geoffrey, living in an unromantic age, had been a romantic from birth. His heroes as a child had been not modern heroes, but the knights of old, the Lancelots with their Guineveres, the Tristans with their Isoldes. It was not, even then, a side of himself he had been accustomed to reveal, and adulthood had driven it even further into the recesses of his most private self. But still, when he fell in love, as even human he occasionally did, it was usually in the fashion of courtly love, in secret and from afar. He was happy, in a strange way almost proud, that it should be thus: it seemed, somehow, to make him one of the olden company, of poets and minstrels, and visor-faced knights riding to battle with their ladies' favours on their sleeves, of the old, sun-dappled England that had been Our Lady's dowry in the days before Anne Bullen had laid her witch's eyes on Harry Tudor.

And now came Alison, English like him, Catholic like him, fitting gracious and golden-haired into the landscape of his dreams, sitting, as he saw her, graceful on a white horse, with bells jangling from the bridle reins. Alison. A beautiful name, an English name. Alysoun. Would Alysoun go with them to Aylesford? Criminal it would be if she did not: as part of the history of the religion they shared in the native land they shared, she must, she would know, as others in the group could not, what Aylesford meant to England. Alysoun at Aylesford. It was the title of a Hopkins poem, a Holman Hunt painting. . . .

'God's teeth!'

There are not many men who can say God's teeth without sounding either fatuous or comic. Francis Upton was one of the few. He strode into the office, as always, without knocking, an erect, ugly man with a magnificently shaped head, a mass of iron-grey hair, and piercing blue-grey eyes, and pushed past Geoffrey's desk to stare out of the tiny, grimy window at Westminster far below. 'If the sodding sun doesn't shine soon, I shall sell my soul to the devil.'

'I thought it was warmer,' said Geoffrey.

'Warmer?' He turned to regard Geoffrey with an incredulity that bordered on contempt. 'You must be in love.' He drew deeply on his cigarette and coughed. 'Or be starting a brain tumour.' He drew again, scattering ash to mingle with the egg stains on his pullover: it was one of his favourite stories that a novice security man at the House had once turned him away for a tramp. 'I should pray for the brain tumour. Where the hell's that jackass Simmonds?'

'I don't know,' said Geoffrey immediately.

'"I don't know,"' mimicked Francis. 'What the hell is this, *Tom Brown's Schooldays*? If the fool's still at lunch tell me the fool's still at lunch.'

Geoffrey shrugged.

'Well, when or if he gets back from lunch, you can tell him that I am waiting in my office to tear him, personally, limb from limb. You can tell him that there's an important job I wanted him to do this afternoon, that I'm flaming fed up with his four-hour lunches, that they're making my life—*my* life—damned inconvenient, and that . . .' He stopped, frowned, and looked at Geoffrey. 'You busy this afternoon?'

'Not particularly.'

'You're not, eh? . . . Well, come into my office.'

He led the way down the stairs, past his secretary, and into his own spectacularly cluttered den, where he carefully closed the door.

'Heard of Margaret Bellweather?'

'Of course.'

'Friend of mine.'

'I know. I've spoken to her on the phone.' Geoffrey smiled appreciatively. 'Not one to be trifled with.'

'Margaret?' He let out a bark of affectionate laughter. 'She's a battleship, always has been. She was at school with my eldest sister, so I probably knew her before I was born. That's my sister Veronica, now Sister Charles, OP.'

'Really?' He had not known that Margaret Bellweather was a Catholic.

'Really. Well, she's not very well these days, getting on a bit, doesn't get out much, you know.'

'Neither,' ventured Geoffrey, 'does your sister.'

'What? Neither does . . . Oh! Good, very good. Yes, neither does my sister. Difference is, Margaret's a nosey number from way back, has to know what's going on, drive you mad. So I write to her sometimes, keep the old biddy happy, you know. Not,' he paused and winked, 'the sort of letters that can be entrustd to HM mail, if you follow me.'

Geoffrey was touched. Who would have thought that Francis Upton would have taken time in his hectically busy life to sit down and write indiscreet letters to an elderly invalid school-friend of his sister's?

'Usually use Simmonds as my carrier pigeon, because he might as well be doing something to earn his salary. But if you're not too busy, I can't see why you shouldn't go instead?'

'Not at all.' Geoffrey rather liked old battleships, and a chance to see where Jack Bellweather's widow lived did not come every day.

'Splendid.' He burrowed in a drawer in his desk, and produced a surprisingly bulky envelope. 'Here's the address. Now, give it to Margaret, remember, not to anyone else, and especially not to her poxy secretary. And if anyone asks, you've spent the afternoon at the dentist's. Got that?'

'Got it.' It was clearly a letter rife with, at best, gossip: and Geoffrey, seeing a new, human side to his leader, only admired him the more.

'Splendid, splendid.' Francis rubbed his hands, his mood brightening abruptly. 'Neither does my sister, very good. Yes, you'll like old Margaret. Can't think why I didn't think of it before.' As abruptly, his mood darkened again. 'And if you see that baboon Simmonds, you can still tell him I'm waiting in my office.'

He actually saw that baboon Simmonds as he was leaving the House: he was strolling across Parliament Square, arm in arm with Sue, with the complete air of one who had not a care, or a hurry, in the world. Poor devil, thought today's mellow Geoffrey, remembering the expression on Francis's face.

'I should watch out if I were you,' he remarked as they drew close. 'Francis is out for blood. Yours.'

'Oh, no!' Sue clasped Nigel, giggling. 'Not . . . blood!'

Nigel drew himself up. 'A man's gotta do,' he drawled, 'what a man's gotta do. Made it, Ma. Top of the world.'

'You won't laugh when he finds you,' said Geoffrey. 'In fact, he had to ask me to do some of your work. He was *not* pleased.'

Sue stopped giggling. 'What work?'

'I am on my way,' replied Geoffrey, looking straight at Nigel, 'to deliver a letter to Margaret Bellweather.'

Nigel's eyebrows rose. 'Are you, indeed?' he commented.

'I am.'

Then Sue started to make a scene. She pushed forward, and spoke more sharply than he had ever heard her. 'You are bloody not,' she said. 'You are *bloody* not.'

It was Geoffrey's turn to raise an eyebrow. Was it really so important to the two empty-heads—since Sue was apparently involved, too—that they, and only they, should be the ones to go visiting Margaret Bellweather?

'Sorry,' he said icily. 'Afraid I am.'

'I'll kill Francis,' she said. 'I'll kill him.'

There was wine on her breath, and her cheeks were flushed. To Nigel's credit, his embarrassment was obvious. 'Sue,' he said, 'just shut up, will you?'

'No, I won't. Look.' She actually clutched at Geoffrey's sleeve. 'Francis wanted Nigel to go, right? So why not let him go?'

'Sue!'

'You see, he knows Mrs Bellweather. They get on well. He . . .'

'Sue!' Nigel put an arm around her, physically hustling her away from Geoffrey towards the roaring traffic that separated them from the House. Over her smooth blonde head, he caught Geoffrey's eye in an expression that was the nearest the two had come to camaraderie. 'Women!'

Women indeed, thought Geoffrey, continuing on his way. Tipsy and undignified, causing a scene like that, and in public, too, over what? Over nothing, over an advantage so marginal as to be barely distinguishable. Women.

Not all women, however. You would not, for example, catch Alison behaving like that. Not Alysoun. Thoughts of how Alysoun would behave kept him more or less occupied until he reached Margaret Bellweather's flat.

Margaret Bellweather still lived in the same flat where she had entertained heads of state when her husband had been Chancellor. It was a politician's flat, all heavy furniture, old bound editions of Punch, and the echoes of long-gone secrets still clinging to velvet curtains that framed a view of the roof-tops of Westminster with the House rising ghostly behind them. There was something fusty, too, about the person who grudgingly let him in, a thin young woman with a squashed face like an early Giles cartoon. She was, more plainly than if it had been stamped over her forehead, the poxy secretary of whom Francis had spoken.

'May I ask,' she inquired with careful distaste, 'what your appointment with Mrs Bellweather is regarding?'

She most certainly, Geoffrey decided, may not. He stared down his nose with distaste of his own. 'Francis Upton sent me,' he replied.

A distinct flicker of something—surprise? respect?—crossed her close-set eyes, as well, indeed, it might. She opened her mouth to reply, only to close it hurriedly as a door slammed and Margaret Bellweather herself, leaning heavily on a stick, limped into the room, a small, snowy-haired woman of whom, Geoffrey noted with satisfaction, her secretary was plainly terrified.

He turned from the secretary. 'Mrs Bellweather,' he began.

'Mr Johnson, it must be.' Her frail hand shook his, and she

produced a smile whose charm had once been legendary. 'Francis told me you were on your way: so good of you to come.' The smile changed to a snarl as she turned to her secretary. 'Well, what the hell are you waiting for? Office is that way, get on with your work, go on, get.'

The secretary got.

'Mr Johnson.' Her smile had returned. 'What a pleasure to meet you. I do hope she didn't give you too much trouble; the girl's a fool.' Turning towards the passage that led to the office, she raised her voice. 'A complete fool. Not that there's any crime in being a fool,' she added in a lower tone. 'But that one's a rogue, too. I call her Matilda because she tells dreadful lies. Well, do sit down.'

Geoffrey sat on a sturdy winged armchair on one side of the fireplace. Mrs Bellweather sat opposite him, rummaged in a capacious handbag, and produced a large silver hip flask. 'Gin,' she commented. 'Only way to survive this bloody winter. For God's sake, don't tell her, because I'm officially off the sauce. Imagine, trying to save my liver at my age. Afraid I'm going to have to ask you to stand up again, and pass me a couple of cups over there. Thanks. Well, cheery frightfully ho, as we used to say.'

There were worse ways, Geoffrey reflected, of spending an afternoon that no one would agree had spring in it, than sitting with an acknowledged battleship, drinking warm gin out of fine bone china. He raised his cup in silent toast to Alysoun.

'Well, Mr Johnson.' Her sharp grey eyes were fixed on him. 'Francis tells me he has high hopes of you. Now what d'you suppose he means by that?'

'Does he?' Geoffrey felt ridiculously, almost schoolboyishly, flattered. 'I suppose you'd have to ask him, really, wouldn't you?' he finished lamely.

To his surprise, she nodded in agreement. 'Quite right, too. Vague. He was always vague. Known him all my life, did he tell you?'

'He said you were at school with his sister.'

'School!' She snorted, the mere word clearly touching a wound that festered still. 'The Bastille, we called it. Hated the place. Hated it.'

'Me, too.' Geoffrey could feel the gin trickling down his throat and into his stomach. He was beginning to enjoy himself.

'You? Tchah!' She tossed her head, blowing down her nostrils like a horse in the cold. 'Your generation doesn't know the meaning of hating school. Breaking the ice on the wash-basins in the morning. One book allowed out of the library a week. Prayers for that bastard Franco every Sunday. And every morning at six o'clock, an evil old nun would come to your bed, drench you in holy water, and say Blessed be Jesus. Blessed be Jesus! Of course, you wouldn't know anything about that sort of thing. You're not a Catholic.'

It was a statement, rather than a question. 'Yes, I am,' said Geoffrey quickly.

'You?' She squinted at him. 'Johnson? Irish mother? No. German mother? Or father—used to be Johansson?'

'Actually, I'm a convert.'

'A *convert*? Good Lord, I didn't know they still had them. A convert, eh? Well, well.' She slapped her knee, poured two more generous slops of gin, and settled back into her chair. 'Tell me. How the *hell* did that happen?'

It was a question which, oddly enough, he was rarely asked. Most non-Catholics felt it to be slightly indelicate, and to most Catholics, the answer was so obvious as to be beneath comment; nor was his usual personal bearing one that promised intimacies. This afternoon, however, was different. This afternoon, he had Alysoun lodged in his heart and gin swiftly reaching his brain; and this was, after all Margaret Bellweather, Englishwoman, Catholic, and character of note, even if a mere footnote, in the century's political history. And the shameful thought did cross his mind that the chances of her having a similar conversation with Nigel or Sue were slight indeed.

So, slowly, over his gin, he began to tell her. About his childhood, adrift in the dreary spiritual nothingness which, when asked its name, would reply, too feebly even to articulate the full title, C of E. About his adolescence, and the bleak isolation of trying, all alone in that barren landscape, to fashion a moral structure sturdy enough to withstand the winds that blew harshly already, and would, he knew even then, blow only the harsher as his life moved on. About his gradual realisation, through observation and reading, that there were such structures already in existence, that his task was not, as he had supposed, one necessarily to be undertaken alone, without word or look of help or encouragement. About university, and long discussions with his college chaplain, about the final joy of being embraced by the rigours of the Church's laws, about the over-whelming, infantile security of surrendering to that stern mother the responsibility of his morals. He told her, which he had told, and had expected to tell, no one, that no matter how long he lived or what happened to him while he did live, he could not imagine that life could hold a day for him more joyous than the day when he was baptised. He told her everything, and she listened sharply, nodding occasionally, and occasionally topping up his gin.

'Extraordinary,' she commented at the end. 'Quite extraordinary. Didn't know it happened any more. Pass your cup.'

Geoffrey passed a none-too-steady cup.

'Of course,' she continued, dividing with a rocklike hand the last dregs from the flask, 'when I was a girl, it was quite the thing. Converts. Father Knox, Frank Longford, that frightful little Waugh man. Always rather envied them myself. They seemed to get so much pleasure out of things that always seemed quite ordinary to me.' She chuckled, malevolently. 'You should have seen that nasty little Waugh's face when they stopped the Latin Mass.' She pronounced the word with a long 'a', as Francis did, the old-fashioned English way. 'I always felt, d'you see, that they had something we cradle Catholics didn't. Knew they'd chosen it. I'll never be too sure myself.'

'Absolutely not.' It was far too late in the day to stand on ceremony now. 'Sorry, but absolutely not. The only reason we became converts . . .' He paused, partly to arrange his thoughts, and partly as an excuse to repeat the 'we' that grouped his own name so casually with the others. 'The only reason we *needed* to become converts in the first place is that one of our ancestors let the side down, somewhere. Henry VIII. Elizabeth. Yours *didn't*. None of them. Don't you see? That makes you . . . I don't think you realise . . .' He fell silent, despairing of ever expressing the rich romance of the heritage that was hers.

'Oh, I realise. . . . Frightful scandal when I married Jack. Prot-estant, d'you see. In those days, that meant you weren't even allowed inside the Church; we had to get married in the sacristy. Horrid, hole-and-corner affair, and six months later, my sister Beatrice went tripping down the aisle, Farm Street aisle, mind, with that Spanish psychopath. Jack's family were furious, of course. About me. Seen as terribly bad for his career. As it turned out, I was rather good for his career. . . . Of course, he never made PM, and you never quite knew whether . . . He did want good things for the country. Care to see something rather special?'

She stood up, hobbled to an old-fashioned tallboy in the corner of the room, and drew out a small package wrapped in cloth. 'Don't keep this on show,' she said, handing it to him. 'Rather old, delicate. See what you think.'

Geoffrey unwrapped it. It was a Fra Angelico: a sallow-faced Virgin, a plump Child, a hill, a stream, a tall tower, and angels' wings.

'I say,' was all he could say.

'Thought you'd like it. Ancestor brought it over from Rome in the bad old days. Priest. They cut his hands off, so when he said Mass, he had a special dispensation to lift the host with his stumps. Or that was the story. And he left us that. Mother Mary Vincent at school used to say—the woman was a complete ass; she wore a monocle if you can imagine such a thing—but she used to say,' uncannily, she dropped over half a century to render a perfect fourteen-year-old's imitation of a woman around the age she was now, ' "One of the great gifts of a Catholic education, girls, is that it encompasses the very cream of Europe's art." Silly ass . . . Well, Mr Johnson, Francis will be accusing me of abduction.' She coughed. 'Did you bring my letter?'

'Oh, my God.' He had completely forgotten. He scrabbled in his pocket, and handed it over. She took it, her manner suddenly stiff.

'I'm an old fogey,' she grunted. 'Don't understand the young any more. Changed a lot since my day, you know. But I must say, I'm . . . surprised . . . at you. Getting mixed up in this.'

Geoffrey bowed gallantly. 'No rule,' he said, 'is above bending . . . when the object is worthy.' It was, he felt, the sort of thing Disraeli might have said to Queen Victoria.

She raised her eyebrows. 'Well,' she said, eventually, 'I'm just an old rogue. Who am I to say? Mr Johnson, it's been a pleasure to meet you.'

They shook hands in an oddly gentlemanly fashion before he left, striding with head held high past the poxy secretary, who sniffed suspiciously at the air as he passed. The afternoon was rapidly turning to night, and a couple of seagulls screaming up from the river promised yet more stormy weather ahead. It couldn't really be called spring, after all, but then, he asked himself, jamming his hands in his pockets and bowing his head against the wind, who cared? He had

had a splendid afternoon drinking gin with a battleship, and in half an hour, he would be on his way home to think long and uninterrupted thoughts about Alysoun.

Anne replaced the telephone receiver, and sat back on the sofa, returning to her solitude. He was nice, Denis, she thought vaguely, to think of Father Bob like that, probably, now she thought of it, the nicest person in the group. Apart, of course, from Stephen, she added hastily. Then she retracted it: because she herself happened to prefer Stephen to anyone in the group, or, indeed the rest of the world, it did not follow that he was, objectively speaking, nicer. Although she had to admit that he was very nice, really very nice indeed.

And just as well she did think so, since they were apparently to spend the rest of their lives together. The rest of their lives. Anne shivered slightly, staring into the gas fire which she had optimistically only half lit on her return home, and repeated the phrase to herself, tasting its vastness, its unimaginability. Two months they had been married now, two months of which she would not change a single bliss-filled second. But so to spend the rest of a life of which, please God, she had yet spent barely a third . . . And to spend it loving so much someone who so much loved her in return . . . She shivered again, and bent to turn up the light on the fire.

The doorbell rang. She sighed, remembering last Friday's nap that had never been, and went to answer it. As she opened the door, she knew she had known it would be Brian.

'Hello,' she said. 'I was just thinking about you.'

'How flattering.' From behind his back, he produced a blue and white blaze of iris. 'For you.'

'Oh, lovely.' Stephen never brought her flowers. 'Didn't the redhead want them?'

'*No*. They're for *you*. To say sorry about Friday night.'

'I know, I'm just teasing. Come in and sit down. They're lovely; I'll find a vase. And get you a cup. You must be able to smell tea all the way from Woodford.' She led him into the sitting-room, noting with surprise how relaxed she felt with him. So this was what it was like to have a brother. 'I don't think Stephen's speaking to you, mind,' she continued, arranging the flowers in an old-fashioned jug that had been a wedding gift from her youngest sister. 'By one minute past seven, he'd had me shipped off to Algeria and the White Slave Trade. As it was, he nearly had me arrested for criminal lunacy in accepting a lift from you at all.'

They both laughed, comfortably, like family.

'How is the redhead, anyway?' she asked.

Brian shook his head, twirling his finger at his brain. 'She's a nurse, you see, and she spends twenty-three hours a day on duty, and believe it or not, she actually would rather spend her hour off in sleeping than being with me. Totally unreasonable, you will agree. So muggins here has to dog the hospital, grabbing her—figuratively speaking, you understand—between the bed pans whenever he can. And they said romance was dead.'

'Well, when do you do your own work?'

'I'm not working.'

'Not?'

'No.' He cast a melodramatic hand to his brow. 'I'm resting.'

'Resting? You mean you can take weeks off at a time?'

'Well, hang on. I worked bloody hard over Christmas, doing that TV thing and the pantomime, and next month I start rehearsals for going on tour, and I don't know why I'm justifying myself to you, *teacher.*'

'Yes, but teachers' holidays are always at the same time. It seems . . . wicked, somehow, to be on holiday in February.'

He leered. 'I'm a wicked person.'

The flowers arranged satisfactorily, she left them on the table and came to sit opposite him on the footstool by the fire. She looked at him, wondering about the life he led that so outraged her good husband, and in the wondering, her stomach sank with delicious guilt, as it had when she was a child, and had whirled herself round in a circle and then suddenly stopped.

'What's it like?' she asked. 'Being an actor?'

'Bloody.'

'Oh, sure.'

'No, bloody. You work stupidly hard and no one thinks you ever get off your backside, you earn no money and everyone thinks you're rolling in it, you never know where the next job's coming from or if it's coming at all, and you'd just better love it while you're up on the stage, or you might as well forget it.'

'And do you love it?'

'Oh, yes.'

'Why?'

'What?'

'Why?'

'Well.' For once, he was silenced. 'It's not something you can explain,' he said at last. 'You have to experience it.'

Anne put down her cup. Suddenly, who knew how or who knew why, it had all become real for her. In one vivid instant, it had flashed across her mind, every compliment her voice had ever received, the applause of the mothers after she had sung at the school's Christmas pageant, the listening quiet that fell over the Friday-night group during her song, all gathered together and multiplied by fame, by faceless multitudes of strangers come to the one place to listen only to her, to love only her. In that moment, it etched itself on her mind and her soul, and looking at him, she saw that he saw.

'If you ever want to talk about it,' he said, 'just to talk about it . . .'

'I don't want to,' she replied. 'And . . . Stephen would hate it.'

'So you do what Stephen wants?'

'No, I do what *I* want. And I tell you that I'm not interested. Can we please drop it?'

'OK,' he said. 'Listen, was I drunker than I thought at your wedding, or do you really have three sisters who look just like you?'

Now why, since she had asked him to change the conversation, should she feel so disappointed?

'Those are nice flowers,' said Stephen when he arrived home.

'Yes, aren't they? Your mad brother brought them.'

'Brian was here?'

'He'd been in Woodford again. He stopped off for tea.'

'Well, I hope he's not going to make a habit of this. Using you as a bloody free tea-house.'

'Oh, he's OK.'

'Listen, just say the word, and I'll tell him to bugger off.'

'He's OK.'

'He's not OK, you'll never get rid of him. Maybe I'll phone him now.'

'Look, if he ever gets to be a problem, I'll let you know, OK?'

'Promise?'

'Promise.'
'OK.'

Tearing herself momentarily from blue seas, white sands, and Conde Arnaldo's ship with silk sails, Maureen looked at her wrist-watch and curled her lip in disgust. It was almost lunch-time. She pulled at her unaccustomedly sober black skirt and sweater—she was lunching with her Head of Department—and felt a school-girlish sinking at the stomach at the prospect of the afternoon ahead.

Wednesday afternoon was a time she usually looked forward to. It was London University's half day off, and she usually devoted it to self-indulgence, to visiting friends, to cycling to the Spanish shop in Notting Hill for cheese from La Mancha and sticky Malaga wine, occasionally, when the weather and her spirits were dark, to slinking home for hot coffee and an old film on television. This Wednesday afternoon, however, was to be different. She was going to tea with Miss Feeney.

She was not, it went without saying, going out of the goodness of her heart. She was going to try to find out, if she could, more about what had happened in Trent Park. Why did she want to know? She could tell herself it was to exorcise the ghost. She could tell herself, and almost make herself believe, that it was to find out that last Saturday she had misheard, or misunderstood, or even imagined it completely. ('My dear Maureen,' she suddenly, longingly, heard the teacher's most tart tones, 'eccentric I may be, but I am not yet quite mad.') But she knew in her heart that it was neither of those things. She knew, beyond optimism, beyond self-reassurance, beyond common sense, that what was driving her to take this journey was something else entirely, something dark and lurking, inside her, something that did not bear examination.

Miss Feeney did not want to talk about her experience, whatever that experience had been. Maureen did not care what Miss Feeney wanted. Maureen wanted to know about it. She needed to know about it. She needed to expose it to the air, in the hope that it might die there, leaving Maureen untroubled, as she had been two weeks before.

And if it did indeed die, what happened in that case to Miss Feeney was Miss Feeney's concern, not Maureen's. Miss Feeney was good. Maureen, preparing herself to trample through her very soul, must and did shut her heart against such goodness.

The teacher, when Maureen had telephoned her last night, had sounded surprised, and, predictably, delighted to hear from her. She had had nothing arranged for this afternoon (since naturally, as Maureen's new savage thoughts had sneered, there was no one else who wanted to see her), and would be only too happy for her former pupil, who would find herself in the neighbourhood, to drop in for an hour. And so it was arranged. Maureen was to spend her afternoon travelling through barren suburbs on a draughty tube train, to wrest, unwillingly, a secret from a sad, mad old woman so lonely she had to invent angels as companions, as a solitary child invents imaginary friends.

'You're mad yourself,' she told herself. 'Loopy. *La loca de la casa.* Mad. You know?' And glancing up at her reflection, ghostly in the library window, she began to pull lunatic faces, gibbering noiselessly, in an effort to render impotent by ridicule the ghastly picture of Feeneybats, poor old sterling-hearted soul, driven, alone in Trent Park, to see what Elijah saw, and Mary, and tattered John fasting in the wilderness.

'Oh, but don't let me interrupt.'

She jumped as a solid expanse of blue denim planted itself on the table in front of her. Then her heart turned over as it sometimes so satisfyingly did. 'Jonathan.'

'The great thing about the academic life,' he continued, 'is the chance it offers to mingle with the country's finest minds. Was that a particularly private moment, or can anyone join in?'

She smiled, and shook her head. 'Moment's over.' She took his hand, large, solid, and sane.

'Can't say black's my favourite colour on you, sweetie.' He ran his free hand over her jumper. 'This in honour of old José Feliciano?'

'Uh-huh. It's to make me look *j*umble over the *jerez*, and *j*ard-working over the *jamón*.'

'Well, I *j*ope you make *j*eadway. And this afternoon, while you're snoring in your siesta, and I'm defending the college's honour on the rugby field . . .'

'No, I'm not . . .' She stopped. 'Hey, what are you doing tonight?'

'Tonight?' Wednesday was traditionally their night off from each other, too. 'I'm seeing my other girlfrie . . . whoops, nothing, forget I spoke.'

'Really.' She pulled lightly at his sleeve: how sweet it would be to come back from mad Miss Feeney to Jonathan. 'D'you feel like a drink later on?'

Jonathan raised his eyebrows. Then he shrugged. 'Why not? Buccaneer about six?'

'Perfect.' She stood up, and began to collect her books. 'Hey,' she said.

'What?'

She hugged him. 'I do love you.'

He smiled into her hair. 'Naturally,' he replied.

And naturally, too, Miss Feeney had pulled out all her pathetic stops for this unexpected mid-week treat, had even, Maureen noticed with a chill sadness, bought a bunch of the season's first sour-smelling daffodils to put in the one vase on the narrow mantelpiece.

'It's nice of you to fit me in,' she mumbled, politely dishonest through a tinned-salmon sandwich. 'I just phoned on the off-chance: thought you'd probably be busy.'

'Oh, Maureen.' Miss Feeney's teeth showed in a gallant smile, and Maureen looked away. 'If you only knew how very *un*busy I was these days. But there. How are the Romances going?'

'Oh . . . they're grand.' It was a cheerful conversational straw at which she was not too proud to grasp; and besides, there were remarkably few people outside the Department with whom she could share this. 'Just grand. I've been thinking about you this week, actually. I've been studying Conde Arnaldo. You know, with the ship that moved to his song, not to the wind? I think it was the first poem you ever read us.'

'Probably. It is a favourite. Do have some more tea, dear. Yes. *Yo no digo esta canción, sino a quien conmigo va.* I always thought those were some of the most . . . romantic lines of poetry I had ever read.' She beamed fondly at Maureen. 'And now, little Maureen Callaghan, who could never get her prepositions straight, is studying them at London University.'

Maureen looked at her plate. It was the moment. The moment to lead the conversation around, subtly and with cold calculation (she who was commonly agreed to have the tact of a bulldozer), pitilessly to pry open, if she could, the door to the soul's innermost chamber of this woman grinning at her with such simple good-heartedness. The Judas moment.

She cleared her throat, preparing herself for her sin. 'They, uh, went in for visions, didn't they?' she said, so casually. 'The Spaniards, I mean.'

'I beg your pardon, dear?' Unsuspecting—and why, after all, should she suspect?—her victim passed a plate of Lyons jam tarts.

'I mean Conde Arnaldo. And John of the Cross. And St Teresa, of course. All so much more ...' How could she most flatteringly express this? 'Well, less rooted in the day-to-day than anyone we've produced, weren't they?'

'Oh, I wouldn't say that.' She actually thought she was being asked her intellectual opinion. 'What about poor Blake and his angels on Peckham Rye?'

'Well, that's true.' Maureen nodded, cunningly letting her feel she'd scored a point. There was a short silence. 'It must,' she said at last, slowly, 'be frightening to see a vision.'

'I imagine,' replied Miss Feeney, 'that it must.'

Was there a hint of repressiveness there? And if so, did that mean she was hitting close to home? She pressed on with treacherous confidentiality. 'I mean, I get frightened when I lose my keys, you know, when I've had them in my hand a minute ago, and now I can't see them. And that's negative, isn't it, not seeing something that you know is there. But to ... actually to *see* something that you know, by all sense and logic and, and *rerum natura* and everything, can't possibly *be* there ... I wonder ... I mean, I can't imagine what it must *do* to you.'

'What it did to Blake,' said Miss Feeney, 'was to produce a madman. And a fine poet. I think we need some more hot water, don't you?'

She rose, still beaming, and stumped into the tiny kitchen. Maureen scowled into her teacup. The old woman was guarding her privacy this afternoon, aspiring, audaciously, to the dignity that belonged to the sane and the loved. But Maureen knew that she had forfeited that dignity, and the black imp that lurked in her mind followed the teacher into the kitchen, prancing behind her with thumb to nose, chanting shrilly like a cruel child, 'Feeney saw an angel! Feeneybats' gone batty! Yah!' No, the woman should not get away with pretending to be as others were. Maureen would expose her, would strip her of every last rag of the pretence of normalcy; she was determined to make her talk.

By the time Miss Feeney returned from the kitchen, tombstone teeth (did she never stop smiling?) still dully agleam, Maureen was ready for her. She fixed on her eyes that she knew had narrowed to shrewd slits beneath her heavy brows. 'How would *you* feel?' she asked directly. 'If *you* saw a vision?'

The world shivered and stood still. Maureen had sinned, a mortal sin. Grave matter, yes, graver far than missing Mass was that question; full knowledge, of the fullest; and fuller consent. She had sinned the ultimate sin, and with a silent thunderbolt her soul was struck dead.

And suddenly, she was fourteen years old, and caught passing a rude poem during the Spanish lesson. The teacher's brow rose, and her voice turned, as Maureen had not for ten years heard it turn, to ice. 'I *imagine*,' she responded, still standing, so that she was able to look down on Maureen fiery-faced in her chair, 'that I should first of all feel frightened. And that then I should pray to God for his guidance and protection. Which I *imagine* he would give me.' As quickly as it arrived, the moment passed. 'Do have another jam tart, dear, or I shall eat them all.'

She stayed another half-hour, drinking tea, and talking about the nuns, and Picasso, and what was to be done about Bernadette. But she did not stay for a glass of sherry, although Miss Feeney was pressing, as if to show that she forgave her for her crude curiosity earlier. But Maureen knew, as Miss Feeney did not, that their relationship had changed, radically and irrevocably; that after this afternoon, and the question she had asked, and the reason she had asked it, she could never, would never, accept in friendship a glass of Miss Feeney's excellent sherry again.

Besides, she had to meet Jonathan at the Buccaneer at six.

She arrived early and sat alone for ten minutes, nursing her red wine and staring ahead, looking, as always when she was lost in thought, rather bad tempered. So the old cow had dodged her, she told herself, coarsening her thoughts in protection against that appalling goodness. A low blow, too, pulling the old schoolteacher rank, coming over posh like that, for all the world as if she were a proper person, a person with rights, and feelings, and standing in the eyes of others, instead of just a Feeneybat, tattered old stick approaching lunacy.

But surely she must know, and she must know now that Maureen knew that she knew, that she wasn't a proper person, not like everybody else—Jesus Christ, what person like everybody else would regularly wash the altar cloth for that bugger Father Mulholland?—and she must know that she was growing less like other people every day. That she no longer had to pretend, now that her mother was dead, and her last pupils had all left school, and even blind old Mother Jeanne d'Arc, her special protégé, had been shunted back off to the mother house in Concarneau; the foundations were cracking, and that when they opened, as they surely would, it would be into a sea of chaos, the chaos of holy virgin martyrs and hopeless candles flickering in age-dark peasant churches, a cold, wide sea, where the only alternatives were to walk on the water, or to drown.

Maureen twisted her grandmother's Claddagh ring on her finger, and drew her brows closer together. God was a shit. He was a shit in the way her bank manager was a shit, a shit with all the power and all the ammunition, a shit head of a corporation too mighty even to hear her voice telling Him what He had done to Miss Feeney, what, if she did not watch both Him and herself like a hawk, He might so well do to her, too. Worse than her bank manager, because if her bank manager proved too outrageous in his shittiness, she could complain to his head office; but who could you complain to about your one living and true God?

'Oh, God,' she groaned, feeling suddenly like discredited Christopher, carrying the weight of the world on his shoulders, 'help me not to believe in you. Just help me not to believe.'

'My darling, raven-clad crow.'

As if in answer to her prayer, there he stood at the door. Jonathan, solid and wholesome, cheeks glowing, hair still damp edged from his shower. She rose to meet him, and they kissed. He smelled wonderful. He smelled of a rugby pitch, ice hard on a raw afternoon, and mist gulped into strong lungs. He smelled of mud washed off by a hot shower, and a clean body slid into a clean wool sweater. He smelled of tea and crumpets toasted over someone's gas fire and wolfed down while outside the afternoon darkened to night. He smelled of sanity, security, a healthy mind in a healthy body, and she loved him so much, she wanted to cry into his broad shoulder.

'You smell good,' she said.

'And you,' he kissed her again, 'smell of the tube. Where on earth have you been?'

'Oh.' No, if she could not tell Alison, she could certainly not tell him. 'Twice round the Circle Line. Don't knock it, it's cheap fun. Did you win?'

'Did we win. We conquered. We vanquished. We kicked sand in their faces, and rubbed their noses in the dirt. It was a draw.'

She laughed. This was how life should be. 'What happened?'

'Well.' He sat down, and pulled at his beer, sighing his satisfaction. 'The bugger of it was that at half-time we were way ahead.'

'Well, what went wrong?'

'Good question. We slacked off. We've done that before. Got to watch it.'

'It could be annoying.'

'It is annoying. And you, my sweet, are not listening to a word I'm saying.'

'I am.' She wasn't, but it was pleasant to let the words slide over her, to feel herself a child again, being told a story she only half understood.

'No you're not. Where did you go this afternoon?'

'All right.' He was right, she wasn't a child any more, and he deserved better than that, too. 'It's nothing, I just went to see my old Spanish teacher.'

'And?'

'And?'

'And why have you got a face like a long way from Tipperary?'

'Oh.' All right, then, he had asked, and he should have the answer. She looked down into her half-empty wine glass, rocking it, watching how the cheap liquid quickly climbed the sides of the glass, and as quickly fell to the bottom, leaving no trace. 'She thinks,' she said slowly, 'that she sees visions.'

She looked up, to catch his eyes fixed on hers. 'She,' he replied as slowly as she, 'has been drinking too much *jerez*.'

Something in her brain turned as icy cold and hard as the earth on the rugby field. 'I shall never forget that you said that,' she said. 'Never.'

'Jesus, will you stop flying off the handle! Look, tell me about it. I want to know, OK?'

She shrugged, a child again, sulking. 'Nothing to tell.'

'Maureen . . .' He stopped and shook his head. 'How do you expect me to know how to react to these things if you won't tell me about them properly?'

'OK.' He was right again, he was always right. She looked back down at her glass. 'OK. She's . . . she's a good woman, right? And she's—she was—a good teacher, she's retired now. And she's all alone, and she's got nothing, *nothing* in her life any more, because she went round being good all the time. I mean, she didn't marry, because, I gather, she was always looking after her sick mother, who I knew, who was a bitch. And she never made any friends of her own, because she was too busy helping the nuns and running the Brownies, and I don't know, I suppose, helping people like me with their homework. Our homework. She was always doing the boring jobs, you know? The ones no one else wanted to do. And everybody kept saying what a sterling soul she was, and she *was, is*, and she's clever, and she can be funny, and she could have enjoyed her life so much more, except that she spent all her time making other people's lives better, and never really bothered with her own. And now, the only life she has *is* her own, and it's just not enough.'

'Poor old thing.'

'Well, not poor old thing, because . . . well, yes, poor old thing. I don't know.' Poor old thing was not quite accurate here, but that was beside the point. 'Anyway, she's old, and she's lonely, and she doesn't have enough to do, OK? And she told me . . . well, she didn't actually tell me, it sort of slipped out. And she's been sort of denying it ever since. But I have . . . reason to believe,' Maureen drew a deep breath, about to express the terrible inexpressible, 'that she's been seeing visions. Of angels. In Trent Park.'

Jonathan winced over his beer. 'Angels.'

'Mm-hmm.'

'In Trent Park.'

'Uh-huh.'

'Well, *poor* old thing.'

Maureen grimaced into her wine, mirroring him unconsciously; she had not looked at him since she began her story. 'Well, no, this really isn't a poor-old-thing situation. I mean, it is, but . . . You see.'

Carefully, she lifted her glass up and down, watching the sticky red circles interweaving on the scratched table-top, nerving herself to voice at last the dread that had dogged her. 'I'm not . . . one thousand and one per cent convinced . . . that she's wrong.'

She looked up. What she saw in Jonathan's eyes told her, colder and more clearly than a sentence of death, that what had been between them was no more.

'Maureen,' he said eventually, 'I know that you're a Catholic, and I know that there are certain things that you believe that I . . . don't, necessarily. But . . .'

'But!' Her anger against her God and herself rose to a boiling head within her, and she flung it at him, inexcusably delighted to have at last found an object that was real, that was sitting not within her nor without her, but opposite her at this old student-scarred table. 'But, is it! I say bugger your buts! Two crazy Catholics, isn't it, two mad Oirish, shure an' begorrah, we have a dhrop of the crature taken, bugger off, Mister Normal Englishman. You do not say "but" to me, not like that.' She paused, stood up, and looked down at him, noticing how his brown hair waved over his temples, how her large hands on the table were dwarfed by his larger, knowing with piercing sadness that she would never again touch the hard body that lay beneath his worn soft clothes. 'It's over, you do know that, don't you?'

'I know.'

'I mean it.' She meant it; Miss Feeney had robbed her of Jonathan. He looked up from under his brows. 'I know.'

'Well, don't you have anything to say?'

He continued to look at her, as solidly inscrutable, as bafflingly calm, as on the day they had met. 'How about—I'll miss you?'

Her sadness washed away her anger, and she kissed the top of his head. 'Be good,' she said.

Feeling old, older than Miss Feeney, older than old Mother Jeanne d'Arc, she left the pub, and stumbled into night-ridden Bloomsbury, bereft of its daytime throng of academics and office workers, its streets now as blank, its high buildings as deserted, its whole aspect as devoid of human life as the surface of an undiscovered planet far from the sun. Hands in pockets against the cold, she trudged down Chenies Street where lampposts of grey granite shed a chilly shadow over black wrought-iron railings outside unlit windows, and crossed to Malet Street to retrieve her bicycle from the fence where she had chained it. Outside the University of London Union was a telephone-box, a bright splash of red in an ash-grey landscape, the yellow light in its ceiling casting a cosy glow over the telephone below. She paused beside it. Did she want to speak to anyone? Not really. Well, perhaps. She furrowed her brow, weighing the relative demerits of silence and conversation. Perhaps Alison. She entered the box, and dialled her number.

After two rings came Alison's cool voice. 'Hello, this is Alison Beck.'

'Alison?'

'I'm afraid I can't come to the phone right now . . .'

Shit. It was her bloody machine.

'. . . but if you'd like to leave a message, I'll get back to you as soon as possible.'

Would she like to leave a message? She shrugged: why not? 'Alison, it's me. Wednesday evening, just rang to see if you wanted a drink. Not important, see you around. Bye.' She left the box, returned her hands to her pockets, and walked on.

Alison at that moment was walking into a wine bar, not the local place, but a rather more up-market establishment on Jermyn Street, new since she was last in London, which Adam assured her mixed a mean Bloody Mary and which was considerably more convenient for dinner at L'Escargot than was anywhere in Knightsbridge. The location also considerably reduced the likelihood of any of her colleagues joining them: the impossibility of holding a serious business discussion in the middle of after-office chatter was so obvious that neither of them had even troubled to bring the subject up. Alison had prepared for the meeting by careful research, and was carrying a businesslike folder under her arm. She also happened to be wearing her best-fitting jeans and an oversized sweater like everyone in Los Angeles had been wearing that winter, of a pastel pink that would have reduced any other girl in dark London to a puffy pallor—and why, she asked herself, briefly checking and finding satisfactory her reflection in the mirrored door, should she not dress like that? Because she liked a client did not mean she had to wear sackcloth and ashes for him, did it?

Adam was already there, hunched slightly over a barely tasted Bloody Mary. He stood up as she arrived, running his eyes in that subtly appreciative manner over her body before homing in on her face, and shook her hand, European fashion. He did not kiss her, which she found oddly attractive; she had had enough kisses from men who barely knew her for no kiss, sometimes, to mean more.

'I'm afraid I've started,' he said, gesturing towards his drink. 'Can I get you one of the same?'

'Looks good.' She reached over to taste it, and gasped. 'Wow! Hot!'

'I was going to warn you.'

'You must have taste-buds like . . .'

'Leather, you were about to say?'

'Actually, I was about to say, like mine.'

After which, the conversation never seemed to stop. Over the Bloody Marys they discussed cocktails: neither had a sweet tooth, but Alison confessed to a weakness for an icy *kir* on a blazing hot day. Strolling unseeingly across Piccadilly Circus to L'Escargot, they discussed Paris: Adam had studied at the Sorbonne, and they discovered they had both patronised, ten years apart, the same tiny, overcrowded family restaurant just off the Rue de L'Odéon. Dinner brought them to memorable meals of their lives: Alison's all-round best ever had been at Maxim's, but her best lobster had been in a hole-in-the-wall dive hanging off a cliff a few miles south of Tijuana. Which led, naturally, to Los Angeles, which they both liked best in the winter, when there were few tourists, and no smog, and you could stand on the sunny beach and see the snow-capped San Bernardino mountains beyond the city to the east. Somehow from there, they passed to school-days: she'd loved hers; he'd hated his. And to families: she was on excellent terms with her parents and younger brother; he adored his mother and one sister, hated the other, his father was dead, and he was not clear about his relationship with his brother since the latter had joined a Tibetan monastery some years previously. And finally, they discussed his wife.

'Where is she tonight?' asked Alison, carefully mopping the last scraps of her trout and almond with her bread: they had established that they both preferred French table manners to British.

He shrugged. 'I told you. It's a very California relationship.'

'Yes, but you didn't tell me exactly what that meant. Most Californians I know are divorced.'

'Aha. And what exactly would your Reverend Mother have to say about that?'

Was it by chance that his feet were pressing lightly against hers under the table? Alison thought of Mother St Vincent, and grinned reminiscently. 'My Reverend Mother would say *exactly* what she thought about that. Which would leave the entire sunshine state feeling *exactly* like something that had crawled out of a rather deep hole.' She paused. 'And we seem to have got off the subject.'

'My dear, stern, convent girl. Very well. My wife.' He poured the last two glasses of wine. 'Let's see. We were very young. We met in Paris. What can I say? We fell in love, it was a sort of student romance, cum holiday romance, cum delayed calf-love sort of an affair. Most people would have lived together a few years and gone their separate ways, but we . . . we were pretty green, and then our families wanted us to marry . . . so we signed a document. We were both twenty.'

'I can't imagine you ever being green. Why did your families want you to marry?'

'Oh . . . respectability . . . and, as much as anything, because her family and mine do a lot of business. And there was, I believe, some sort of grossly dynastic idea that Our Child would Unite the Two Families. Except that Marcia and I were far too selfish ever to think of having children.'

'Mm-hmm.' Marcia, eh? 'So why do you stay married?'

'Oh, we have a good life, don't misunderstand me. She's a beautiful, charming woman, and a very dear friend. And that's not bad at all, for a marriage. It's just that we don't, well, pry too deeply into each other's private lives.' He smiled at her with a sudden delicious warmth. 'And will you please start looking less like your Reverend Mother, and more like a young woman who has been around the world?'

'Oh, I wasn't . . .' To her fury, she felt herself blushing. 'I mean, I'm just curious, really. What do other people think, the people you get involved with?'

'Ah, now, there is an interesting question. What do the people we get involved with think? What, ah, what indeed?'

And his smile widened with unmistakable meaning.

It was time to make a point.

'I think,' said Alison, slowly, 'that you should know that I don't do cocaine. And I don't do windows. And I don't do married men.'

'I thought you didn't.' He nodded. 'It's not usually very classy, is it?'

'It's never very classy. And that's not the point.'

'No, of course it isn't. I'm sorry.' He held up his wine, squinting appraisingly at its clear, straw yellow against the restaurant's white walls. 'Always look at your wine against a light, plain surface, or you distort the colour. The only piece of advice my father ever gave me . . . Supposing you met a man who was not . . . *married* in the sense of any deeply exclusive personal commitment, but not exactly single, either? What then?'

He looked at her with raised brows, and the soft light caught the mole on his cheekbone. He was a really very attractive man. Unfortunately.

'Unfortunately, there's no such thing as not married and not single either.'

'Divorced?'

'Counts as single. *After* the divorce.'

'Heavens above, what *will* Reverend Mother say? . . . OK. Supposing this, this man . . .'

She laughed, she could not help it. 'This Mister X.'

'Precisely. Supposing this Mister X told you, no, promised you, that there was no danger in the world of your breaking up a marriage that was anyway so minimal as to be scarcely worth the breaking? And supposing he added that he had liked you—not just been attracted to you, mind, *liked* you—from the moment he had met you, and believed that the two of you could make each other really rather happy? What then?'

What, then? Married men were taboo, that was a fixed, a given; not always immediately easy to carry out—Adam was by no means the first attractive married man who had been attracted to her—but nevertheless an unquestioned and unquestionable tenet of her day-to-day life. Alison was not a young woman much given to introspection, and rarely found it necessary, rewarding, or indeed anything other than a mildly guilt-inducing self-indulgence to examine too closely the motives for her actions. In most of the situations which had so far arisen in her life, she had tended to follow what she referred to as her horse sense, a blend of roughly equal parts common sense, survival sense, and sense of fair play. Horse sense, on the whole, stood her so far in excellent stead. Horse sense said that married men were, simply, not on.

This, however, was a different situation. They were neither of them green any more, nor, apparently, was the shadowy Marcia whom he had loved in Paris; there was really no reasonable reason why she and Adam should not have the chance, as he said, to make each other happy. Was it horse sense that stood in the way? Or was it an echo of the old, strict teaching which had shaped her childhood, which taught that a vow was a vow and must be honoured, that what God had put together, no man—or woman—should tear asunder?

'I'm very much afraid,' she replied, 'that the answer would be the same.'

'OK.' His eyes met hers, disappointed, but reassuringly friendly. 'So now we know. If you should ever change your mind . . .'

'Believe me, Mister X would be the first to know.'

'Good.' An unexpectedly companionable silence lay between them for a moment, as if they had fought together through the first skirmish of a war. 'You see that waiter over there? The one carrying the two huge brandies and the two tiny coffees?'

'Mmm.'

'Well, we have a choice. We could call him over for two huge coffees and no brandy, and discuss the whatdoyoucallit.'

'The account!' Lord, she had completely forgotten.

'That's right. Or we could call him over for the same as he's carrying now, and I could bore you into an early grave with the day I met Chagall. In which case, I warn you, we'll have to meet again before my board meeting on Tuesday.'

Luckily, it was not a choice at all, since it was obviously far too late, and the meal had been far too good, for her to deal anything like competently with business matters. Besides, he had not yet seen the lemon sweater, and God knew, her tan would not last forever.

'I hate Chagall,' she said. 'Can't you pretend it was Picasso?'

When he saw her into her taxi, he kissed her warmly on the cheek, which she liked even better than she had liked the handshake.

Maureen should not have been surprised: she was not surprised, and neither, she imagined, was he. They had both known from the beginning that it had been only a question of time until they ended it, and now that it had happened, it brought in its way its own dull relief at the final acknowledgement of a separateness too wide to be travelled, too deep to be joined. Jonathan was, after all, so blessedly different a being from herself, so happily matter of fact, so luckily without shred of imagination or . . .

Not true. She pulled herself up. Not fair, and not true. Jonathan had imagination enough, but his was tempered with common sense, and rightly so, rightly so. Monstrous of her, aloof in the arrogance of her unwilling spirituality, to condemn him for common sense! As monstrous, too, to expect him to adapt to her way, the way that had produced—what? Mad Miss Feeney, and twitchy Denis, and poor, crushed, nonentity Kate. No, he was well out of it was Jonathan, well out of the doomed relationship, between the sick and the healthy, the warped and the straight.

For herself, however, she mourned. She was not gifted at happiness: having little in her life overtly to sadden her, she had nevertheless been born with her race's curse of natural melancholy, a melancholy she would carry with her, unless she were given a specific reason to put it aside, for all of her life. She knew that and expected no great lasting joy, reckoning that if she were avoiding actual sorrow, she was keeping at least one step ahead of the game. There had been exasperation, it was true, with Jonathan, but little sorrow, and much, yes, looking back very much, merriment. She mourned the merriment, as she mourned the temporality which she longed so desperately and had failed so utterly to achieve, the inner life that Jonathan took so completely for granted, that for her, it appeared, was as impossible as for a cripple to walk, or a literate person to look at a printed page and not read.

There were so many things about which she could not bring herself not to care. And yet on the other side of the fence, the committed Catholic side, was so much folly, so much hypocrisy, so much self-deception, that she could not belong there, either. She was left alone, in the middle, neither Catholic nor non-Catholic, as she was neither Irish nor English, saying '*This* is not wrong, but *that* is not right, either.' And alone it seemed she would stay, rejecting one side, rejected by the other, the loneliest person in the wide, lonely world.

Reaching her bicycle, she peered down the bleak wastes of Bloomsbury and shivered, needing crowds, human activity. She would cycle home, not the quick way, past the Park, but the jolly way, down bustling Oxford Street, around the death-defying circle of Marble Arch, and up Edgware Road to Kilburn and home. Perhaps first, she would stop off at Claude Gill and buy herself a book; God knew, she could use a treat.

Unlike most of her colleagues, she usually rather liked Claude Gill; she liked the shop's cheerful vulgarity, so sharp a contrast to the musty gloom of Dillons and the higher floors of Foyles; she enjoyed the crude covers of the paperbacks, glaringly vivid after the muted colours of the Colección Austral, among which she spent most of her time. Tonight, however, it was all different; hollow, tawdry. Tonight, the brash displays were merely cheaply commercial, the bright lights a distrustful warning to shop-lifters, the other customers poor, lost souls like herself, the lonely, the cold, those with ten minutes or a lifetime to kill.

She wandered through and stood against the far wall, next to someone who might or might not have been a prostitute, staring glazedly at the New Fiction and trying vainly to decide between something uplifting like the new Muriel Spark, or comforting like the new P. D. James. She knew, but could not help herself, that the longer she debated the more impossible the choice would become, that it was irrelevant anyway, since no matter which one she chose now, she would have inevitably changed her mind by the time she arrived home, and that to buy both would be worse still, because then she would spend the evening grasshoppering from one to the other, enjoying neither. She wished Barbara Pym were still alive. She stood there for a long time.

Suddenly, she blacked out. Rather, she felt she had for a moment, because the lights went dark, and her mouth was filled with a strange taste of old wool. Then the sky cleared, and she realised, dimly, that all that had happened was that the possible prostitute had moved away, and someone tall had walked into her.

'Sorry,' he said.

'What?' she blinked, feeling herself still a long way away.

'I said sorry. I walked into you.'

'Oh. Oh, that's OK.' She nodded, and prepared to dismiss him from her thoughts.

But he did not go. 'Um, this sounds silly. But don't I know you?'

Too right. It did sound silly, and she was really not in the mood. 'I doubt it.'

'No, I mean it. Haven't we met?'

He actually sounded as if he did mean it. She abandoned both Muriel Spark and P. D. James alike, and for the first time looked at him properly. He was the sort of person she might well know, bespectacled and slightly bewildered looking; with unkempt hair and a shirt that even she could see was buttoned wrongly under a heavy, and not noticeably clean, sweater.

They inspected each other for a moment, and then his face cleared.

'Weren't you Maureen?'

'I still am. Maureen Callaghan. You're . . . ?'

'Daniel Greenberg. Remember I used to go out with Miriam Jason down the corridor from you?'

Down the corridor. A student phrase, like living in hall, like shopping at the Buttery, a phrase from five endless, ageing years ago.

'Oh, yes. You were always trying to blow yourself up in the pantry.'

'Never got the hang of those gas rings. And *you* . . .'

'Please, I'm trying to forget. How's Miriam?'

'Fine, I think. She married Manchester Pete, remember him?'

'That idiot?'

'That's what I said.'

They fell silent, awkwardly, each wondering whether to continue the conversation, or, if not, how gracefully to wrap it up.

'So,' he said at last, 'what are you doing here?'

'Well . . .'

'And don't say waiting for a bus.'

'I wasn't going to. Actually, I'm trying to decide between Muriel Spark and P. D. James, and it's killing me. What about you?'

'Pretty much the same. Between William Boyd and Chaim Potok.'

'I don't like William Boyd.'

'Well, I don't like Muriel Spark.'

'Well, that just about settles it, doesn't it?'

They paid together, and left together into the chilly night air.

'So do you, um, work around here?' he asked, lingering by the shop's entrance.

'Uh-huh. Well, work, I'm a postgrad. You?'

'Me, too. I mean, I work at a publisher's, just up the road. . . . Would you like a drink?'

Maureen thought. Would she? It seemed wrong, somehow, to be accepting a drink from a more-or-less strange man not half an hour after you had broken up with your boyfriend. On the other hand, an injection of alcohol over a gossip about old friends might be just what she needed. Certainly, she was not looking forward to returning home. 'All right,' she said.

There was a pub just on the other side of Oxford Street, long, deep, and surprisingly quiet. Maureen sank into a cracked plastic armchair, and closed her eyes gratefully while Daniel went to the bar for gin and tonics. He returned with two double measures.

'You looked like you needed it,' he said.

So it showed, did it?

'It's the time of year,' she said quickly. 'I hate this bit, don't you? It's been winter forever, and there are still three months till spring.'

'Yes, I know. Well, here's to spring when it does arrive. Actually, you were just an excuse for the double: I rather wanted a stiff one myself.'

'Yes?'

'Yes.' Behind his glasses, he opened his eyes wide and blinked, like someone emerging from a long, dark tunnel. 'I've just spent half an hour on the phone to my mother, explaining why I can't be home for Pesach.'

'Pesach?'

'The Passover? Next month?' Of course: he and Miriam had been Jewish. 'It turns out there's a big do at work, which I really should be at.'

'Well, can't you get out of it?'

'Well, I could, but . . .' He stopped and blinked again. 'You see, it's a really very important do, and they really want me to be there. And I'm not orthodox any more, so Pesach, for me, is just self-indulgence anyway. But trying to explain to your orthodox mother that you've decided the right thing to do is *not* to celebrate Pesach . . .'

'Jesus, don't I know it.'

He paused, raised an eyebrow at her. '*You* are Jewish?'

'Try Catholic parents for size, mate.'

'I don't know many Catholics, actually. Don't you find an awful lot of people you come into contact with tend to be Jewish?'

'*Really?*' That was so interesting that for a moment she actually almost forgot both Miss Feeney and Jonathan; she hooked a foot under her chair, and leaned forward over the table. '*No! I* find an awful lot of people tend to be brought up Catholic!'

It was the sort of conversation that happens rarely, and by definition only once in any given relationship, when two strangers meet who find themselves in some way or other so startlingly similar that they bypass the conversational appetisers of usual first acquaintance and plunge, unexpectedly and with appetite undulled, straight into the meat of intimacy. They talked, of course, about religion. They talked about the uncertainty of overthrowing their parents' faith, and the seeming impossibility of replacing it with one that was as good in the good parts while lacking in the bad. They talked about the hopelessness of trying to convince those parents that the way they were living was not a lapse from duty, but a duty itself, not a moral weakness, but a striving for moral strength. They talked about isolation, about the loneliness of knowing—and knowing they knew when others did not—that they were, in a way that was as difficult to vocalise as it was impossible to ignore, not quite as the others were. They talked about Catholicism and Judaism, and Judaism and Catholicism, they raised their voices and waved their hands, they questioned and answered and questioned again. And at last did not so much leave the pub as were thrown out, dazed and hoarse, into an Oxford Street alive with cinema-goers streaming to the tube stations and home.

'We should do this again,' said Daniel.

Maureen looked at him and smiled, she who had thought she would never smile again. 'I think we should,' she agreed.

They should; they exchanged telephone numbers promising that they would; and what a pity it was that they would not. People simply did not follow up on these things: the weekend would arrive, and then the weekend after that, the moment for establishing contact would come and go, the sharp memory of the evening would dull, and the two telephone numbers would sit in the two separate wallets, becoming more ragged and less significant with each passing day.

A pity indeed, but Maureen, cycling home through a London whose lonely streets held now no terrors for her, thanked God for the evening. She thanked the deity whom she would not insult or flatter by asking for signs, for having sent her a sign nevertheless, a sign that, while unusual, she was not, as she had thought alone, that there were others, all over London and all over the world, who were experiencing what she was experiencing, feeling as she felt. She thanked him, scrupulously careful, since she would not ask for such things, always to acknowledge them when they arrived, for saying to her, that evening, through Daniel, exactly what she had needed to hear. A pity that she and Daniel would likely never see each other again, but that was not the point of the evening at all. She acknowledged what could not be, and thanked God for what had been.

Why, then, as she reached the top of the stairs that led to her tiny flat off West End Lane, and heard her telephone ringing, did she all but batter down her own front door to reach it before it stopped?

'Hello.'

'Maureen?'

'Oh, hi.' Alison. Well, who else was she expecting?

'I just got your message. Are you OK? You sounded strange.'

'You don't sound too normal yourself, chum.' She didn't, either. You been out on the razzle?'

'Me? No. Well, sort of. I've been out with sort of a client.'

'Sort of a client.'

'Sort of half a client, and,' she paused, 'sort of half a, a *man*, you know?'

Alison. Barely through Customs, she had said herself, just a couple of weeks before. But Maureen, whose own loves were always so hard won, invariably so fraught with pain, did not feel the shameful envy she usually felt at these times: on the virtuous contrary, she was interested. 'Clientman, is it? Tell me more.'

'Well, it's rather complicated. Look, what did you ring for, anyway?'

'Oh. Oh, that.' The early evening seemed suddenly so very far away. 'I broke up with Jonathan.'

'Oh, no.'

'Yes. Like, *per omnia saecula saeculorum*. It was coming.'

'Well, yes, but . . . Are you OK?'

'No, I'm lying on the *chaise-longue* in a decline. Of course I'm bloody OK, I told you, it was coming.'

'Well, let's meet, anyway.'

'Damn right. I want to hear all about Clientman. Tomorrow night?'

'Fine. No, blast, I have to go to a reception.'

'Oh. Well, Friday's mad Catholics, and you presumably don't want to go there again. So . . .'

'Hang on. What the hell do you mean, I presumably don't want to go there again? I wish you'd bloody stop telling people their opinions, I really do.'

Maureen was taken aback: she actually sounded quite ratty. 'Sorry,' she said mildly.

But Alison was not appeased: she had clearly touched some quite unexpected nerve. 'I was baptised just the same as you were, and I probably believe more than you do when it comes to it, so just cut it out, will you?'

'Look, I only . . .'

'You're like bloody Hitler. You talk about priests being dogmatic . . .'

'I'm sorry, OK?'

'OK.'

There was a pause.

'Would you like,' said Maureen eventually, 'to come to the meeting on Friday?'

After another pause, she heard Alison's chuckle. 'I suppose I can't really get out of it now, can I?'

On Friday, Kate took an extra long lunch-hour to go to the hairdresser, and returned to the shop with her hair blown into gleaming chestnut waves around her small face.

'You look nice,' said Elaine, who had wandered into the office in search of Liz.

'It's Mummy's birthday tomorrow,' said Kate. 'I'm going home for the weekend.'

'Are you? Bearming-gum, right?'

'Outside Birmingham.'

'Oh, yes.' She wedged ample hips against Liz's desk, and Kate, whose battle for charity had not been going well lately, tried hard not to observe that she was wearing a skirt similar to the one Liz had worn last Friday, and that the style suited Liz rather better than it suited Elaine. 'Where *is* the girl, anyway? Poor old you, it's a cold night for a train journey, isn't it?'

'Oh, I'm not going till tomorrow. I hate the train on Friday nights.'

She paused. 'Besides, I'm seeing some friends tonight.' And even charity was forgotten as her heart pounded in the mixture of dread and hope that Elaine would question her further, would want to know about these friends, would perhaps link them with the friends she had seen last Friday, with Tuesday's telephone call, with . . .

But the moment was shattered as Liz swept in, fresh from the sale at Bally's, triumphant in positively the last pair of exactly the sort of boots Elaine had been hunting high and low for all winter, and Kate's affairs were lost in cries of envy and admiration.

Kate looked at the clock. Three and three quarter hours to go. Well, two and three quarters until the end of the day, and an hour on top of that; it made it seem less if you broke it up. And thank God, oh, thank God and whoever it was who had arranged the calendar that last year had been a leap year, or her mother's birthday would have been on the Friday, and if that had happened, she really did not know what she would have done.

Unobtrusively, she slipped from the office to the bathroom, locked the door, and stared at herself in the smeared little mirror. Vanity was a sin, of course, but she had to admit that today she looked nice. Marilyn had done her hair just so, shaping its natural unruliness in a way that would last at least until the next time she washed it; the red and white striped shirt, instead of the cream one she usually wore with this outfit, added a touch of daring; and today, her mouth did not look disapproving at all. Not as interesting, of course, as Liz, or, goodness knew, as pretty as that friend of Maureen's. But nice all the same.

Something must happen tonight. It must. After that phone call . . . Kate's eyes glazed over, and something warm wriggled inside her, as it had at odd moments through the last three days, whenever she remembered the call. He had phoned her. He had thought about where she worked, had looked up her telephone number, and had phoned her. And that must, surely it must, if there were any justice on earth or mercy in heaven, lead to something, some further sign, tonight.

Just what it was that might happen, she did not quite know. He might, unseen by the others, give her a word or a look that would say, clearly and beyond a shadow of doubt, 'Yes, I am yours, yes, wait for me.' He might, casually, towards the end of the evening, suggest they meet later in the week, for lunch or a drink: he did, after all, know her telephone number. He might stay after the others had gone, to clean the bar, and she might stay to help him, and he might look into her eyes and take her by the hand, and . . . and there, Kate's imagination balked, dissolved, shattered into a thousand kaleidoscopic fragments of love and tenderness and eternities of happiness piled one on top of the other, and all in the one person of Denis.

Then the door rattled, and she hastily and unnecessarily flushed the toilet, and washed her hands, waiting for the stars to dim in her eyes.

'Well, tell her, Father,' said Mrs Mullins.

Bob sighed, and looked at Mrs Mullins' eldest, Deirdre, who crouched, pink eyed, at the very end of the presbytery's sturdy old sofa.

'I think,' he replied, 'that Deirdre knows by now what she should and should not do.'

Mrs Mullins rumbled. She had made small secret of her disappointment at finding Father O'Dowd not at home that evening.

'You don't know the half of it, Father,' she said grimly.

The sorrow of it was that he did know, had known since they had arrived some half-hour previously.

'What's the real trouble here?' he asked. 'Apart from staying out late and shouting at her father? What is it really?'

'Tell him, Deirdre,' thundered Mrs Mullins.

Deirdre whimpered.

'Then I will.' She rose to her feet and pointed a finger, her voice sinking all at once to a whisper. 'She's pregnant.'

Thank God it was out at last.

'Oh, dear,' said Bob. 'Oh dear, oh dear. Well, how are you feeling, Deirdre?'

The girl looked up at him, warily, out of the corner of her eye. Bob continued.

'I remember my sister feeling just terrible for the first three months. But then,' he turned to the mother, 'I believe it gets better, doesn't it, Mrs Mullins?'

Mrs Mullins was staring at him.

'Father,' she repeated, as if he had not heard. 'She's pregnant. She's going to have a baby, Father.'

'Yes, I know. I know.' He smiled sympathetically at Deirdre. 'Her life's going to change quite a lot, isn't it? But I think she did the right thing in coming first of all to her mother, don't you?'

They were both staring at him now, openly agape. With a spurt of exasperation, he wondered just what they thought he heard in the confessional every week.

'A baby, Father,' said Mrs Mullins. 'A baby.'

'And little James hardly out of nappies himself. Well, at least she's had practice, haven't you, Deirdre?'

They continued to stare at him with expressions whose similarity, were the circumstances not tragic, would have been comic.

'I know what you're thinking,' he said suddenly. 'You're thinking, here is he, a priest, lives with another priest and a housekeeper, no idea what it's like to have a baby around the place, and to top it off, he's a man. What on earth does he know about it? That's what you're thinking, right? Well, I'll let you into a secret. You're absolutely right.'

For the first time that evening, Deirdre made a sound that might just have been a giggle.

'However.' He crossed to the desk, and wrote a number on a piece of paper. 'Here are some people who aren't men, who don't have housekeepers, and who do know a bit about babies. Will you phone them?'

He held out the paper. Both women reached for it, but Deirdre took it.

'Thank you,' she mumbled.

'Well, come and see me after you've seen them, and we'll talk again. I don't suppose you're in contact with the father, are you?'

She shook her head. Girls who were in contact with the father did not look as she looked.

'Well, I'll say a prayer for you. Now, will you do something for me?'

She looked up at him.

'When the baby's born—may I baptise it?'

'Baptise . . .' She rolled the word in her mouth as if it were a new flavour, and unexpectedly sweet. 'Oh, yes, Father.'

'Father.' Mrs Mullins grabbed his arm. 'Father, she's pregnant. Pregnant, Father.'

'I know, Mrs Mullins.' Their eyes met, adult to adult. 'But I always think that, whatever the circumstances, there's something just a little bit magical about a new life, don't you?'

'Even a bastard, Father?'

'Like St Martin de Porres, Mrs Mullins? . . . I realise that Deirdre has sinned. But I think she's being fully punished, don't you? And what a lucky girl she is to have a mother she can turn to at this time, especially when you consider . . . some of the alternatives she has these days.'

Mrs Mullins sniffed. 'My Deirdre,' she said, 'would never consider murder.'

'Then you've raised her well, haven't you? Say a prayer for me both of you, and come back and see me soon.'

Mrs Mullins yanked Deirdre to her feet with a rough maternal hand.

'We'll take the bus home,' she stated. 'You've got to start taking it easy.'

As the door closed behind them, the smile left Bob's face. It was a sad affair, a life shadowed, if not darkened entirely. Fifteen years old was Deirdre Mullins, and bright: she would be heavily pregnant when she took her 'O' levels this summer, and there was, of course, no hope of 'A' levels now. A strangely severe punishment for so small a thing as lust—but then, God's ways were not his ways.

Nor, he must remember, was his flesh as other men's flesh: it was, and for many years had been, consecrated to God. Sins of the flesh, for most men, were sins of the flesh, and while that in itself was plenty enough sin to be coping with, it was, on the other hand, all that they were. For himself, such a sin was—rather would be, in the unthinkable event that he were to commit it—would be what? Would be beyond words, a cataclysm of betrayal, an infidelity worse than Peter's that morning before the cock crew, would be no less than adultery to his Creator and the One most high. Other men may abuse their flesh, but that flesh at least belonged to them. Bob's belonged to no man or woman, but to his God.

Preparing himself to leave for the Friday-night group, he wondered idly how different his life would have been had he been born fifty, or even thirty, or possibly even fifteen, years later, after the Church had changed—as inevitably in the near future it must change—its teachings on the celibacy of the clergy. It would certainly make life simpler if he were able occasionally to think without guilt about girls . . .

'Girls!' he added, aside, to his Boss. 'Who am I kidding? Not You, anyway. I mean, girl.'

He meant Alison, the thought of whom had followed him pitilessly, since last Friday night.

'It's not getting any easier,' he felt justified in mentioning: one night's wrestling with temptation was one thing, but the strain of seven was beginning to tell. 'I know it's a test of faith, and I know I said bring on the heavy guns. But can we please just remember that You're not dealing with St Jerome here?'

He looked up at the twisted figure on the crucifix, and was immediately ashamed.

'OK, Boss,' he said. 'Point taken. Sorry. And it's Ash Wednesday next week too.'

As a penance, he made a deliberate point of not checking himself in the mirror as he left the presbytery. But he hoped all the same that she would not be there that evening.

'So what you're saying, Bob . . .' began Maureen.

Geoffrey and Stephen groaned, and Denis let out a hoot of laughter.

'What you're saying,' she repeated, 'is that every time I spend Sunday morning sitting at home happily reading the Sunday papers like nine-tenths of the population does, instead of standing like an idiot in a draft in that great barn of a church in Quex Road in a bad temper, I'm committing a mortal sin?'

'I'm saying that if you don't go to Mass on Sunday, you break a fundamental rule of the Church.'

'And Mass on Friday doesn't count?'

'Well, of course it counts . . .'

'But for this fundamental rule, it doesn't?'

'It doesn't fulfil the Sunday obligation, no. I'm sorry, Maureen. I'd love to say yes, do as you please, go when you feel like it. But a rule is a rule is a rule, and the Church is run by rules.'

'But suppose I don't accept those rules?'

'Then leave the Church! Look, you want to play tennis, but you don't like hitting the ball over the net. So you take the net down. Fine. Grand. I hope you have a good game. But you can't call it tennis, now, can you?'

'OK, but . . . supposing the net's too high. Supposing it's so high that *no one* can reach the top, that to play properly, you have to have a . . . a deformed wrist . . .'

'A *what*?'

'Wrap up, Denis. Supposing a normal person simply cannot hit the ball over. What do you do then?'

'You have a very odd-looking Wimbledon.'

Stephen snorted, and even Kate's mouth twitched.

'Wrap *up*, Denis. Do you lower the net so that people can play, or do you keep it up there till the game dies out entirely?'

'And let's not forget the Club-Foot Cup Final.'

'Denis! Look, all I'm saying here, and God knows it's not exactly a novel theory, is that the Church makes demands that are pretty well impossible to carry out, and utterly unreasonable to ask in the first place.'

'I don't find them either,' said Anne.

'Well, either you're lying, or you don't realise how lucky you are.' She squinted at Bob. 'What about you? The . . . some of the *stupid* things the Church asks of you. Don't you resent them?'

'No.'

'Oh, sure you don't.'

'*No.*' He paused. 'They're . . . not always necessarily easy. But I believe there is a reason for them, and I trust that that reason is a good one.'

'Surely that's all you can do?' Denis weaved back into the conversation proper. 'Trust. There are some things you just can't imagine any reason for or justice to. All you can do is—trust that there's a plan somewhere.'

'And if you don't trust that plan?'

'Then you've got a problem, haven't you?'

'I agree with Denis,' put in Kate. 'Trust is quite often all you have.'

Anne and Stephen exchanged glances.

'If it's full trust,' said Stephen, 'it's enough.'

Maureen stared at Kate. 'Do you mean to tell me,' she demanded, 'that you really and truly believe it's all part of some great Scheme? That you, Kate, what is it, Waters, are going to wake up some day, in heaven, on earth, wherever, and say, "Aha! I see it all! It was all—wars, plagues, pestilences, all—for the greater good of mankind! Thank you dear God, for wars, plagues, and pestilences?"'

'Yes,' said Kate.

Maureen shrugged.

In the short silence that followed, Geoffrey closed his eyes, opened them, and prepared to speak. 'Maureen,' he began, 'have you ever actually tried, ah, playing tennis without any net at all?'

'Yes, I've tried. I've tried several times. And the reason why I'm here tonight instead of down at the pub with the rest of the Department is . . .'

'No, you haven't.'

'Well, thanks very much, there's no answer to that, is there?'

They glanced at each other, and the hostility that was usually latent between them spluttered into life and died like a match lit in a high wind.

'What is it about these rules anyway?' asked Alison, for the first time joining in the discussion. 'I mean, the thing that seems to me—seemed to me—slightly unfair about them was that they kept changing. Like, oh, fish on Friday. First you mustn't eat meat, and then I remember it was sort of OK but not really, then it was really OK. And I remember the nuns taking us on school trips, and the rules would change completely depending on which country you were in. And that's fine. Except that I don't see you have the, the right to be so *rigid* about these rules when you know perfectly well that in fifty years' time or a couple of hundred miles away, they'll have changed completely.'

'At-ta-*girl*!' said Maureen. '*Adelante, amiga.* Up the rebels.'

Bob frowned. 'The thing about the rules,' he replied. 'The—do shut up, Maureen—the thing about the rules is that they are the Church's interpretation of God's will. And part of belonging to the Church is accepting that it has the best interpretation going. I'm not saying the only interpretation. But the best.'

'Broadminded of you.'

'And I'm saying that whatever the issue—blasphemy, mass murder, fish on Friday—we simply have to put our faith in it. And that's all there is to it.'

'But what about you, Bob?' Alison looked straight at him, blue eyes into brown. 'You're young and you're intelligent. You surely can't not believe that, for instance, in a few decades' time, priests will be allowed to marry . . .'

'What the Church requires of me now, and what the Church will require in the future are two separate issues.'

'Yes, but what about *you*? If it won't be wrong for you to . . . to marry in the year two thousand and whatever, when you're old and grey and don't want to, then it surely can't be all that desperately wrong for you to do it now. When you might want to. You might even think it might make you a better priest, or a fuller person. But you're not allowed to because of the rules. Doesn't that make you . . . a bit *sore*?'

A curtain fell over Bob's face. 'No.'

'Bob doesn't have any quarrels with the Church,' said Maureen. 'His spiritual life is one long sunny Saturday afternoon.'

Anne and Stephen looked at each other, remembering in the same instant the Saturdays of the far-away last summer, and smiled.

'I think,' said Alison slowly, 'that if there were something I wanted to do—not mass murder, but something that really and honestly didn't seem to do anyone any harm, and might even do a . . . a couple of people a bit of good, or make them happy, anyway—and I were stopped from doing it just by a *rule* . . . I think I might become quite bitter.'

'And I,' said Denis, 'would become a dentist. Because I've always wanted to see the bitter bite.'

It was the end of the discussion.

'You know,' said Maureen, after the Blessing, while Denis was pouring the drinks, 'I'm surprised you don't hire yourself out to the IRA. As the ultimate deterrent.'

Denis laughed. 'I like it. Stand in a pub as an unattended package . . .'

'And just carry on precisely as you usually do. The entire British Army would be on the next boat home.'

'Speaking of which,' said Bob. 'I think I'm going home myself; it's been a rather hard week. Good night, all.'

'What's the matter with him?' said Stephen, as the door closed.

'He looked tired,' said Anne. 'Well, Denis, that was a bit of cloak and dagger work for nothing, wasn't it?'

'Me talents is wasted,' he agreed. 'But anyway, have we pretty much decided on a crucifix? Because if so, and you'd all like to chip in now, Mister Money here can buy it.'

Bending into a beggarly crouch, he went around the circle. 'Spare a penny, sorr? Ah, 'tis you have the good heart, God bless you. Annie, me darlin', thank yeh, and Missus Callaghan, is it yourself would put the money into me own deformed wrist . . . Alison.' He stopped, and straightened up. 'Well, you don't really know Bob. But are you coming with us anyway?'

'Sorry?'

'Are you coming? Didn't Maureen tell you?'

'Oh. No, I didn't.' Maureen dug into a packet of potato crisps, and handed them around. 'I forgot. Sorry.'

'You *what*?'

She looked up, startled: his tone had changed completely.

'Forgot. I'm sorry. Let's ask her now.'

'No, hang on a moment.' No one in the group had seen Denis angry before: he was angry now. 'You *forgot*? You forgot to ask her?'

'*Quia peccavi nimis, cogitatione, verbo, et opere.* Yes, Denis, I forgot. Oh, forgive.'

'Which just goes to show,' put in Geoffrey, but his eyes were fixed surreptitiously on Denis, 'what comes of playing tennis without the net.'

'Yes, but I did all the spadework!' His knuckles were actually white. 'I trekked around bloody Westminster pricing crucifixes. I phoned everyone up. I phoned Geoffrey, I phoned Anne, I phoned Kate—' he stopped. 'I did phone you, didn't I, Kate?'

Under the new hair-style, Kate blushed a deep crimson. 'Yes, you did,' she said quietly. And the colour ebbed, leaving her paler even than usual.

'Yes, of course I did, and *you* said you'd do one lousy thing, and you forgot.'

'I hate to butt in,' said Alison, 'but what are we talking about?'

'Denis will tell you,' said Maureen. 'I can't be trusted.'

'We're going to Aylesford for the day,' said Denis. 'On St Patrick's Day—which I've just discovered is Bob's birthday. Maureen and I were wondering if you'd like to join us. Would you?'

Alison looked at Maureen. Maureen shrugged. Everyone else looked at Alison.

'Well,' she said. 'Well, yes. Yes, that would be lovely.' Not, she felt, for the first time with this group of people, it was the only answer she could possibly have given.

Denis's Saturday passed pretty well as three out of four of his Saturdays did. He woke late and slowly, and stumbled into the kitchen of his dark little flat in Herne Hill for a mug of Nescafe, a bowl of cornflakes, the *Daily Mail*, and Capital Radio. He did Mrs Jennings' shopping, and had a cup of tea with her afterwards, duly admiring her new pink cardigan, Fred the canary's latest trick with the ladder, and the new photographs of her granddaughters in Australia. He treated himself to a late lunch of fish and chips and an individual fruit pie over an anonymous western on his jumpy black and white television, then made a pot of tea and read *The Big Sleep* for an hour. Then he had a quick bath, and went out to dinner with Philip and Ruth.

And in all that time, not five minutes went by but he thought of Alison.

She was everywhere, filling everything, surrounding it with her glow. She was in the one grudgingly optimistic ray of sunlight on his cracked formica kitchen table. She was in the early crocuses, pushing their purple and gold heads through the wet earth in a magical ring around Mrs Jennings' bird-bath. She was in the first spring-like breeze that tugged at his coat in the chilly sunshine outside the Express Dairy. She was in the thundering horses and the artificial sun beating on the streets of the studio back-lot. She was in the motion of the tube train, in his footsteps echoing down the dark North London street, in the ringing of the doorbell, the greeting, the plop of the cork leaving the bottle of wine. She was Alison, she was forbidden to him, she was everywhere. He raised his glass in a secret toast to his monumental task of abnegation.

'Are you all right, Denis?' asked Ruth, as Philip went to the kitchen in search of peanuts.

'Me? Fine. Why?'

'I don't know. I never feel you eat properly.'

He looked at her with sudden affection.

'You,' he replied, 'never feel anyone eats properly unless you've cooked what they're eating.'

'Bossy to the last,' she agreed instantly. 'That's why . . . Oh, hang on.'

The doorbell rang again. It was her friend, Charlotte.

Denis was relieved to note that Charlotte was fully as horrified to see him as he was to see her.

'I didn't know,' he said to Ruth, with all the jocularity he could muster, 'that you were going to invite *people*.'

'I'm not people,' shot back Charlotte. 'You are.'

'People?' Philip had wandered back into the room. 'Who's talking about people? Don't hold with them myself, never did. Hello, Charlotte, how are you?'

'Fine, thanks. How are you?'

'Better than he was on Thursday,' said Ruth. 'And Denis too, from what I hear.'

They groaned, simultaneously.

'What happened on Thursday?'

'It happened on Wednesday,' said Philip. 'We got plastered.'

'You got plastered,' corrected Denis. 'I was a model of sobriety.'

'Oh, yes? Tell it to that chap you tried to sell your shoes to.'

'I'd forgotten that.'

So many things you forgot when you were drunk: it flitted across Denis's mind to wonder whether he ever in that state had said anything, had given any clue . . . but no. Drunk as he had been, he would never be so drunk that he would do that.

'They had one of their stupid leaving parties for someone in the office,' Ruth told Charlotte. 'And they all got drunk, and most of them staggered off to find something to eat. Except for these two, who staggered off to find something to drink.'

'We got lost on the way to the restaurant.'

'They got lost between the Wig and Pen, and the bottom of Chancery Lane. Twenty yards, would you say? Phil rolled up here at 3.30 in the morning, smelling like a whisky still in a brewery, and couldn't understand why I wasn't very friendly.'

'I'd had a frightful journey, actually,' said Philip. 'First I couldn't find a taxi, and by the time I did, I was so cheesed off with every taxi driver in the world, that when he asked me where to, I wouldn't tell him. God knows how Denis got home.'

'I walked,' said Denis.

'Walked?'

'It seemed like a good idea at the time. It really wasn't too bad. The only difficult part was crossing the river: I couldn't find a bridge.'

'How were the Marx brothers?' said Ruth suddenly. 'Charlotte's a fan, too, aren't you, Charlotte?'

'Well, I'm not going to say I'm not, now, am I?' said Charlotte. 'What, me? Sense of humour? No—I hate laughing.'

'He went to a festival at the NFT,' added Ruth. 'You're a member of the NFT, aren't you?'

Denis grabbed for the first diversion that came to hand. 'I was surprised how crowded it was, actually,' he said. 'I mean, they're obviously flavour of the month at the moment. We arrived quite early, and it was quite a fight to get good seats.'

'Who did you go with?' said Ruth; he had known as he said it that the 'we' had been a mistake.

'A bloke I know.'

Ruth looked at him, and something flickered in her eyes. It would be galling, if restful, if she were to decide he was gay. If only it were so simple. Denis shelved for later amusement, which he just might, but probably would not, share with Maureen, the idea of Geoffrey as his secret lover.

'What are we eating, anyway?' he said. 'I worry about Philip: I never feel he eats properly.'

'Spaghetti.' Ruth pinched Philip's ruddy cheek. 'I make-a da pasta for-a da man.'

For an instant, Denis's mind was flooded with Italian images: his school-friend Angelo's steaming, olive-oil smelling, holy-picture-hung kitchen; the hills outside Florence; the milling crowds in St Peter's Square as the Pontiff lifted his white, omnipotent arm to bless the city and the world.

'Good,' said Charlotte. 'She's terrible to live with,' she added to Denis. 'But she is a good cook.'

'The thing to do,' said Denis, 'is to arrive as she puts the plates on the table. And to leave as she carries them off.'

'Of course, the ideal would be if she started a take-away service.'

'If you've all quite finished being funny,' said Ruth, 'I think we might even start to eat.'

They sat down at the comfortable old table, and Ruth passed the unmatched dinner plates of unmarried couples. Denis, trying not to see Alison's face smiling up at him from the white china surface, wondered whether other people had as many things to juggle in their inmost minds as he had in his own.

'Now, tell me honestly,' he said, turning to Charlotte. 'Is she really chatty in the mornings?'

* * *

'I thank God,' said Mrs Waters, 'that I have a daughter like Kate.'

It had been a birthday of which any Catholic mother would have been proud. Her children had both been there, Kate arriving in time for lunch, Michael soon after it; she had had Mass said at the local convent by her cousin Gerald, who had travelled up from Farm Street specially; and the day had been crowned by a slap-up meal at the Crown Hotel, with her husband (and how good God was to have sent her, in Brendan, a rare Irish-born Irishman who was neither a drunk nor a fool) at her side, and her children and Gerald across the table. And if, later in the night, over the whiskey, voices had been raised between Michael and Brendan, well, men were men and would fight, and she had lain in bed saying her rosary, and thank God Michael had been to early Mass (being old-fashioned, she did not regard Saturday-evening Mass as fulfilling the Sunday obligation) before he had left.

Now here she was, back from the 10.30, sitting in her gleaming living-room, enjoying a drink with her own good friends: Dr Howard, the backbone of the parish pilgrimage to Lourdes; the sweet Misses Flanagan, Irish of course, but like herself, so far back that it didn't count; Joan Precieux; and dear Jack Barry, still indomitably cheerful, with fifty years of ill health keeping him from the priesthood. And, of course, Brendan and Kate.

Mrs Waters laid a hand over her daughter's. 'When I look around,' she continued, 'at some of the other young people you see today, leaving the Church, taking drugs, living in sin, I don't know what . . . well, I just thank God for Kate.'

There was a buzz of approving agreement.

'She is a credit to you, Peggy,' declared Carmel Flanagan.

'Refreshing,' added Dr Howard.

Even Joan Precieux unbent so far as to lean her long, mauve body towards Kate's chair. 'Always hold on to your innocence, my dear,' she whispered. 'It is the single most precious gift you have.'

'Innocence,' sighed Carmel Flanagan. 'It seems to have been thrown out of the window these days.'

'The permissive society,' nodded her sister Patricia.

'I don't know,' said Mrs Waters. 'All this permissiveness. I know Kate finds it very difficult—don't you, Kate?—with all the shocking things that go on. There's so much *talk* around these days, isn't there? I don't see why we have to talk so much. I have a husband and a son and a daughter, and my children both have good jobs and they both still go to Mass. And I never needed to *talk* about anything.'

Jack Barry shook his head. 'I don't know what's happening to young people these days,' he said.

'I blame the changes in the liturgy,' said Mrs Waters.

They settled back over their glasses. It was a familiar theme, and one whose delight was inexhaustible.

'Modern music,' shuddered Joan Precieux.

'Relevant,' mumbled Jack Barry.

'Making the Mass meaningful,' snorted Dr Howard.

'And as for the sign of whatever they call it, the sign of peace . . .'

'All this nonsense about brotherly love . . .'

'I said to Father White, I said, "Listen, Father, I don't come to Mass for brotherly love. I come to Mass to save my soul."'

Dr Howard was an acknowledged card.

Just then, the telephone rang in the hall, and Brendan went to answer it.

'Hello.' His voice drifted through the open door, its dreamy Galway accent by now almost completely obliterated. 'Yes, this is he. Yes, she is, who is this, please? O'Leary? Oh, hello. Yes, no, think nothing of it. I'll get her now.'

He returned to the living-room, a roguish smile on his broad face, and looked straight at Patricia Flanagan. 'Mrs O'Leary from the presbytery. Some entirely indecipherable emergency about the apples for Father White's pie.'

Laughing—because Mrs O'Leary's emergencies were famous in the parish—Patricia Flanagan got up and hurried to the telephone, closing the door behind her. Brendan refilled the glasses, sherry for the women, whiskey for the men, and they all continued with their conversation.

Denis lay in bed, debating whether to go to the 12.15—which meant getting up more or less immediately, but would on the other hand get it over and done with—or to wait for the 5.30—which meant more time in bed, now, but one of Monsignor Van Der Kamp's interminable sermons later on. He was hung over, not much, but enough to make it pleasant to stay between even month-old sheets; but then again, his thoughts did stray so during the Monsignor's sermons, which was dangerous at the best of times, and positively foolhardy at the moment.

He lifted his head experimentally off the pillow. The experiment appeared to be successful. He groaned. He had it badly this time. Practised as he was at shutting off other thoughts, he was generally remarkably adept at not allowing himself to become too seriously attracted to a girl, applying to his thoughts of the entire female sex the distance of centre-fold girls, of women beyond human reach or possibility. It was the only way he could possibly live the life he did, and he was good at it: for sheer survival's sake, he had to be.

Alison, however, now, she was a tricky one. She was so pretty. And her smile was so warm. And blithering idiot that he was, he had actually wanted her to spend the full day with him, at Aylesford, in less than a fortnight, had even shouted unfairly at poor old Maureen simply for forgetting to ask the foolish question for him. . . .

Maureen. He sat up—a bit suddenly, but it was no more than he deserved—remembering how grossly, how unwarrantably unpleasant he had been to her a couple of nights before. Poor old Maureen, he thought, being not too proud to distract himself from his own troubles by means of the troubles of others; he had really come down unnecessarily hard on her. And she'd probably been having a lousy time lately, hating the cold the way she did, and then having to put up with that assinine boyfriend (Denis and Jonathan had met twice, and had both separately assured Maureen that that was twice too often), and all he could do was shout at her because something had slipped her mind. At his friend.

'This must stop,' he said aloud, and not, weakling that he was, a moment too soon. He should have said it two weeks ago, should not have allowed himself even the leeway he had allowed himself, since this was where it had already led him. 'This must stop,' he repeated, and he knew, iron self-disciplinarian as he could be, that it would stop. He had decided so. And he could begin by ringing Maureen, apologising, and asking her out to lunch one day next week.

Wrong. He sat up straighter, scratched at his chin, and groaned again. He could begin by getting out of bed now, shaving, and hot-footing it down to the 12.15 to ask for help. Yet again, he groaned, deeply, satisfyingly—no one after all had ever claimed self-discipline for a noticeably joyful task—threw off the bedclothes, and staggered to the bathroom.

'Let me be slow to do my will,' he sang as he shaved.

'Prompt to obey,
'Help me to mortify my flesh,
'Just for today.'

He sang loudly to drown Alison's voice which made his heart leap so deliciously as it sang in the rushing water: but he knew that, if he put his mind to it, he could soon stop singing altogether.

'I suppose,' said Maureen, carefully laying a large casserole on the small table, 'you've forgotten all about Sunday lunch. I suppose you're used to brunch by the pool with cocktails to match your bikini.'

Alison nodded. 'But your policemen are wonderful.'

'Funny.' She lifted the lid of the casserole, and the room in the dull daylight was filled with a rich, evening-like, Sunday smell of chicken, wine, and garlic. She poked at its contents with a slightly surprised spoon. 'I hope this is OK. It's a rather strange mixture.'

'You always say that. And it's always delicious.'

It usually was: Maureen was a good cook.

'Hmm. Well, *que te aproveche.*'

'So what happened about Jonathan?' asked Alison. 'You seem cheerful enough about it, anyway.'

'Do I? I suppose I am, really.' She reached for the salt-cellar. 'Needs more salt. We—just—you know. It was coming. Funny, I always used to be rotten to him on Sundays, whether I'd been to Mass or not. . . . It was pretty depressing at first. I mean, if you can't get on with Jonathan, who can you get on with? But . . .'

She stopped, and shrugged. She certainly wasn't going to tell Alison about that evening in the pub. What was there to tell, anyway? She could barely articulate to herself what it was that had happened. If she tried to explain it to Alison, she would either think she was mad, or start leaping to conclusions about Daniel.

'But,' she continued, 'I've just got to get on with that, haven't I? To thine own self be true and stuff. And that's OK, you know?' It was OK, too, or if not OK, nearer to it than a week ago she would have ever dreamed possible. She had met a stranger, and she knew now, as she had never thought to know, that in the cosmic sense she was not alone; and if, in her sad bodily self she must stand alone, well, that was the way it must sadly be. She ran her hands down the sturdy denim that encased her thighs. 'The only thing is, I didn't half fancy him, you know . . . I mean, I know that's not everything but it's not nothing, either, is it?'

Alison nodded in sympathy. 'Bloody men.'

'Bloody men. Anyway.' She shook herself, relegating kind and funny Jonathan to her past. 'What about you and Clientman? What's going to happen there?'

'Well, nothing much. What can happen? He's married, and that's the end of that.'

'Is it?'

Alison looked up, sharply. 'Isn't it?'

'*I* dunno, I'm just a poor bog Irish Catholic.'

'What the hell,' said Alison, 'is that supposed to mean?'

'You know. Sanctity of marriage and all that.'

'Oh, for God's sake!' She laid down her fork. Maureen had really gone too far: she always went too far, but this was too far even for her. 'Do you really and truly think that Catholics—and you still don't seem to believe that I am a Catholic. . .'

'Well, you aren't, are you?'

'Whether I am or not, I think you've got a jolly nerve to comment, and what I was trying to say was that Catholics aren't the only bloody people in the world who take marriage seriously.'

'I'm not saying that.'

'Yes, you are. You don't have a copyright on morality, you know.'

There was a silence, while they chewed their chicken.

'Good chicken,' said Alison at last.

'Hmm. I wasn't saying that. I was brought up in a . . . an anachronistic way you couldn't *believe*, and I sure as hell didn't choose it that way, but that's the way it was. And part of this upbringing is that certain . . . precepts are, whether I like it or not, ingrained. And one of them is that, for me, married men, even men with marriages like your Clientman says he's got, are—taboo.'

'Well, for me, too, Miss Sanctity of Marriage! Otherwise. . .'

'Yes, but why? Why is it so very wrong? For you? I mean, it's not as if she's stuck at home with twelve kids, thinking he's God Almighty. If it really is part of the relationship that they have the odd fling, then what the hell's stopping you?'

Alison ground pepper, watching the black specks settle on the amber sauce of the chicken. What the hell was stopping her? They had dined on Wednesday, spoken on Thursday, lunched on Friday, and planned to dine again on Monday. He liked her; she liked him; where was the problem? Was it that Adam had made a bond, a commitment that, lightly as he himself appeared to take it, she could not bring herself to help him break? Was it some atavistic instinct of sexual solidarity with the unknown, beautiful, charming woman he had loved in Paris? Or was it simply that, as every single girl knew, messing with a married man meant, eventually, nothing but trouble?

Or was there at least partly another reason?

'Partly,' she replied, her eyes still fixed on the chicken, 'that, if it happened, it wouldn't, for me, be . . . necessarily . . . just a fling.'

'Aha.'

'I could like him, you know,' she continued. 'I mean, really like him. I mean, it's ridiculously early days yet, and I don't think he's Warren Beatty and Bonnie Prince Charlie rolled into one or anything, but he feels . . . right. I can see . . . this is purely hypothetical of course, but I can see that, in time, there are things about him that would even annoy me, but I can see that they're . . . the right things. The things I could cope with.'

'Oh, boy.'

'Oh, boy is about right. Can I have some more wine?'

'Sure.' She paused. 'Um, this is none of my business or anything . . .'

'But . . .'

'OK, but. But if you do really feel like this . . . and if he's going to go on giving you the pressure he's giving . . .'

'Oh, he's not . . .'

'Come off it. If all this is going on . . . do you really think it's a good idea to carry on with the account?'

'I've thought about that, too,' said Alison. 'And you're probably right, it's not a good idea. I probably should talk to Barry about it, work out some kind of swap with Sally.'

'Sounds sensible.'

'Well, it's the only way, really.'

'So will you do it?'

'No.'

Their eyes met, and they laughed together, the age-old, lewd laugh of women friends.

'Here's to men,' said Maureen, raising her glass. 'Who needs the buggers, anyway?'

They drank and the telephone rang. 'Bugger,' said Maureen. 'Bloody uncivilised time to call. No, don't move. I'm quite good at this.'

With practised ease, she slid past Alison and waded through drifts of discarded Sunday paper into the living-room.

'Hello.'

'Hello?' the voice was unfamiliar. 'Um, may I speak to Maureen, please?'

'You are.'

'Oh, hello.' There was a pause. 'This is Daniel.' Another pause. 'Daniel Greenberg, remember?'

Remember. Maureen felt the warmth begin in the pit of her stomach; she felt it travelling up her body like mercury up a thermometer, until it erupted in her face into a great, cheesy, lolloping, shiny-cheeked grin. For the first time that year she noticed that one valiant ray of sunshine had made its way through the window, and was gleaming on the Andalucian tiles propped on her mantelpiece.

'Oh, hello,' she said. 'Nice to hear you.'

'Yes, it is.' He was nervous, she noted, her grin spreading until her cheeks bunched over her eyes. 'You, I mean, nice to hear you. How've you been?'

'Me?' Come to think of it, she wasn't too confident herself. 'Oh, fine. Well, you know, fine, really. How about you?'

'Me? Er, OK, actually.' He paused. 'Yes, OK.'

'Good.'

There was another pause. It was a dance, she thought, something rather stately and Tudor, with steps forward, steps back, and intricate, sedate twirls to the sounds of viols and recorders, while outside the castle walls noddy lumpkins were tumbling greasy Joans in the new stacked hay, and corn kings and May queens were ducking Mother Demdike for a witch, and . . .

'I was wondering . . .' he began.

Which, of course, was what they were dancing towards.

'Yes?' she said.

'If, that is, you'd . . .' He stopped. 'I enjoyed our talk, you know.'

Step forward, step back. They were the same age, but Maureen was older than him, older than his father, than his grandfather's grandfather. 'Me, too,' she said.

'Good,' he said, and stopped yet again. 'Would you, um, like to get together again next week? Talk some more?'

'Oh.' Step forward. She was young again, his age, back in the dance, and her chest was hot with joy. Smoothly, her voice glided to the correct position, the mixture of surprise and pleasure, up a bit on the surprise, down a bit on the pleasure. 'Oh, that would be nice, yes. When were you thinking?'

'How about Wednesday?'

'Wednesday.' Wednesday was Ash Wednesday, the day of mortality, the fasting, first day of sorrowful Lent. 'Wednesday would be perfect,' she said.

After she put the phone down, she stared at herself for a full minute in the mirror, still grinning, head hanging to one side, tongue protruding idiotically. Then she composed her face and returned to the kitchen.

'Who was that?' said Alison.

'Oh.' She shrugged. 'Just a friend.'

Alison's ears pricked up. 'Just *what* friend?'

'Just a college friend.'

'Called?'

'My God! Daniel. Nobody you know.'

'Mm—hmm. Married?'

'No, he . . . oh, wrap up. Look, I've known him for years and years, and we bumped into each other on Oxford Street, and we're having a drink next week. Happy?'

'And she calls me a fast worker. And not married, either.' She nodded. 'Well done.'

'Will you wrap up?'

'Here's to—how did it go again? Here's to men. Who needs the buggers anyway?'

'Oh, go and . . . Jesus Christ.' The telephone was ringing again. 'That toast has a curse on it.'

'It's probably Warren Beatty for you.'

'Or Bonnie Prince Charlie for you. Look, I know I'm good, but you might just budge up a little bit, OK?'

This time, the voice was sharp, darkly accusing, and richly Irish. 'Have you been to Mass?'

'Aha.' She perched herself precariously on the narrow window-sill. 'Is it yourself, Denis O'Leary, is after saving me soul from the devil, and he coming for it this Laetare Sunday, as well you know, God bless the mark?'

'Ah, 'tis a terrible hussy y'are . . . Hey, Maureen, how's it going?'

'Denis. Well, it's been so long, I really don't know where to begin.'

'No, really, how are things?'

'OK. I mean, the court case comes up on Tuesday, and my blood tests haven't come back yet, but apart from that, fine. How are you?'

'Good. Oh, I'm fine. Listen, I wanted to say sorry about Friday.'

'What about Friday?'

'Well, you know. Shouting at you like that. I, um, had something on my mind.'

'Did you? I'd forgotten.' She almost had: she was so used to people losing their temper with her that much of the time it barely registered. 'Oh, that's OK. Did you really ring up just for that?'

'Yes. Look, I want to . . .'

'*Did* you?'

'*Yes*. And to hear the sweet sound of your dulcet voice, of course. Listen, can I take you to lunch? Next week? To apologise?'

'Can you . . . oh, you great eejit, you don't have to do that.' She was genuinely touched. 'Well, let's meet, anyway. Thursday?'

'OK. Spaghetti House? My treat, though.'

He was a nice guy, she thought, such a nice guy. And what an absurdity it was that he should be sitting at home now alone, while Alison was getting herself tied up with . . . She had an idea. 'Hey, d'you feel like a corny film this afternoon?'

'Do I sound like a corny film? What film?'

'Ha ha ha. Only Alison's here, and we thought we might bugger off to the cinema later on. If we can find something she hasn't been to the Hollywood première of.'

'Oh.' His voice changed. 'I don't think I can make it, you know. Things to do.'

'What things?'

'Oh . . . laundry and stuff.'

'That doesn't sound much fun.'

'No, but society tends to encourage it. Well, I'll see you on Thursday, shall I?'

'OK. Hey, Denis. Thanks for ringing, that was really sweet.'

'Oh, shucks. See you.'

'Well?' said Alison when she returned. 'Which was it, Bonnie or Clyde?'

'You've been working on that. Actually, it was Denis. He rang to say sorry for ticking me off on Friday. Wasn't that sweet?'

'Did he? Oh, that was nice, yes.'

'He's a nice guy, Denis.'

'Yes, he seems it.'

And he's not married either, thought Maureen, but of course, you couldn't say that sort of thing.

It wasn't the passion that made the marriage, Anne decided. It was the quiet times like this, when they curled—rather, she curled, he sprawled—on the sofa, two bodies in perfect harmony one with the familiar other, lightly leaning together in the sweet torpor of a Sunday afternoon, while a half-watched spy film flickered an endless succession of short-barrelled guns and long-legged women on the television screen in front of them.

'Would you like to be a spy?' she asked her husband idly.

'Love it,' he replied. 'All those beautiful women. Ow!'

She had pinched him, hard, on the leg.

'What was that for?'

'Just testing your pain resistance. It's not very high, is it? ... Stephen?'

'Hmm?'

'You know what we were talking about on Friday night? Trust? Would you trust me—whatever?'

'Anne! What a question!'

'No, really.' She pulled away from him slightly to look him in the eye. 'Suppose I ... suppose I really wanted to do something you really didn't want me to do?'

He shook his head, his eyes blank.

'I can't imagine that.'

'Well, just suppose.'

'I don't want to suppose.'

'Well, I do.'

So, of course, they supposed.

'Suppose I wanted to paint the bedroom purple and orange? What would you say?'

'Well, if it meant an awful lot to you, I suppose I'd have to say yes, wouldn't I?'

'I see. And suppose I found a boyfriend, and wanted to move him into the spare-room . . .'

'Anne!'

'Well, what would you say?'

'Well, you wouldn't, would you?'

'Aha! And I suppose you think I would paint the bedroom purple and orange?'

'Well.' He scratched at his beard, delighted and exasperated. 'What's this all about, anyway?'

'Just wondering.' She dropped her head back onto his shoulder. 'Just wondering.'

'Well, don't. You don't have to wonder about me. You know that, don't you?'

'Yes,' she said after a moment. 'I know that.'

The doorbell rang, and they looked at each other in dismay.

'Maybe I can make whoever it is go away,' said Stephen, getting up.

'Growl at them.'

'Grrr.'

But she knew before he opened the door, before she heard the now familiar voice that was like and yet not like Stephen's, that it was Brian, and that he would not go away.

'Oh,' said Stephen. 'It's you.'

''Allo. Been to Woodford again, 'aven't I?' Brian stepped past Stephen into the living-room. 'Hallo, Anne.'

'You've met my wife, have you?' said Stephen. 'Oh, of course —she's your tea-time pit stop, isn't she?'

'Stephen!' said Anne. 'Hello, Brian, it's nice to see you.'

'So that's why you married him,' said Brian. 'His irresistible charm.'

On balance, Anne decided not to laugh: polite or rude, her loyalty lay with Stephen.

Brian dropped into a chair, never imagining that anyone might not be delighted to see him.

'Indulging in a little intellectual entertainment, I see,' he said, nodding at the television screen.

'We're very intellectual people,' said Stephen.

'It's a good film, actually. I like him. Terrible actor, but a very nice chap.'

'Do you know him?' said Anne.

'Brian knows everyone,' said Stephen.

There was a pause.

'I went to Basingstoke the other day,' said Brian. 'Love sent all round. You,' he pointed at Anne, not so much imitating as becoming his mother, 'are a sweet girl and a good little wife. And you,' his finger swung to Stephen, 'should be down on your knees every night thanking God for the blessing he's given you.'

Anne laughed and even Stephen smiled.

'Let's go for a walk,' said Anne.

'Walk?' Brian frowned.

'Yes, you put one foot in front of the other, and go all sorts of places. Stephen and I do it all the time. Come on, we'll show you the park.'

'The park?'

'P-a-r-k.' She turned to Stephen, who was no longer smiling. 'Tell me, were you two brought up on the same planet?'

'I sometimes wonder,' said Stephen, but he unwound himself anyway, and stood up. 'Come on, mate, we'll show you the park.'

Together, they set off down the road, the two tall men with the short girl between them. It was pleasant for March; there was even a hint of warmth in the air.

'You should have brought the redhead,' said Anne.

'You'd be lucky,' said Stephen. 'You never get to meet Brian's girlfriends.'

Unexpectedly, Brian seemed hurt. 'Well, I never met any of yours.'

Stephen squeezed Anne's hand. 'I only really had one.'

It was a pleasant park, well-kept with wide paths between orderly flower-beds, and a tiny local museum in the restored Elizabethan manor-house.

'Well, this is rather nice,' said Brian, as they strolled around the redundant sundial and through the Garden for the Blind.

'It's hardly Hampstead Heath,' snapped Stephen.

'Actually, Hampstead Heath gives me the creeps. All that nature. I like a park to be a park. Remember playing cricket in the park when we were kids?'

'Yes. You never let me bat.'

'Well, I was bigger than you then. Anne, if you have children, always warn the first that the second might be bigger than him one day, because . . . hey!'

A football flew past him, narrowly missing him. Stephen caught it and bounced it until two boys, fair haired, spectacled, and identical but for a couple of years in age, ran to claim it.

'Can we have my ball?' said the elder.

'*My* ball,' said the younger.

'*My* ball. It was my birthday present.'

'You kicked it offside. That makes it mine.'

'But if somebody picks it up, that makes it a new game, and it's my ball.'

'I'll tell you what,' said Stephen. 'I'll throw it at that tree over there, and whoever gets it, keeps it, OK? On your marks—get set—go!'

The two boys ran after their ball, the younger marginally ahead.

'I don't care if he gets it,' said Stephen. 'He'll never get to keep it.'

'Well, that's my point,' said Brian. 'In just ten years, he'll be twice his brother's size, and then watch out, brother.'

'Serve 'im bleedin' well right, then, won't it?' said Stephen.

They wandered amiably enough around the duck pond, past the bandstand, and sat on a bench to watch the ducks.

'Remember Miss Holly?' said Stephen suddenly.

'The Duck Lady? God, yes.'

'She lived at the bottom of the road,' Stephen told Anne, 'and she was always taking us to the pond to see the ducks. I mean, always. Whether we wanted to or not. We used to dread walking past her house because she'd pounce on us and carry us off.'

'Would you like,' Brian bent down, baring his teeth, maniacally, 'to come and see the duckies? Nice duckies? You *would* like to come and see the duckies, *wouldn't* you?'

'The woman was mad,' agreed Stephen. 'Mum always made us go with her or we'd hurt her feelings. I mean, bugger our feelings. I never got out of going; did you, Brian?'

'You're kidding. I think Moira did, once. Now you mention it, I think that's when Mum started calling her Your Ladyship.'

'They're all the same, aren't they?' said Anne. 'Parents. You do one thing once, and a label's hung round your neck for ever. My sister Claire, for instance. She ... she was a very good little girl, really. Except that one day, she said a rude word.'

Brian whistled. 'Rude word, eh?'

'Something scandalous, like blast. Anyway, for ever after that, every time she opened her mouth . . .'

'Excuse me.'

A teenaged girl was standing in front of them, pink of face, and grey of tooth. Anne stopped speaking. The girl looked at Brian.

'You're him, aren't you?'

'I beg your pardon?'

'Him from the telly. Detective Bunney.'

'Oh, him.' Barely perceptibly, Brian sat straighter on the hard bench, and barely perceptibly, his voice deepened. 'Yes, I suppose I am.'

From a plastic handbag, the girl produced a grubby slip of paper. 'Could I have your autograph? For my friend Valerie?'

'For Valerie? Yes, of course.' He rummaged in his coat pocket, and turned on Anne a brilliant, unseeing smile. 'Do you have a pen I could borrow? I'm always losing mine,' he confided to the girl, whose face turned from pink to beetroot.

'Valerie thinks you're smashing,' she blurted.

'Does she? Well, that's nice. Tell her I think she's probably quite smashing, herself, OK? There you go. To Valerie, with love. Come here.'

By now speechless, the girl approached. He kissed her lightly on both cheeks. 'For Valerie—and for you. You take care, now, won't you?'

The girl croaked something which might have been an affirmative, and ran off, clutching the paper, to the telephone-box by the park entrance. Brian watched her, his smile fading.

'Bloody typical,' he said, as almost out of view she reached the box and scrambled inside. 'Bloody typical. You slog your guts out trying to be a good actor and nobody knows you from Adam. And you do a couple of guest shots on a crummy cop show to help pay the rent, and bingo. Fame.'

'I thought it was all rather sweet,' said Anne.

'Oh, yeah, yeah, it's sweet. Sweet. It's just that . . .' He picked a stone from under the bench and tossed it in the pond, watching the ripples spread in the brown water. 'Oh, well. Sorry about that, folks, it's what you get for going out with a professional show-off.'

'Anne was speaking,' said Stephen.

'What?'

'I said,' repeated Stephen, 'that Anne was speaking.'

'Was she? Oh, yes, of course, sorry. Sorry, Anne, what were you saying?'

'I can't remember,' said Anne.

'You were telling us about your sister Claire,' said Stephen.

'Was I? Well, it can't have been anything very interesting because it's gone now. But talking of sisters, I must mention you to Michelle, Brian. She's always up on the latest heart-throbs.'

'I don't want to be a heart-throb,' said Brian.

'Like hell you don't,' said Stephen. 'Let's go home, it's getting cold.'

In near silence, they walked back through the park, and down the quiet street to the flat. Brian hovered at the entrance.

'You're coming up for tea, aren't you?' said Anne, and received an elbow in the ribs from Stephen.

'Thank you, Anne,' said Brian. 'That would be very nice.'

Still in silence, they trooped up the steps and into the flat. Stephen picked up a piece of the Sunday paper and immersed himself in it, while Brian wandered to the bookshelves and stared aimlessly. Their quiet reached into the kitchen and washed over Anne like an icy shower as she boiled the water for the tea.

'No song, then?' said Brian, when she returned with a trayful of tea things.

'Didn't I?' She had not realised, that she, too, had been quiet.

'She's not a bloody gramophone,' said Stephen from his paper.

'Your wife,' said Brian, 'has a fabulous voice, you know. Truly fabulous.'

'I know,' said Stephen, still from the paper.

'And I still say that it's a, a crime that she doesn't at least try to do something with it. Share it with people.'

Stephen laid down the paper, and looked his brother in the eye. 'What,' he said, 'and get like you?'

'Well, would that be so very terrible?'

'Yes.'

'Oh, sod you.' Brian stood up and reached for his coat. 'Rude little bugger. I've been trying to be pleasant all afternoon, and you can't even . . . Goodbye, Anne. It was nice seeing you.'

He swung out, slamming the door behind him.

'Well, you weren't very nice,' said Anne.

'Tough.'

'But you're not like that with anyone else.'

'No one else is Brian.'

'He was being OK.'

'OK! Barging in like that with no warning and no invitation. He'd go mad if we did that to him.'

'We weren't doing anything special.'

'And being rude to you like that.'

'What?'

'Oh, don't tell me you didn't notice. We were talking away for hours about our family, and then the very minute you start to talk about yours, there's an interruption.'

'Well, he couldn't help that.'

'No, you'll find he never can. But you'll notice, if you hang around him long enough, that you find out an awful lot about Brian, and yet the instant the . . . the *spotlight* is off him, something mysteriously happens to swing it back on him again.'

He stopped, scowling. Looking at him, Anne remembered suddenly his once telling her that as children, he and Brian had been very close.

'Well,' she said, going over to sit next to him. 'He's gone now. And if anyone else rings at the door, we just won't answer, OK?'

'OK,' he said.

'No worst, there is none.' The dreary week long, Hopkins' words had been echoing in her head, scratching at her brain like an itchy sweater worn too long. Hopkins, who had hailed the spring in dappled Oxford quadrangles and wild wet Wales and the gardens outside Farm Street, had also known that, also hailed that. 'Pitched past pitch of grief, more pangs will, schooled at forepangs, wilder wring.' No worst, there was none.

It was unfair, cried out the core of her being, unfair. She had been good, been faithful, tried so hard. She had done all of the right things, and none of the wrong. She had been to Mass, rain, snow, or shine, good temper, bad temper, or period pains, on Sundays, on feast-days, on days in between. She had been to Lourdes, she had been to Rome, she had been on retreat. She had been a good Catholic, in fair weather, and foul, she had asked for so little reward, and had received, as it turned out, no reward at all.

And now here came Alison, lovely and laughing, who had taken from the Church precisely what she had wanted to take, and had given back not one iota of what was not convenient for her to give, and what was Alison's reward? The whole world, it seemed, and, on top of the world, to which she was welcome, the one thing that Kate herself wanted. Denis. Unfair.

And what was most unfair of all was Denis himself. Because Denis was not like Alison, one of the spoiled, the spectacular. He was like Kate herself, a good and faithful servant, the prodigal's dull brother, a labourer in the vineyard since dawn. They were two of a kind, she and Denis, they spoke the same language, they walked the same road. And he could not even remember whether or not he had spoken to her on the telephone.

Unfair, cried Kate's soul, as she saw herself with nightmarish clarity as she was, and ever would be, a good woman as the Misses Flanagan were good women, a woman with no love or joy, with nothing but good works, a clear conscience, and the Church.

The Church: that was the common denominator. Somehow, Kate realised, it all led back to the Church, why she was the way she was, and the Misses Flanagan were as they were, and why Michael drank so unhappily and so much, and said those terrible things to their father every time they met. So many things that were wrong, all wrong, and they all, she saw suddenly, vividly, led back to the Church.

Yet the Church was a good thing, that was a given. It had produced St Francis, and Mother Teresa, and you didn't, as Dr Howard was fond of pointing out, find too many humanists running leper colonies. And it had produced her. And if the Church could take such great and glorious credit for its successes, then surely, in justice, it must accept some responsibility for poor, lost Kate as well?

Sitting on a wooden bench in Bedford Square, she closed her eyes against the ineffectual midday sunshine, and tried to remember the Sermon on the Mount. Blessed are the meek; blessed are the pure of heart; blessed are the peacemakers; blessed are those who mourn. But was she blessed? She was meek, surely; she was, yes, even her pitiless Catholic conscience reluctantly conceded that she was, on the whole, at least reasonably pure of heart; she had tried at the weekend to be a peacemaker, and even—since Michael had finally agreed to go to Mass on Sunday—succeeded; and God knew, God knew, she mourned. She had kept all the rules, and where was she left? Sitting solitary on a bench, feeling her soul turn pinched and sickly inside her with envy of one who—whatever her other attributes—was surely not meek, and surely did not mourn. Alison, who broke the rules, was blessed, not she. It was wrong, her soul shrieked. Wrong.

The Church was wrong. Kate opened her eyes, clutched her handbag, and stroked the splintering warped wood of the bench beneath her as, all in a flash, a familiar country turned into a terrifyingly alien land, with speech and customs that were unaccountable, foreign. The Church was wrong. Yet the Church could not be wrong, it was your Mother. It was your mother's Mother; it lay upon and around you with two weighty millenia of maternity, of love, of nourishment, of knowing what was best. To think the Church was wrong was the way madness lay: worse than madness, annihilation. Because if the man who married your mother was not your father, then you were someone other than you had thought. But if the woman who carried you in her womb was not your mother, then who, and what, and whence, and whither, and *why* were you?

Lost, lost in the darkness by stormy winds driven, her mind groped for the familiar, the comprehensible. Confession? The monthly rota of mumbled sins, in a list barely changed since childhood, a bored absolution, and prayers for penance—how could that help her now? But there was more to be had from confession for those who needed it; for all of her life she had known that, when she was truly in need, it would be there, like a fairy-tale gift whose magic powers became effective only when all human resource was exhausted.

But was she, truly, in need? The comfort of confession was repentance: she had surely not sinned to deserve that solace. Into her head ran Sister Benedict's words, echoing from a far-off rainy summer. 'Confession is for souls in trouble. For those who would otherwise despair of God's forgiveness.' Selfish, then, surely of her to take up the priest's time with her own small doubts when possibly behind her in line was a mortal sinner, was someone who was, truly, in need?

Selfish—or merely needy? Kate was not, unless doubts were a sin, a grievous sinner, but she was most surely in need. In need of the quiet of the dark box, of the priest, anonymous and unshockable behind the grille, in need of someone to explain—as priests surely explained a dozen, a hundred times a week—why she was feeling what she was feeling about the Church, and the world, and herself. The good and faithful servant was in need. She would go to confession.

Kate stood up, straightened her skirt, and with uncharacteristically determined step, made her way down Tottenham Court Road, in this world that was suddenly enemy terrain, to St Patrick's, Soho Square.

'Bless me, Father, for I have sinned.'

There was silence from beyond the grille. How many times had she said those words? Two hundred? More? But that was the routine opening, that was for ordinary confessions. It did not matter today how long it had been since her last confession, how many uncharitable thoughts she had had, how often her attention had wandered during Mass. She drew in her breath, and abandoned the routine words.

'Father, I'm finding it very difficult to be a Catholic, and still live in the modern world.'

There was more silence. Kate hurried on, saying, here where anything could be said, things she had never thought she would ever say.

'I mean, I love the Church, and I do, I do want to stay with it, but it's so difficult! I know so many people who were brought up Catholic, my school-friends, my, my cousins, all sorts of people, and almost all of them have left, and I—I can see why.'

Still beyond the grille was silence.

'I can see why, because the demands the Church makes are—yes, they are, some of them—unreasonable, and I don't want to leave, Father, but I don't see why I should be the only one to stay, and I'm all mixed up, and I don't know what to do.'

At last, the voice came. It was the voice of authority—of a deeply offended authority.

'If that is how you feel about the Church, then you do not have an obligation to be a Catholic. You can be something else, if you choose.'

It was as if her mother had, without anger, spat in her face.

'The Church, you know, was never meant to be easy.'

'But it must be possible, Father, surely.'

'As, indeed, it is.'

'But for who? Father, most people I know . . .'

'That depends on which sort of people you know. Now, I don't know what sort of circles you move in. But in some parts of Ireland, regular Mass is attended by ninety-five per cent of the population.'

'But not here. Not here, Father. Here . . . well, I sometimes feel that the only people left in the Church are . . . I don't know . . . freaks . . .'

'Indeed! I would not consider myself to be a freak.'

'Oh, no! I didn't mean . . .'

'Listen to me, my child. Look into your soul. I think you will find that what you're saying is a camouflage for some . . . sin you would like to commit, some deed that you know, deep down, is only wrong.'

'No, Father. Honestly, no.'

'Honestly. Try to *be* honest. Try a little harder to look for the root of the problem.'

'Father, that *is* . . .'

'And talk to your parish priest at home. People should talk more to their priests, they are quite accessible, you know. Now go in peace, and pray for me.'

'Thank you, Father.'

Kate left the confessional box, left the church, and crossed to sit in Soho Square. She sat and stared at the first blazing tulips in the square, at the office workers sharing sandwiches from greaseproof paper bags, and the pigeons squabbling over the crumbs at their feet, and knew herself to be alone, not only in this world, but the next.

Father Bob's thumb sketched the cross in holy ashes on the foreheads of the congregation of Midday Mass. 'Remember,' warned his voice, to each one who approached the altar, 'that thou art but dust, and unto dust thou shalt return.'

'OK,' ran his thoughts. 'I surrender, Uncle. It's not getting any easier, You know that, don't You?'

He dipped his thumb again into the ashes. 'Remember,' he told the shrivelled old woman, who looked as if she needed no reminding, 'that thou art but dust, and unto dust thou shalt return.'

'I agree,' he added, 'that I was getting a big smug. I admit that, when I said bring on the heavy guns, that was a whacking dollop of spiritual pride right there. But, You know, I'm not proud any more, I promise You I'm not.'

'Remember,' he told Geoffrey Johnson (who surely usually went to the Cathedral?), lifting his arm from the old woman's wrinkled forehead to Geoffrey's lofty brow, 'that thou art but dust, and unto dust thou shalt return.'

'I know what You're going to say,' he thought. 'You're going to say it's good for me. No pain, no gain, right? I know—well, You know I know—that in that case, I'm probably earning myself great massive mansions in heaven for this.'

'Remember,' he told the burly labourer, who stood with work-calloused hands reverently crossed, 'that thou art but dust, and unto dust thou shalt return.'

'But, You know, I'd swap, I really would, for a medium-sized mansion then, and you to take this away, now.'

Behind the labourer was a young blonde girl, younger than Alison, a student, or possibly—she could be German, or Dutch—an au pair. Her forehead was smooth, cool, and moist without dampness. To get to it, he had to push aside her hair with the joint of his thumb: it was heavy and silky, and as it moved, it caught the light of the sanctuary lamp behind him in glints of sunshine-yellow gold. He had never touched Alison's hair.

'Remember,' he told her, 'that thou art but dust, and unto dust thou shalt return.'

'Abba, Father,' he thought, 'You have the power to do all things. Take this cup away from me. But let it be as Thou would have it, not as I.'

How else, anyway, could it ever be?

Denis would have to be watched where Alison was concerned. Not, obviously, that he was in any sense a threat, a shrimp of a chap like that, all nervous twitches and embarrassing jokes, and generally looking as if he were still going through his own personal potato famine. No competition, then, for Geoffrey, one of Alysoun's kind, a compatriot, fashioned from the clay which had fashioned the bowmen at Agincourt and Crécy, while Denis's forefathers had been running half-naked through the bogs murdering each other. No, he was a nice enough chap, was Denis, but no competition at all. All the same, he would have to be watched.

Geoffrey had not, for instance, phoned him all week. He had been tempted to a couple of times, in fact on Monday had almost given in to the temptation, but so far had resisted, and was glad of it. Denis would probably be wondering what was up, but that was just too bad. Two men could not be friends and rivals at the same time, and if Denis must lose a friend, well, that was the way it must be. The right thing was not always the most pleasant thing: but it was what must be done nevertheless.

It was 2.30 in the afternoon, the Speaker was about to enter the Commons, and Parliament was stirring slowly into its post-luncheon life. Geoffrey, his head swept clean by a walk through London made more invigorating by the awareness of curious eyes on his ash-marked forehead, was sitting at his desk, half reading Hansard, and occasionally glancing in vague suspicion at Nigel and Sue, who even at this hour, were sitting at their own desk, ostentatiously sober, and ostentatiously diligent. Something appeared to be up, and if the disgruntled expression on Nigel's face and the self-satisfied twist to Sue's prim little mouth were anything to go by, whatever it was was Sue's doing. Perhaps Francis's talks were having some effect on her at last: there had, now he thought of it, been more of them than usual lately, and he had even caught her a couple of times coming out of the inner office looking really quite upset. He looked at her, savouring the distaste that still lingered from the memory of that extraordinary exhibition outside the House last week, and since he had worked hard all morning, he allowed himself a short indulgence in what was becoming a favourite pastime of comparing her unfavourably with Alysoun.

She looked up and caught his eyes on her. 'You've got a smudge on your forehead,' she said.

'Those,' he replied with dignity, 'are my ashes.'

Sue looked at Nigel, and they exchanged shrugs.

'I think he's flipped,' she said.

'Driven mad by your beauty,' he suggested.

Beauty, maddening beauty.

'It's not *your* beauty,' Geoffrey could not resist telling Sue.

But she did not appear to hear him. The manner of both of them was uneasy, almost abstracted, as if they were waiting for something to happen that might or might not be momentous.

All that did happen, however, was the arrival of Francis, blustering in like the March wind outside, to stand in the middle of the room and survey them down the length of his ugly, distinguished nose.

'Well, well, well,' he observed. 'Barely the middle of the afternoon, and everyone's back from lunch. Let's see: Simmonds; the very lovely Miss Townsend; and, yes, of course, Johnson.' His eyes flickered towards Geoffrey, and Geoffrey saw that he registered, although he did not comment on it, the ashes. He himself was wearing none. 'All here, and all at least pretending to work. This must indeed be a red-letter day.'

'As you see, Francis,' said Sue meaningfully, 'we are all here.'

'Indeed you are, my dear. All here, and apparently all there, too.' He chuckled heartily at a joke of his own. 'And what a coincidence that you should be here today of all days, because it is today that I happen to have another letter to deliver to our very good friend, Mrs Margaret Bellweather. Now, which of you three is going to take it to her, h'm?'

So that was what was up. Geoffrey shook his head at the pettiness of the intrigue, and out of the corner of his eye saw Sue stare hard at Nigel.

'I will,' said Nigel.

'You will indeed,' said Francis. 'But the question is, shall you?'

Nigel shrugged.

'I think he should,' said Sue.

'Certainly someone must,' agreed Francis. 'But I was thinking perhaps Geoffrey . . .'

'Perhaps Geoffrey's busy.'

'*Perhaps* Geoffrey can speak for himself!'

Since it was, after all, Ash Wednesday, Geoffrey tried not to derive too much satisfaction from Sue's wince at the party leader's tone.

With elaborate courtesy, Francis turned to him.

'*Are* you busy this afternoon, Johnson?'

'Not particularly.'

'Then would you, when you have a moment, care to step into my office? I have a small errand I would like you to run.'

He swept out, and Geoffrey swept in his wake, past the careful indifference of Nigel and the open fury of Sue. It was stooping to their level fully to enjoy the moment. But briefly, Geoffrey stooped.

'Oh, it's you,' said Margaret Bellweather. She was clearly in a bad mood, and seemed surprised to see him.

'Didn't Francis warn you?'

'Yes, but I thought he said you . . . Well, never mind, you're here now. Well, what are you gawping at?' She turned to the poxy secretary, more squashed and Giles-like than ever in the tentative sunlight. 'Get to your work, girl.'

Once again, the secretary got.

'No gin today, I'm afraid,' muttered Margaret Bellweather, ill-temperedly tapping her stick on the floor. 'Not what it was, though. Ash Wednesday. Don't suppose you'd remember it in Latin, hmm?' She sketched a cross in the air with her thumb. '"*Memento, homo, quia pulvis es, et in pulverem reverteris.*" Sent shivers down your spine. . . . Well, as the nuns used to say, *tout passe, tout casse, toute lasse.*' She grunted, and settled herself back in the chair, seeming this time much older than the last. Suddenly, she squinted up at him from under her brows. 'Francis going to make a habit of using you as his messenger?'

Geoffrey was taken aback. He had thought she liked him. After all, she had shown him the Fra Angelico, hadn't she?

She must have read his face, because her own changed. 'Don't mind me, Mr Johnson, I'm a cranky old stick today. Change in the air, you know. And a bit of withdrawal symptoms too, probably. And you see, the last time you came, I thought . . . I thought it was just the once.' She looked straight at him, her eyes beady. 'A word about Francis. He's vague, you see, always was. Clever. But vague. He starts to use you as an errand-boy, he'll think that's what you really are. You get on with your own work, don't let him push you around. Hmm? 'Nuff said. Did you bring my letter?'

Astonished, Geoffrey handed over the package. She took it without thanks. 'Well, run along, Mr Johnson, run along. Back to your own office, do your own work.' She turned towards the office, and raised her voice. 'Don't want to end up like Matilda, nothing to do but sneak around, eavesdropping on other people's conversations.'

Poor old thing, thought Geoffrey, striding down the stately street towards the river. Awful to be old, to turn crotchety with the change of seasons, to get eccentric, unshakeable notions about people and situations, to feel your body and mind failing and know they would never rally. To know you would never again fall in love, as he was in love, and look up at the blue sky, even on this day of death with the mark of his own mortality dark on his forehead, and thank God who had made the spring, and the daffodils, and the first bird's song, and Alysoun.

Denis chewed his cheese sandwich slowly and with meticulous care; even so, it was depressingly soon gone. He had had his main meal at lunch-time, but since the reason for that lunch was to interview a local councillor who was, it transpired, willing to talk about anything in the world but the local council, he had been unable to do the meal full justice. However, a meal it had been, and left him, therefore, with only a collation to fill in this long, hungry evening.

'Welcome to Lent, pal,' he muttered, picking sliced white bread-crumbs from his plate with a wet finger. He planned a busy Lent, with daily Mass, Stations every Friday, and possibly trying to do without the Mars Bar that had lately become an integral part of his journey home from work. He stared into the electric fire for a while thinking about it, then stood up and raised a rakish eyebrow into the dim mirror above the fireplace. 'You sophisticated devil,' he told himself. 'Giving up sweets for Lent.'

He sat down again. The important thing, of course, was to keep busy. To keep very, very busy. Maybe he should look in at the children's home, see if they wanted any work done, anything built or mended. The nuns were always grateful enough, God knew, for a handyman.

It was a good idea. He'd give them a ring tomorrow, before he met Maureen. That should keep him busy.

Daniel finished his drink and looked at his watch, a matter of form since it had stopped several hours earlier. 'Fancy an Indian?' he said.

'Fine.' Maureen realised with surprise that she had not even realised she was hungry. 'Of course,' she added, while they struggled into their coats, 'officially speaking, I'm fasting.'

He snorted: she had already explained the Church's fasting rules to him. 'You call what *you* do, fasting?'

'*I* don't do it.'

As they left the pub and made their way through the lonely back streets to Charlotte Street, she half thought he might put his arm around her, but he did not. Which was just as well, because it seemed they both needed both hands for talking, anyway.

Anne shook the chips in one pan, and threw fish into the other, watching the hot butter sizzle. 'Just think,' she said, 'last Ash Wednesday, we'd barely met.'

'And now, here we are,' said Stephen. Under his fading ashes, his eyes kindled. 'Together. For ever.'

'For ever,' repeated Anne.

'No sign of Brian, then?' asked Stephen after a moment.

'I think you scared him away.'

'Good.'

'Brotherly love. Well, what did you decide on, beer or puddings?'

'I thought I might do something positive instead of just giving up. Weekday Mass. Read the Bible. Catholics don't read the Bible enough.'

'Well, it's still sugar for me.' She patted her spreading stomach. 'I'm getting as fat as a pig.'

'You're beautiful,' said Stephen.

High above Archway Road, Geoffrey speared the last piece of boil-in-the-bag cod onto the last frozen sprout, and sat back with a grunt of satisfaction. The necessary interruption of eating now over, the rest of the evening was his own, to do with as he chose. And this evening, as last evening and the evening before that, his very first choice was simply to sit and think long and unwavering thoughts about Alison.

Alison, Alysoun. What was she doing now, as he thought of her? He saw her, perhaps, sitting sadly, like a Pre-Raphaelite beauty, staring into a sorrow that no one could understand. Or perhaps busy with some deliciously mundane task, shelling peas, or stitching a hem onto something that was blue and cool.

Perhaps, perhaps: what did it matter in the end what she was doing? What mattered was that she *was*, was part of the world, part now, like Francis and the Party and the Church, of his life. And she was going to Aylesford with them. She would travel with them, gracing their raggle-taggle group as the Abbess had graced the Canterbury pilgrims, and he would see her, it occurred to him, for the first time in the daylight, with the soft Kent sun on her hair, and under her feet myriad flowers of early spring thrusting through the damp earth.

He picked up his plate, his knife and fork, carried them to the sink, washed up, and cleaned the kitchen table. Then he went through into his bare tidy sitting-room, sat down on the not-particularly-comfortable armchair his mother had given him when he had left home, closed his ears to the roaring traffic below, and continued to wonder what Alison was doing.

'Well, I think,' said Alison, finishing with heroic effort the very last scrap of her red mullet, 'that we've done jolly well. We actually managed to talk about the account.'

'And it's only our fourth meeting,' he agreed. 'I think it calls for a celebration. Some wickedly luxurious dessert.'

'I couldn't possibly.'

'They have fresh strawberries.'

'Oh, well, in that case.'

'It's strange, isn't it?' she added when the strawberries arrived. 'In Los Angeles, they have strawberries all the year round, but they didn't mean a thing to me there. Whereas here, they're a real treat. I think it's that they're so rare that makes them a bit special.'

She looked up, and caught his eye.

'I said nothing,' he protested.

Bob had known that the night would come, but that did not make it any the more welcome when it did. He said good-night to Father O'Dowd at the usual hour, climbed the narrow stairs to his bedroom, and, slowly and with relentless unsleepiness, prepared himself for bed. He took his clothes off and hung them in the old-fashioned wardrobe, carefully resisting the temptation to check himself in the spotted mirror for further signs of ageing. He averted his eye, too, from the mirror over the wash-basin while he was brushing his teeth, but as he climbed into his pyjamas could not help pinching his stomach for signs of flab. He was not sure that he liked what he felt, and wondered briefly whether he should take up jogging himself. Then he said his prayers, switched off the overhead light, and got into bed.

He picked up Thomas Merton from his bedside table, but did not open it. 'Not making it easy, are You?' he commented. Keeping in shape was one thing, but even Father Joe hadn't jogged twenty-four hours a day. Then he shrugged. 'I suppose You know best.'

He decided to give Thomas Merton a miss, turned off the bedside lamp, and lay down for the long night's struggle.

The flat was so small that, even though Caroline and her naval lieutenant were talking in whispers, their voices carried through from the sitting-room and straight into Kate's bedroom.

'I tell you,' said Caroline, 'something's wrong.'

'Nothing's wrong. She said she was fine.'

'She didn't look fine.'

'She never does.'

'Well, I'm going to check. Look . . .' and the whispers died from earshot until Kate heard a groan, soft but unmistakable, from the naval lieutenant.

'Just this once,' whispered Caroline.

Three seconds later there was a knock on the door, and Caroline's face peered through. 'You all right, Kate?'

'Yes, I told you. I'm fine.'

'You sure?'

'Well, I have a headache, that's all.'

'Oh. Listen, Richard and I thought we'd go to the pub. D'you feel like coming?'

'No. No, thank you. I think I'll go to bed. I'm fine, really.'

'Well, OK. Shout if you want something.'

The door closed. Richard said something that Kate did not catch.

'That's a shocking thing to say,' said Caroline, but she sounded amused as well as shocked.

'I must say,' said Maureen, expertly twirling a hefty forkful of spaghetti, 'this is really very nice of you.'

'I'm a really very nice person,' Denis told her.

'No, I mean it. People are always shouting at me, and they hardly ever apologise at all.'

'That's because you're such a holy terror.'

'Probably.'

For a few moments, they concentrated in companionable silence on their spaghetti.

'So how's life?' said Denis at last.

'Oh, good.' She thought about it, and felt the little spark of warmth that had been lurking inside her all morning grow and spread. 'Life's *good*.'

'Sounds interesting.'

'Could be.' She gulped at her inky red wine. Maybe half-way down the carafe, she'd start to tell him about Daniel; but not yet. Instead, she heaped extra Parmesan cheese onto her plate, and smiled a smile that tried not to be enigmatic. 'Could be.'

'How's Jonathan?'

'Jonathan?' She was startled at how little the question upset her. For so many months, he had been so vivid a part of her present; in just a week, he had already faded almost to the sepia-coloured past. 'Didn't I tell you? We split up.'

'*What?*'

'Yes. Oh, it was coming, everybody kept saying, even we kept saying, it was coming, and it came. He was awfully . . . Protestant, you know.'

Denis frowned. 'He probably still is.'

'Chances are good. And you're right, he wasn't Protestant. I was Catholic.'

'Ah, I told ye. What you need is a decent Irish b'y.'

'Absolutely.' Laughing, hugging her secret, she poured more wine. 'That's exactly what I need. Anyway, we sort of made it official a week ago yesterday. *Finito.* You know?'

Denis laid down his fork. '*What?*' he repeated.

'What?'

'It happened last week?'

'Yes.'

It had happened last week. It had happened and he had not known, not noticed, had snapped at her even—he being so selfishly wrapped in his own flirtation with the impossible—had been unfriendly at a time when more than any other she needed friends. It just showed. It just showed.

'Listen, I'm *sorry* about Friday. Jesus, if I'd had any idea . . .'

'Denis.' It was pleasant to be so considered, but enough, Maureen felt, was enough. 'I don't know if you'd noticed and all, but I don't actually shatter into a thousand tiny fragments every time someone shouts at me.'

'No, that's not the point.' She did not understand, could not possibly understand what had happened to him on Friday, what, if he relaxed his control for one second, might happen to him again and again and again. 'You don't understand,' he said.

'OK.' Maureen shrugged. So much for his consideration, then. She decided to make trouble. 'Well, she agreed to come, anyway.'

'Who?'

'Who! Alison.'

'Did she?' He had taken too large a forkful of spaghetti, and bent his head to untangle it. 'Yes, so she did. Hell, I forgot to go crucifix shopping.'

Maureen watched him with interest. 'Can I ask you a question?' she asked his crown.

'Do you have to?'

'Yes. Why is it that whenever Alison is mentioned, you leap three feet into the air, and turn the colour of rotgut Chianti?'

Denis looked up. 'Because I'm languishing slowly from an all-consuming passion for her. Can't you see me pining?' He filled his mouth with spaghetti.

'You like her, though, don't you?'

'You say everybody does.'

'Yes, but . . .' But it was all so ridiculous, she realised with the sudden clear intensity of the third glass of wine. Denis mooning miserably over Alison, and Alison mooning miserably over what-was-his-name, while only she, by nature the most miserable of the three of them, seemed as if she might, just possibly might, be conceivably about to . . . 'Why don't you do something about it?' she asked Denis, hastily squashing the thought before it bloomed into providence tempting life. 'Ask her out for a drink or something. She doesn't bite, you know.'

He looked at her thoughtfully. 'You know, you could do something to help,' he said.

'Can I? What?'

He beckoned to her until their heads met confidentially in the middle of the table. 'You could,' he whispered, 'mind your own business.'

Maureen drew back, and poured more wine. 'Never let it be said,' she remarked, 'that I can't take a hint. And in that case, I shan't tell you about Daniel.'

'Who's Daniel?'

'Never mind.'

'OK.'

He meant it, blast him. 'Daniel's a man. I mean, he's a guy I was at college with, and we hadn't seen each other since, but we bumped into each other just last week, and . . .' She stopped, and shrugged.

'And? And is he the reason for the spring in your step and the light in your eye?'

'Well, sort of. I mean, if you really want to know, yes, he is.'

'Aha! You see, I did tell you so. Oh, Danny boy, the pipes, the pipes are ca-a-alling . . .'

'Actually, his name's Daniel Greenberg.'

'Oh. Well, another theory bites the dust. What's he like?'

What was he like? Maureen allowed herself a vacuous grin. 'He . . .' Abruptly, she stopped, her mood making one of its lightning, 180-degree-turn changes. 'No, you mind your own business this time. I'm sick of you.'

'What?'

'I tell you things because I've got a great loud mouth, and you sit and listen, and you never tell me anything. I'm fed up with it.'

'Do I?' He was taken aback: he had always felt himself to be more open with Maureen than with almost anyone. 'Don't I?'

'*Yes*. And *no*.'

'Oh.' He sat blinking for a moment, assimilating this into his picture of their friendship. 'Well—what d'you want to know?'

'*I* don't know. Anything.'

'OK. Denis Joseph Patrick O'Leary. Sex: male. Marital status: single. Age: . . .'

'I know what I want to know.' Of course she knew. But she knew, too, that it was the one question that not even she could acceptably ask. But then again, she asked herself, her mind warmed by wine and the thought of Daniel, why not? Why the bloody hell not? 'Why is it,' she asked, 'that you never, ever have a girlfriend?'

'Why . . . ?' Denis puffed air through his cheeks, and divided the last of the wine. 'Because I'm madly in love with you, what do you think? Another carafe?'

'You see, that's what I mean. I ask you, and you make a joke. Yes, let's, but this one's on me. That's really rather offensive, you know, when you always do it.'

'Well, it's a really terribly personal question.'

'Of course, I'm a complete stranger.'

'Well, maybe, in this particular area of my life, I want you to be.'

'Well, maybe I don't want to be.'

'Well, maybe that's just tough.'

'Fair enough.' The second carafe arrived, and Maureen attacked her glass angrily. 'If that's the way it is. We'll finish the wine, and we'll talk about the weather, and I'll see you on Friday night. Oh, and thanks for the lunch.'

Shit. He had really hurt her feelings. Perhaps even friendship was beyond him, then.

'I am not,' he said at last, slowly, 'good ... at emotional involvements.'

'News flash, Denis. Not many people are.'

'But I ...' He stopped, estimating just how much of an explanation he either owed or dared to give her. 'I'm a good bloke, really, until you get to know me. But the closer you get...' His words trailed off, and he shook his head.

'But how do you know,' she asked, 'unless you let anyone get close?'

'It's in the blood,' he said.

Denis's mother was mad. It was hereditary, apparently, a genetic defect, had been in the family since before the Famine. She had known of the weakness all along, indeed had revelled in it, was boasting of it in Denis's first memories of her, a wild-haired, beautiful young woman, delighting him and his sister Kathleen with ever more outrageous tales of the magnificent Dunmores back in County Tipperary, they whose rich eccentricities contrasted so cruelly, so amusingly, with the lace-curtain respectability of the O'Learys of Camden Town. But that was when he was a child, when his father was still alive, before the disease had properly set in. You could not go mad while you had a husband to feed and young children to care for.

She had lasted out as long as she could. But as he and Kathleen reached the age where they could fend for themselves, and as his meek, industrious father had died, fading first, it seemed, into a grey nothingness of which his actual removal from this life was merely the final stage, her grip had relaxed. Her fiery Dunmore temper, her rich Dunmore imagination, had become more pronounced, less susceptible to control. She had gorged herself on fantasies, enraged herself on fancied offences. She had blurred generations, confusing Denis with his father, Kathleen with her own mother, erecting around herself, slowly but all too surely, an impregnable fortress of eccentricity, giving, as the years passed, fainter and fewer signs of just where in that crazily baroque establishment was hiding the once charmingly colourful Rosemary Dunmore. One day, when Denis was sixteen, he had looked into her eyes, and seen in them nothing, or rather, a closed curtain hiding whatever might be there, and had known that she was gone.

There was nothing to be done. Even at sixteen, Denis had known that help was impossible unless she were to seek it herself, and that she would never do. Nor was there family he could turn to: they had been brought up as isolated from the O'Learys as if they had lived across the globe rather than across London, and there would be no help coming from County Tipperary. As for Kathleen, she simply would not accept that her mother was less than sound, would fly into a rage whenever Denis brought the subject up. It was not long before Denis became aware that Kathleen was inching, ever so slowly, towards madness herself.

The two women lived together now, and would until one of them died, Kathleen supplementing their income—hardly necessarily, since Denis's father had left the family amply looked after—by a little secretarial work at the local convent. They lived well, ate the best foods, and were always in magnificent health. How happy they were, Denis had never been able to establish. He visited them one weekend a month, uneasy visits, in which his mother would tell her fantastic stories of the Dunmores, and Kathleen would sit, as she had as a little girl, perched on the very edge of her chair, her eyes glistening, watching her mother's lips with rapacious intensity. There was nothing he could do for them, locked out of their shared world as he was by his maleness and his sanity; they were strangers, alien beings, the woman who had given birth to him and the big sister who had tied his shoelaces; they were exotic, extraordinary creatures, Dunmores, while he was his poor, drab, dead father's son.

But that was the added horror of it. He was not his father's son, not exclusively, and he knew too well that the flawed blood of the Dunmores ran in his veins every bit as strongly as it did in Kathleen's. And the horror of the horror was that he felt it, late at night, or when he was off his guard, felt the pull of that path where truth blurred with fantasy, what was with what should be or might have been. He knew that, if he allowed it to happen as his mother and Kathleen had, he himself could all too easily be led, step by oh so attractive step, down the sweet road to insanity.

The way to deal with it, he had long ago concluded, was to deny it. To exert unceasing self-control, fixating himself on the down-to-earth, the passionless, allowing himself no love, nor rage, nor even introspection. Emotions were very well for others. For him they were as sure a disaster as sugar for a diabetic or one drink at Christmas for an alcoholic. It was what he had always done—checking his sanity constantly, as a cancer patient in remission checks his bodily health—and it was what he would go on doing until he died. It was the only way.

How, though, to convey this to Maureen? How to explain to her the life he lived, the road he must always travel? How to make her understand as she wanted—deserved, damn it, as his friend—to understand?

'My mother,' he told her, 'is mad.'

'Whose mother isn't?' she replied.

He looked at her across a gulf too wide ever to hope of bridging.

There was no biscuit with Anne's tea today. She looked with longing up at the top shelf of the kitchen cupboard where, thoughtfully out of her reach, Stephen had stored all the sugary snacks, and sighed, reminding herself that the first few days were the worst, that to conquer her sweet tooth would do her nothing but good, that she really was putting on far too much weight.

· Not that Stephen seemed to mind. She could be as fat as a pig for all he cared, or as thin as a rake; she would still be Anne and, simply for that reason, he would continue to love her with all his goofy, good heart. She took her tea into the living-room, sat on the sofa, and held it cupped in her hands as she pondered his seemingly limitless love.

How lucky she was—how lucky she must never forget that she was—to have such love. And how wicked to wonder, as she wondered now, if there were indeed limits to it, and if so, exactly where they were. Once, as a child, during an outing to Longleat, she had somehow been separated from the rest of the family, and had wandered for what seemed like hours, days, years, in a wilderness that stretched nightmarishly in every direction further than the eye could see. But even Longleat had its walls, its boundaries, even the Queen knew where her country ended, the Pope himself held no sway over—for instance—her own lapsed Methodist father. Stephen's feelings for her . . . thinking of Stephen's feelings for her, she began to grow dizzy with agoraphobia, as when she tried to imagine the universe, or eternity, or to pinpoint precisely what the thing was that inhabited the body and mind of Anne Collins.

It came, then, as something of a relief when the telephone rang, shattering her thoughts. She crossed the room eagerly to answer it: it was the time of day when her mother often rang. But it was not her mother. It was Brian.

'Oh, hello,' she said.

'Anne,' said his voice. 'Oh, thank God you're still speaking to me.'

'Well, why wouldn't I be?'

'I don't know. I just had a horrible thought after last Sunday that maybe your family was the sort that was nice to each other all the time.'

'Oh. Well, you needn't worry about that.'

'Oh, good. Listen, I'm in Woodford. Can I look in just for five minutes to say sorry?'

'Oh, Brian . . .' she paused, thought about it, sighed. 'Do you really think that's a good idea?'

'Why not? Do you think I'm going to leap on you and ravish you on your spanking new sofa?'

'Oh, don't be daft. But . . .' But what? He had been rude to her husband in her living-room: why should he not apologise to her? Stephen would not approve, but then Stephen had been even ruder to him. 'You spend a lot of time apologising, don't you?'

'It's one of my most irresistible expressions. Wait till you see it. Please.'

'Oh . . . all right.'

'Terrif. I'll be ten minutes, and don't get any biscuits out because I'll bring a huge, gooey cake.'

'But . . .'

But it was too late. He was gone.

Twenty-five minutes later, he was at the door, his eyebrows raised, his mouth turned down, a large cardboard box in his hands.

'It's my apologetic look,' he said. 'How d'you like it?'

'It's utterly repulsive,' she told him.

'Oh, Oh, well.' He thrust the box at her. 'Cike.'

It was the first time he had included her in the Cockney joke: Lent or not, she would have to share his cake now.

She led him into the living-room, poured tea, cut the cake.

'It's good,' she mumbled, through a mouth full of sponge, nuts, and cream. It was good, too, wickedly good—and she had been off sugar for barely thirty-six hours.

'Well, I am sorry,' he said. 'Honestly. And how about this?—we'll even save a slice for Stephen.'

'You know, I don't think Stephen's very keen on you coming here.'

'Then he's bloody inhospitable, isn't he?'

'He's also my husband.'

'Sorry. *Sorry*.'

'Well, anyway. How's the redhead?'

'Siobhan?' He shook his head. 'Don't talk to me about Siobhan, she's crazy. Just . . . out of her box and climbing up the wall crazy.'

'Siobhan? That's a good Irish name.'

'And don't talk to me about Irish names. Jesus.' He slapped down his cup and rubbed impatiently at his chin; Anne noticed for the first time how like Stephen he looked. 'Never be Irish,' he told her. 'Never. You leave school, you leave home, you don't go near a church, or a pint of Guinness, or even Kilburn, for God's sake, for years, and there are however many million nice, normal, sane English girls in, oddly enough, England, and who do you find yourself driving to Woodford to see?'

'Siobhan?'

'Siobhan red-headed bloody state of grace O'Malley. She was the one who told me to come and apologise, incidentally.'

'Well, that was very nice of her. Are we going to meet her?'

'I don't know. I was going to phone you anyway, because I wanted to talk to you.'

'Oh? What about?'

'Guess.'

He picked up his cup again and the resemblance to Stephen dimmed. Anne hated guessing games.

'I couldn't possibly,' she said.

'Oh. Well, have you seen that thing on television, *Gonna Make You A Star*?'

'The talent show? With the terrible man and that awful giggling girl?'

'That awful giggling girl happens to be a very good friend of mine, and you shouldn't judge by appearances.'

'Sorry.'

'Well, I was talking to that awful giggling girl who also happens to have a name, which is, Andrea, the other day. About you.'

'Oh, were you?' So that was the game. 'Brian, how many times do I have to tell you?'

'Just talking, *belle-soeur*.'

'Even so.'

'Well, anyway. Siobhan and I are having a drink with her tomorrow week—because she's so bloody busy these days you have to book her months in advance—and we're meeting at that wine bar in Wells Street and . . .'

'Yes. And.'

'What do you mean, yes, and?'

'Well, what do you think I mean?'

'Oh, come off it, Anne, what do *you* think you mean?' He set down his cup again; it rattled angrily. 'Can we just cut the sh-sorry, cackle here, please? You know you're interested, and you know I know you know.'

'Oh, do I?'

'Yes.' His eyes, Stephen's eyes, their mother's eyes, met hers. 'Yes, you do.'

She was silent. The truth was that he was right. Stephen's elder brother had found and touched a nerve in her that, in all her years of singing, no one before had found. She, who had never thought to be interested, was interested. Not tempted, true. But interested.

'Stephen,' she said at last, 'would hate it.'

'Stephen.' He raised his eyes. 'Let me tell you something about Stephen.'

'Do.'

'Sorry. But I know him quite well, too, you know. Anne.' Forgetting for once to be charming, he grabbed the teapot, and refilled his cup, ignoring hers. 'Anne, if you only *knew* how you sounded . . .'

'Oh, I know that,' she told him.

'Do you?'

'Yes.' Of course she knew; she had always known.

'Well, I'm afraid I think that's disgracefully selfish. I mean, people are always telling me I'm selfish, because, well, because they are, but I think that to have what you've got, and to know you have it, and not to be willing even to try to share it around, well, I just don't understand it.'

'I didn't ask you to understand it. I didn't ask for your comments at all.'

They glared at each other for a moment, two eldest siblings, both outraged at the challenge to their authority.

'My God,' said Brian at last. 'The women we Higgins get tied up with.'

Anne laughed, and filled her own cup. 'Who is Siobhan, anyway? I mean, how did you meet her?'

'Oh, listen,' said Brian quickly. 'Don't tell Mum she's Irish, OK?'

'Why not?'

'Because it would make her very, very happy.'

'Oh.' She understood: her own mother after all, was French. 'OK.'

'You're my favourite sister-in-law. Look, I've got to be somewhere. I just dropped in to . . .'

'To make a bit of trouble.'

'And to apologise.'

'Thank you, Siobhan.'

'God. Women. Well, say hello to that rude bugger Stephen for me. And look.' Half-way into a battered tweed jacket, he stopped and looked down at her from his height. 'Friday week. If you change your mind . . .'

'You don't give up, do you? If I change my mind, I'll let you know.'

'It's a damned nice wine bar. And you'd get to meet Siobhan.'

'Goodbye, Brian.'

'And I don't suppose you'd even thought that there's no guarantee in the world that you'd even get into the show, anyway.'

'Oh, very subtle. Anyway, believe it or not, I'm busy that night. *Goodbye*, Brian.'

At last, he was gone. She stood by the door listening—because he was capable of coming back again and again—until she heard his car lurching down the quiet street and around the corner. Then she went and sat by the fire, absent-mindedly cutting herself another slice of cake as she did so.

She was interested, there was no getting around it. She was interested, of course, in Brian—and natural enough to want to know about the man who had grown up with your husband; and she was interested in the life he led—who wasn't interested in the life of an actor? But it was not Brian she was thinking about now, as she stared into the orange points of the gas fire: it was herself.

It had stung to be called selfish. Was it so very selfish of her so little to want to share her voice? To keep, as she had always intended to keep, the wonderful gift that God had given her so close a secret between herself and her family, and the gift's giver? It was the way she had chosen, the way that had seemed right for her to choose. But what if Brian's way were the less selfish way after all? And if that were the case—and she felt again the delicious, guilty dipping of her stomach as she wondered—how much would she, Anne, really and truly dislike that way?

Munching her cake, she looked into the fire, and fantasised, not the mild acknowledgement that Brian knew, but extravagant, ridiculous fame. She fantasised thunderous applause at the ends of her concerts, records with her face on the sleeve arriving in shops to sell out within the day. She fantasised herself, grown magically tall, slim and clear-sighted, sweeping out of taxis and into restaurants where she was always charmingly, apologetically, laughingly late for lunch dates with interesting people; she fantasised the other lunchers nudging each other, and whispering her name; teenaged girls shyly approaching her for autographs. She fantasised arriving at star-studded parties amid the glare of a thousand clicking camera lights, she dressed in something floating and silver, and Stephen, looking at ease as Stephen never could, in a made-to-measure tuxedo. Stephen.

'He'd hate it,' she whispered to herself in awe. 'He'd hate it.'

'Well, I call it unfair,' said Sally. 'Here am I drudging to work at the crack of 10.30, and all I find is a stroppy message from Barry. While Madam waltzes in twenty minutes later, and *her* desk is groaning with several hundredweight of the most beautiful flowers I have ever seen.'

Alison raised her nose from the massive bouquet. 'Should have swapped then, shouldn't you?' She buried her nose again. 'Mmm. Spring.'

'What, honest Sal, a gal's best pal? Now, I wonder who in the world they could possibly be from?'

Alison began to open the note. 'He likes what I'm doing with the account.'

'Sure. Well, go on, what does he say? You're blushing!'

'Shut up.' Hastily, she replaced the note in its envelope. 'Anyway, he's married.'

'Oh, very.'

'No, he is. He . . .' She dropped to a chair, and frowned at the flowers. 'He shouldn't be doing this, actually.'

'The man's a cad. Want to swap accounts?'

'I've got to talk to him. Straighten some things out.'

'I *know*. Sending you flowers, the rat.'

'You know, I should call him now. I really . . .' She drew the phone towards her, and glanced at Sally, who had become suddenly immersed in paperwork. 'Sally?'

'Mmm?'

'Don't you have something to do?'

'What? Yes. This.'

'Something somewhere else?'

'She was sharp as a tack, was Miss Beck. No fun, mind. But sharp as a tack.' Half-way to the door, she paused. 'I hope you get hay fever,' she said.

After she had gone, Alison sat for a while, looking at the telephone. Adam Pilkington was married ('Oh, very,' echoed Sally's mocking tones in her head), and it simply did not do for a married man to send a single girl flowers for no other reason in the world than that each time their eyes met, enough electricity to fuel London seemed to pass between them. Yet how could he have known how she loved freesias?

Sitting there, she heard Sally's voice somewhere down the corridor, doubtless regaling the rest of the office with a highly coloured version of the morning's event, and felt, suddenly, lonely. The truth was that, hide it with all the grace that she might, when it came down to it, she was not quite like most people she knew, and that the difference lay in her religious upbringing. She was, of course, no Maureen. But then again, neither was she Sally: there was, would always be, a secret facet of her that could never fit comfortably into the society she usually moved in, the facet that was her childhood, that had shaped her first eighteen years to a world of miracles and mortal sins, of May Day processions, hymns to saints, and an unquestioned God-made man who had died bleeding on a cross to save the world and Alison Beck.

Usually, it was not an aspect of herself to which she devoted much attention, only occasionally, bringing it out at carefully chosen moments, as a surprise weapon, or, more occasionally still, feeling with a little pang the sadness that what had once been so fundamental a part of her should, not ten years out of its native habitat, be wasting so quietly and with so little struggle, almost towards death. Lately, however, her thoughts had been drifting towards it surprisingly often, and she was not quite sure why. Perhaps it was seeing so much of Maureen after so long a time. Or perhaps it was this business with Adam. The shreds of her Catholicism were not helping her with the Adam situation. But then, now that she came to think of it, neither was Adam himself. She looked at the flowers, and frowned again. Unfair of him, knowing how she felt, how he had claimed to respect how she felt, now to send her flowers. Alison hated unfairness. She picked up the receiver, and dialled his number.

'Adam?'

'Ms Beck.' His warm voice embraced her from the earpiece. She shut her eyes, and tried not to see the mole on his cheekbone. 'Hold on.' There were voices in the background, and then a door shut. 'How are you, Ms Beck?'

'I'm fine, thank you, Mr Pilkington. Thank you for the flowers.'

'Ah. You don't approve.'

Damn. How dare he, in two short weeks, grow to know her so well? 'I think we'd better have a talk.'

'Now, *there's* an interesting proposition.'

'Adam . . .'

'I'm sorry. You're pulling your Reverend Mother face, and it was just my little joke. Sorry.'

'Sorry.'

'Didn't you really like the flowers?'

'No, I hate flowers. Of course, I loved them. I just think we'd better have a talk about them.'

'I'm sorry, truly. I just couldn't resist them. They . . .'

'If you say they reminded you of me . . .'

'I wouldn't dare, Reverend Mother.'

They were laughing together down the cold telephone wires.

'I still think,' she said, 'we'd better have a talk.'

'If that's what you'd like. Tonight?'

'Tonight?' It was Friday night, and she had vaguely assumed that, as on the previous three Fridays, she would go to the Catholic group. But then, because she did something three times did not necessarily mean that she would do it a fourth.

'Tonight's fine,' she said.

'We adore thee, Oh Christ, and we praise thee,' said Father Bob.

They knelt, awkwardly, because it was the seventh station, and they had turned half of a circle to face the back of the church. 'Because by thy holy cross, thou hast redeemed the world.'

Bob had never been big on the Stations. The way of the cross, the step by step retracing of the dolorous way, the formality of the prayers, the ponderousness of the medieval hymn, always had seemed to him dull, lifeless, a harking back to the barely remembered grim days before Vatican Two. Besides, this Lent he needed less than ever before to be reminded of that melancholy journey to Calvary: he had his own way of the cross to stumble through, his own crown of thorns to wear.

'Consider,' he said, 'the second fall of Jesus under the cross, a fall which renews all the wounds of his head and members. My most sweet Jesus, how many times have you pardoned me, and how many times have I fallen again, and begun again to offend thee. By the means of your second fall, give me the necessary help to persevere in your grace until death. Grant in all my temptations such assurance that I may always commend myself to thee.'

Moving slowly to the eighth station, he crossed the aisle at the back of the church, passing a row of girls from the convent, there for the devotion or the privilege of being allowed to go to lunch ten minutes early. As he walked by, his stiff robe, purple for suffering and majesty, almost brushed Bridget Fahey. Marie Therese O'Donnell,

173

standing next to her, nudged her, and Bridget blushed, and frowned. She was a good girl, and knew that it did not do to be in love with a priest while he was performing his priestly duties. Bob, sending up a brief prayer that she would grow up good, and healthy, and happy, wondered what sort of woman she would become. A good Catholic wife and mother most likely, married to a man she had met through her college chaplaincy, raising just the two children (since, sadly, few even pretended to take seriously the Pope's teaching on birth control) in the faith, and sometimes looking back with a mixture of mortification and amusement on the days when the world had known her passion for Father Bob Power. Bob occasionally had a drink with the Anglican curate at St Jude's, who had a fund of similar stories of girls, and women, too, who fell, or fancied themselves to fall in love with the clergy. But an Anglican priest was different in that way: if he was celibate, it was by choice, while Bob's celibacy was God-imposed, a divine requirement. No one was as untouchable as a Catholic priest.

And she was touching him, his thoughts, the desires of his weak flesh, every hour of every day. So much a part of his life was she becoming that a pattern was beginning to develop. He would see her on Friday, and Friday night would be, pure and simple, hell. Saturday would be not much easier, nor Sunday, nor Monday; Tuesday would bring a slight dimming of the image, which by Thursday would be almost a relief; Friday morning would be positively manageable, and that was the worst of all, a tantalisingly brief glimpse of a world in which the cross might be lifted from his shoulders, the cup taken from his lips; and then on Friday evening, he would see her again, the innocent temptress, the unknowing occasion of sin, and it would all start all over again. It was as it had been last week and the week before; as it would doubtless be this week to come.

'I don't suppose,' he suggested, 'You'd consider giving her an alternative engagement, just for tonight?'

But he asked without hope, for form's sake. She was his via dolorosa, his athlete's wall, his make-or-break factor. She was the temptation he could not flee, the cross he was given no choice but to carry.

'OK,' he said. 'If that's how You want to play it. Thy will be done. Thy will be done.'

He moved on to the next station, singing in the voice that the choirmaster at Ware had never trained to carry a tune.

> Bruised, derided, cursed, defiled.
> She beheld her only child.
> All with bloody scourges rent.

> *Vidit suum dulcem natum,*
> *Morientem, desolatum,*
> *Dum emisit spiritum.*

Stephen preferred the words in plain English, but Ely Place was the most convenient to the office, and he had a heavy workday today. He had not, in fact, made himself popular by leaving the office at all, and he knew it: the glances askance by his desk-bound colleagues as, muttering about an engagement that simply could not be broken, he had slid outside, had been hard to miss. Not, of course, that it would even have entered his head to explain where he was going. One just did not, in non-Catholic circles, refer in any way to the spiritual unless one were forced, and then only with considerable embarrassment. Stephen had once shared an office with another Catholic for nearly two years before either had guessed at the other's Catholicism.

'We adore thee, Oh Christ, and we praise thee.'

'Because by thy holy cross, thou hast redeemed the world.'

He knelt and stood and knelt again, the contortions that were difficult for most people made almost impossible for him, and, briefly catching sight of Denis on the other side of the church, for once envied the other's lack of height. He surreptitiously wiggled his knees, in a vain attempt to fit eighteen inches of leg under fourteen inches of pew space, and tried to feel Lenten. And that was another near impossibility. How could he—who, having found Anne, was not supposed even to be married to her yet; who, promised a lifetime's happiness, had been granted a four-month jump even on that—how could he possibly feel Lenten?

> *Eja, mater, fons amoris,*
> *Me sentire vim doloris,*
> *Fac ut tecum lugeam.*

The hymn helped, though. The solemn, simple tune that you only heard in Lent, that sounded throughout Lent, the connecting cord drawing it from now, winter's end, to Easter and spring's beginning, that he had heard Friday after Friday in raging gales, pelting rains, and finally, primrose yellow sunshine, meant Lent; to an extent, for him, it was Lent.

Before he could stop himself Stephen snorted with laughter. Swimming up from somewhere in his unconscious had rushed with merciless vividness into his mind a picture of Brian, nine years old and wearing a table-cloth, doing a wickedly accurate impression of old Father Dwyer saying Stations, while he and Moira and little John had laughed until the tears had run down their cheeks. It had been a funny impression, although he had not thought of it for years; Brian had been a funny elder brother.

He had not been very nice to Brian on Sunday. Anne had said so, and if she had said so, she must be right. But then, he had not felt particularly like being nice to Brian for some years now. Brian and he had been inseparable as children, the way close brothers are inseparable, the one the master, the other the willing slave, sometimes barely even individuals, but two halves of a greater Brian and Stephen whole. It had been so through childhood, through early adolescence, could not, then, conceivably be otherwise. Then—and Stephen could still, at times, feel the pain of the betrayal—Brian had deserted him. It had happened quite suddenly. He had gone away to drama school, a funny elder brother who had loved to do imitations of Miss Holly the Duck Lady and Father Moriarty the maths master; he had come back a few weeks later a young man about town, unrecognisable, who had demanded coffee rather than tea in the mornings, who, when Stephen, hungry for Father Dwyer jokes, had asked him which Mass he would be going to, had repeated in an incredulous tone 'Mass?' and had laughed a laugh that had cut Stephen to the quick.

Stephen had blamed the theatre: he still did. Brian had once told him, laughingly, that centuries ago, actors were regarded as men without souls. Stephen had laughed too, politely, but the image had stayed with him long after the conversation which gave birth to it had been forgotten. Men without souls, buried like dogs, outside the churchyard in the chill moonlight, lost, damned. Straw men, hollow men, their hearts turned inside out for the passing amusement of strangers, leaving them, ultimately, dry as an empty coconut left in the sun. Men without souls. Stephen did not think he could bear it if anyone, anywhere, ever, had thought of accountants as men without souls.

Not, of course, that many people thought of accountants as anything—certainly no one's eyes had ever lit with interest when Brian had revealed Stephen's profession, as they did when Stephen revealed Brian's. Yet Stephen's contribution to the community was fully as valuable; and it was not Brian that relations, and friends, and relations of friends and friends of relations, came to for investment advice and help with tax problems. That was what Stephen dealt in, the solid, the stable, the long-term, while his brother's dealings were of the here and now, the immediately glamorous, the charming today, leading tomorrow to—where?—to the burial outside the churchyard while the owls hooted and no priest prayed.

On the other hand, Anne had said he had not been nice to Brian, and he probably should apologise to God for that. Sorry, God, he muttered, and determined—because this was, after all, the twentieth century, and even Brian probably had a soul tucked away somewhere —to try harder next time.

'Glory be to the Father, and to the Son, and to the Holy Ghost, as it was in the beginning, is now and ever shall be, world without end, Amen.'

At last it was over, and not, Stephen's calves told him, before time. He genuflected hastily and left, arriving in the little courtyard, in the gusty wind that was March coming in like a lion, at the same time as Denis.

'Misther Collins,' the other greeted him. ''Tis you have made a grand start to Lent, and 'tis meself will be telling St Peter so on the Day, God help us.'

Stephen laughed through his beard. He liked Denis: he was always the same. 'Is it my imagination, or does it get longer every year?'

'I don't think it's your imagination as much as your legs.'

'Jesus,' said Stephen with feeling. 'Never be tall. Never.'

Denis laughed. He was a rare short man who appeared comfortable with his size. 'Chance would be a fine thing. Feel like a drink?'

'My God. Don't you journalists ever do any work?'

Denis frowned in puzzlement. 'Work?' he queried, sounding, coincidentally, eerily like Brian.

'Believe it or not, some people do it all day long.'

'Well, you live and learn, don't you?'

They walked up Charterhouse Street and separated, Stephen hurrying up Farringdon Road to the City and the covertly disapproving faces of his fellow workers, Denis wandering, shoulders hunched against the wind, down Farringdon Street towards Ludgate Circus.

Usually, he felt restored coming from Stations, having found in the grim procession, untroubled by hope, from Pilate's court to the cross at Calvary a sort of gloomy peace, even a comfort. He had not found it; today he was depressed as he rarely allowed himself the indulgence of being depressed. Not even Stations of the Cross could cheer his innermost heart today.

The reason for his depression was, of course, yesterday's lunch with Maureen. It was not her lack of understanding of the situation that had depressed him: naturally she had not understood, how could she possibly have been expected to? It had been a mistake —but a man was allowed a mistake, after all—a mistake brought on by the treacherous wine and the more treacherous demands of her friendship even to try to open up at all. It was the implication of the mistake that depressed him, that laid its lion's paw on his spirit, stilling it to a deadness from which he felt he would never break free.

He had tried, and failed, to explain himself to another human being. He had had all along a fantasy, a secret, abject hope that somehow, somewhere, some day, he might bring himself to expose his sorrow to another who might just conceivably understand it. Not to a lover, of course—he knew that a lover was not for him; he was even, thank God and blast it, winning the battle against thoughts of Alison—but to a friend, possibly to a friend. Maureen was as close a friend as he was ever to be allowed to have, she had wanted to understand—and she had not understood. He had shot his bolt, had his chance, he was alone, Denis O'Leary, barren end of the line, last of the tainted Dunmore stock, undeserving of propagation, and he would stay alone until at last, alone, he died.

And on top of everything, he had forgotten yet again to buy the crucifix.

'I say, I say.'

He had reached Ludgate Circus, and had almost walked into

Philip, coming up from the river. Denis stopped, raised an imaginary hat, and adjusted his tie. 'What do you say?'

'Who was that gentleman I saw you with this morning?'

'That was no gentleman, that was my editor.'

'You thirsty?'

'That's funny, I thought it was Friday.'

'That's funny, so am I.'

'So how's life?' Denis asked five minutes later, as they sat in an unexpectedly quiet corner of the King Lud.

'Fine, thanks. The kitchen ceiling's just fallen in, but there you go. Oh, and Ruth wants to know when you're coming over to fix those shelves.'

'Ah, Ruth. She only loves me for my Black & Decker.'

'Well, you'd better make it soon, or we'll have to buy our own. So what are you doing roaming the streets alone on a Friday lunch-time?'

'Me?' Denis swallowed his Guinness, swallowing with it the natural impulse to tell the truth of where he had been. 'Oh, I've just been for a walk. I begged the others to let me join them at the Clachan, but you know how it is when you're a pariah.'

'Well, you can't really blame them.'

'Wouldn't dream of it. What about you?'

'I,' said Philip loftily, 'have been meeting a source.'

Denis groaned. 'You've seen *All the President's Men* again.'

'Actually,' Philip looked over his shoulder and lowered his voice, 'I couldn't tell you before, but I think I might be on to something good. Another spy scandal.'

Another spy scandal. Denis addressed himself once more to his Guinness, momentarily tired of this world where it was acceptable to discuss treason but not to discuss his church. 'Double bill, was it? *All the President's Men* and *The Spy Who Came in from the Cold?*'

'You don't believe me, do you? I've just had a disgusting lunch at Peter Jones with probably the most poisonous woman in the Western World.'

'Oh, you've met my aunt, then.'

'Shut up. Listen, she's in a pretty powerful position, and she's spent a year collecting information, which she's just decided it's time to put to the public. Via the *Sentinel*.'

He sat straight and stopped talking, as a couple of secretaries teetered past on clacking high-heeled shoes. Denis stared into his drink, and realised that the week was nearly over. It was his weekend to visit his mother and Kathleen.

'Anyway,' the secretaries had gone, and Philip was talking again, 'she's the private secretary of an extremely well-known political widow, and there is dirt. I mean dirt. Her employer. A foreign power. All sorts of people, including the leader—mind you leader—of one of our smaller political parties.'

'Which party?'

'Aha, oh ye of little faith. Mind your business.'

'Which party?'

'For God's sake, pipe down.' He reached in his pocket, produced his notebook, and scribbled a word in it. Denis read, and wondered, and hated himself for wondering, why he had not heard from Geoffrey all week long.

It was extraordinarily felicitous for Geoffrey that the two most gratifying things in his life, his work and his love, were not in the least degree a distraction one from the other. Here he was, having been up late last night and early this morning thinking of Alysoun, about, he sincerely hoped, to see her in the very flesh in just a few hours' time, and yet he was still able to work with as intense a concentration as if he had nothing on his mind but the weather, the traffic, and the notes he was making for Francis's speech on the homeless.

He was a good researcher, accurate, yet possessed of an instinctive ability to ferret out facts whose significance had hitherto gone unnoticed. The notes on the homeless were coming along well, really very well indeed. It was almost three o'clock, and he had been at his desk for almost an hour—since, unlike many of his colleagues, he saw no excuse for working any less hard at the end of the week than he did at the beginning—had, indeed, accomplished more in that one hour of quiet than he would in two with Nigel and Sue around. He had done well, he told himself, allowing himself a brief glance out of the window at the round moon-face of Big Ben. Five to three. He would give himself, now while it was still quiet, five minutes alone with Alysoun, and then he would go back to work. He was doing well. Meanwhile . . .

'Woolgathering, Johnson?' The clock struck and simultaneously Francis was in the room, filling it with his presence. 'Nothing better to do, eh? Be turning into Simmonds if you don't look sharp.'

Geoffrey looked around, trying to wipe the smile off his face. 'I was just enjoying the sunshine,' he apologised.

'Sunshine? Where?' He squinted out of the window at the deceptively bright day. 'Oh, yes. Much overrated, I always thought. How are the homeless?'

He craned over Geoffrey's desk, reading without effort even Geoffrey's roughest handwriting. 'Interesting,' he said. 'Bloody interesting. Be a few red faces in the House over this one, eh? Good work.'

It was his highest accolade. For a split second it seemed to Geoffrey that they were united, crusaders, one, albeit in their trivial way, with the barons who had forced the Magna Carta, and Cromwell's stiff-collared generals, and all the statesmen who had even walked the corridors of the House and dreamed of a better land.

'Where the bloody hell,' said Francis, 'are your, for want of a better word, colleagues?'

The moment passed. 'I don't . . .' began Geoffrey.

'You don't know, of course. God's blood.' He paused, stooped to inspect the *Telegraph* lying open on Sue's desk. 'How anyone reads this rag . . . I say, Johnson.'

'Yes?'

He was still scrutinising the newspaper. With anyone but Francis, you would have said he was embarrassed. 'You did give that letter to Margaret Bellweather, didn't you?'

'What? Yes, of course.'

'And you didn't mention it to anyone?'

'No.'

'Not a soul? You're sure?'

With anyone but Francis, Geoffrey would have been offended. 'Certainly not,' he said rather coldly.

Francis looked up at last, and examined him. 'No, of course not. Well, when you see those other buffoons . . . Ah, talk of the devil.'

Nigel and Sue had arrived.

'We've been at lunch,' said Nigel.

'So I see,' said Francis. He opened a window. 'Or rather, so I perceive.'

Sue giggled.

'I want to see you both,' said Francis. 'Now.'

He led them out, as Big Ben sounded a quarter past the hour. Geoffrey sat back. The day was going remarkably well. There would be no more time for quiet thoughts this afternoon, but then, it really was not so long until he would see her again, even—who knew? —snatch a quiet word alone with her. And the unaccountable thought struck him that, rivals or not, it would be rather good to see Denis again: there had been times this last week when Geoffrey had really almost found himself missing him.

Meanwhile, the homeless were waiting. Whistling softly between his teeth, he set to his afternoon's work.

It was a strangely depleted meeting: Kate was not there, and neither was Alison.

'Where's your friend?' Geoffrey asked Maureen.

'She couldn't come,' said Maureen. 'Had to see a client, or something.'

'Ah, the hussy,' said Denis. ''Tis out meetin' fellas in the bars she'll be.'

'And she a Child of Mary,' tut-tutted Maureen.

Geoffrey looked from one to the other, and said nothing.

Bob, too, said nothing, at least outwardly. Inwardly, his heart was singing a paean of joy. 'Thanks, Pal,' he was saying, silently, over and over again. 'Thanks, Pal.'

'Well, I hope she's here next week,' said Anne. 'Tomorrow week's Aylesford, remember.'

'No chance,' said Denis. 'Bad companions, leading to neglect of spiritual duties. This time next week, she'll have been hit by a bus and gone straight to hell.'

Geoffrey continued to look at Denis.

'Didn't I tell you?' said Bob. 'There's no meeting next week. The Hopkins Society are having their St Patrick's Day party here.'

'No meeting?' said Stephen. 'Oh, well.' He looked at Anne. 'That means I can go to that party, then.'

'What party?' said Anne.

'That stag night. That chap from work, Roger. I told you.'

'No, you didn't.'

'It's always the wife,' said Maureen, 'who's the last to know. Looks like you're going to be a free woman next Friday, Anne.'

'Yes,' said Anne, quietly. 'So it does.'

'Well,' said Maureen, 'I'll check up with Alison about Saturday. Where's Kate, anyway?'

Nobody knew.

'I suppose she is coming. Anyone got her home number?'

Nobody had.

'Well, I'll ring her at work on Monday. Since I seem to be on attendance duty. And now,' she finished her drink and stood up, 'I'm going to be dead boring and go home to bed. I've been rather short on early nights lately.'

'I'll go too,' said Bob. 'I've been short on early nights myself.'

'Now, Mr Johnson,' said Denis quickly, as they all prepared to depart, 'ye would not refuse an oul' pal in one for the road, would ye so?'

Geoffrey raised his eyebrows, but still said nothing as Denis poured the drinks. He raised his glass in answer to Denis's muttered '*slàinte*', and for a few minutes they drank together in silence.

'I haven't spoken to you all week,' said Denis finally. 'How's work?'

'Fine,' said Geoffrey.

'Good. How's Francis?'

'Fine.'

'Good.'

There was more silence. Geoffrey watched Denis; Denis watched his drink. 'I'm glad,' he said slowly, 'we've got a chance to talk.'

Geoffrey smiled. 'Are you, now?'

'Alone, I mean.' He continued to study his drink. 'I want to . . .' he broke off. How the hell did he begin to say the sort of thing he had to say? He glanced at Geoffrey, who was sitting, inscrutable, offering no help or clue, and took a breath. 'I had a drink today with a friend. Journalist. Reputable bloke, not a scandalmonger. He seems to think there's some trouble brewing. In your neck of the woods.'

'Does he?'

Geoffrey's voice was neutral. Denis began to feel very slightly foolish. Then he reminded himself of the lunch-time conversation: whatever Geoffrey's involvement, Denis could not as a friend refrain from alerting him.

'Politics, I mean. Heavy stuff. I mean—this is dead confidential, right?—he's talking about . . .'

Again, he stopped. How could he seriously, sitting over a pint with a friend, articulate the short word that belonged not in the here or the now, but in extravagant adventure films, in creaking historical romances? Yet it was the word Philip had used, and it was the correct word to describe the activity involved.

'What,' said Geoffrey, 'is he talking about?'

'He's talking—he might be wrong of course, and I hope to God he is—but he's talking about . . . about spying.'

It was out, and, out, irretrievable.

'You surely,' said Geoffrey after a pause and in tones of ice, 'aren't expecting me to comment?'

'Oh, God! No, I'm not pumping you, Jesus! I'm trying to . . .' Once more, the words died on him.

'Yes? Tell me—precisely what are you trying to do?'

'I suppose I'm trying to warn you. And I shouldn't, because this is just deadly, deadly secret, but . . . My friend—I just pray that he's wrong, but he's not usually, and he . . . Francis's name was mentioned.'

There was a knock as Geoffrey put down his drink half-finished and stood up. 'Do not delude yourself,' he said, 'that I am not on to your pretty trickery. I've seen many things in my life, Denis, but I must say I'm disappointed that someone like you could stoop quite so low as that.'

He picked up his coat, and walked out alone into the Soho night.

'Thanks, Pal,' repeated Bob as he undressed.

'Thanks, Pal,' he muttered as he cleaned his teeth.

'Thanks, Pal,' he said, as he finished his prayers and climbed into bed.

It just went to show that if you had enough faith in your heart, it would see you through in the end. True that, back there, there had been a sticky bit. True that he, brought it seemed to the very limit of his endurance, had even wondered, God forgive him, whether he were not to be pushed over the very edge into the abyss below. That he poor, weak mortal that he was, had been straying in his minor temptation all too dangerously close to the edge of the grievous sin of despair.

But he had, thank God, found from somewhere the strength to stick it out, and at the last minute, God had given him a break. He had taken up his cross, he had walked on the water, had resigned himself to all that was or might be. And, when he had done so, God had come through for him.

Thanks, Pal.

He wasn't out of the wood yet. The temptation was still there; he still, he acknowledged, reaching for Thomas Merton, had and would for some time have to keep all too close a guard on his thoughts and desires. But oh, the contrast between this Friday night and the sweating torment of the last, when he had lain here, minute by minute, self doing battle with self until dawn! As he opened Thomas Merton, he felt settling over him the delicious lassitude of a sickness conquered, of the beginning of a pleasingly self-indulgent convalescence. He closed the book, turned the light out, and lay down, smiling to himself in the darkness. For this week, at least, he was in the clear. And by the time he saw her again, he would have a week's prayerful preparation under his belt, and, besides, he would be there. He would be thirty.

Thanks, Pal.

So that was Denis's little game. Geoffrey stared out at the black night from the yellow depths of the bus, and sadly contemplated the extremes to which love, or rather the wrong sort of love, could drive even a fundamentally decent chap like Denis. Granted that they were rivals, and therefore, in this area at least, competitors rather than friends.

And granted that even Denis, seeing the odds stacked so very heavily as they were in Geoffrey's favour, might understandably be tempted to redress the balance, even if it involved deceit. But this was too much. He should know, had no excuse for not knowing, what the party meant to Geoffrey, what Francis meant, what the country meant to Francis. To use Francis, and above all, Francis's national loyalty, as a weapon to shake Geoffrey's self-confidence was, quite simply, unacceptable. Beyond—as the expression went that was born in the Plantagenet colonisation of Ireland—the pale.

But there, of course, Geoffrey realised, lay the clue. What could an Irishman know about patriotism? Look at Ireland, after all, barely a country, a tiny island of warring tribes that had come to England for help all those centuries ago, that had taken the help and caused nothing but trouble in return, that was even, in those ridiculous few square miles of the North that still clung leechlike to England and would not let go, causing trouble to this very day. No, Denis had shown, in his choice of this particular method of warfare, not only bad sportsmanship, but also an ignorance of what England meant to an Englishman and that had doomed his plan from the very start.

Poor Denis, thought Geoffrey as the bus swung down Kentish Town road, forced into selling his soul like that, and selling it, doubly, in vain. Because, even if his scheme had worked and Geoffrey were put out of the picture, he didn't stand a chance, ugly nervous little Irishman that he was, didn't stand a snowball's chance in hell with a girl like Alysoun. Two creatures of a different breed they were, barely the same animal, what possible chance did the fool think he stood? Whereas he . . . Well, she would as like as not turn him down, too, but at least he would not be ludicrous in the asking. He stared out of the window, thinking Alysoun thoughts, and ignoring what in a lesser man would have been the pain of friendship betrayed.

'Let us proclaim the mystery of faith,' said Father Conway.

'Christ has died,' they replied. 'Christ is risen. Christ will come again.'

There were always running in Maureen's mind during Sunday Mass three strands of thought. One was a more or less cursory attention to the routine miracle that was being performed on the altar in front of her; another was a review of minor practical tasks she would need to complete today and during the week; the third, and most important, was a confrontation with herself, an assessment unhampered by any distractions physical or social of just how she was coping with the task of being Maureen Callaghan. It was the last which governed how often she went to Sunday Mass. Given that the results of such an introspection were likely to be tolerable, she was perfectly happy to spend an hour of her weekend in contemplation, if not in worship, of a deity. The results, however, were not always tolerable.

She had not, for instance, until now even considered Sunday Mass since that first visit to Miss Feeney, not merely missing it, but actively avoiding it. Enough she had felt, that what she had heard on that Saturday afternoon three weeks ago should have had access to her in her every unguarded waking moment. Even she was not quite such an idiot as to sit herself down in church, with nothing to think about but God, his angels, and the whole sick, saintly business, and actually invite it in. But that was until last week, when she had still been angel-ridden; this week, things were different. This week, Miss Feeney had been deposed, had been plucked, it seemed, by God's unexpectedly kindly hand, from the focal point of Maureen's perspective, to be replaced, in the most delightful fashion, by Daniel. Thank you, God, she said, with her usual careful politeness, in between reminding herself to stop at the off-licence on her way home, and remembering her grandmother in the Prayer for the Dead. The image flitted across her mind of how she would have felt by this stage of the Mass, had she, just last Sunday, been mad enough to attend it, and she felt herself physically shudder. Thank you, God.

Daniel. Three times she had seen him that week, on Wednesday evening, on Friday lunch-time, and on Saturday evening, and each time they had drawn closer to each other, known more about each other, than human beings had the right to dream could possibly be drawn or known. Less than twelve hours, all told, spent together, and already she recognised him, knew that his mental shape fitted into hers as snugly as hers into his, outrageously comfortable, unforesee-ably felicitous. Physically, too, she recognised him, big and like an Irishman, yet not like an Irishman, with sallow skin and slightly slanting eyes, urban, throwing up in contrast her own crayon-coloured, peasant potato-face, like herself and yet not like herself, in the most important of ways not like herself at all.

'This is the Lamb of God,' said Father Conway, 'who takes away the sins of the world. Happy are they who are called to his supper.'

'Lord, I am not worthy,' they replied, 'to receive you. But only say the word, and I shall be healed.'

Maureen waited a few moments, rose to her feet, and shuffled her tingling body into the communion line. Her mother would most certainly regard it as a mortal sin for her to receive communion when she was not in a state of grace, and it was as incontrovertible that someone who had missed Sunday Mass for so many weeks would be well out of that particular state. Luckily—or perhaps even unluckily, since her mother's way seemed to make for so restfully few conflicts of right versus wrong—she had her own soul, not her mother's, to care for.

'The body of Christ,' said Father Conway, handing her the Host.

'Amen,' she replied, receiving it.

The body of Christ, she repeated to herself, walking back to her seat. Did she believe that what she had swallowed was really the body of Christ? Could she, could anyone, truly believe, as they were asked to, that what every physical sense proclaimed to be a small, round, mass-produced wafer of bread, was, in actual and literal fact, the very body and the very blood of the God-made-man? She reached her place, and shook her head as she slid to her customary kneeling slouch. Impossible. Unimaginable. And yet, she believed unimaginable things. She believed in Australia, although she had never been there, and in Uranus, Neptune, and Pluto, and that the press of a switch could lighten a darkened room, and that trees turned from brown to green in the spring. And angels? she found herself adding. Did she believe in angels? But that was the joy of this Sunday, that the most unimaginable thing of all had happened—Daniel. If Daniel in this world were real, then that left her free to believe in the other worldly goods, in God, and Our Lady, and the angels and saints, and whatever the hell it was that poor, good, Danless Miss Feeney had seen that day in dreary Trent Park.

'The Mass is ended,' said Father Conway, after the blessing. 'Go in peace.'

'Thanks be to God,' Maureen, who usually responded with at best a mutter, found herself saying, joyously, aloud. What a joke it would be if she were to be led back to Holy Mother Church not by Father Bob, or Miss Feeney, or the nuns, or her parents, but by a Jew! Well, after all, it was a Jew who had started it in the first place.

She scuffed out of the church, past the line of freckled men sitting, Irish fashion, on the stone wall outside, and home under a grey sky whose promise of rain for once did not so much as dampen her spirits. It was a fine soft day, an Irish day, a fit day for Mass here in Kilburn where every second face you passed had Munster or Connacht stamped over it, where not to have been to Mass was more remarkable than to have been. These were her people, after all; not Daniel's, certainly, but by extension, not Jonathan's either; not the Irish in Ireland, but not the English. The immigrants and their children, dabbling in two races, belonged to neither, just as, in his way, Daniel did not belong.

She arrived home and, since Alison was coming to lunch, immediately started cooking, feeling, as always when she did so, like her mother, capable and slightly matriarchal, having nourishment of the spirit attended to, that of the body in process. Like her mother, she poured herself first of all a drink—sherry, rather than Guinness, however, from her somewhat depleted bottle (she would have to pay another visit to Notting Hill); with her mother's clumsily expert action, she selected and began to chop onions; like her mother when the sun shone or some other piece of unexpected good fortune arrived, she felt cheerful and wondered why she could not always feel so.

She switched on the radio, and began instantly to sing over it, carefree warblings that wandered innocently from octave to octave. She was trying to find a song for Daniel, since, ever since she could remember, she had had a song for everyone she was fond of. Alison, for instance, in some forgotten association from a singing lesson on a long-ago summer's afternoon, was 'Lavender's Blue'. Denis, for reasons she could not begin to articulate, was 'Kevin Barry'; her mother was 'The Mountains of Mourne'. Daniel was—what? 'Danny Boy' had been taken early by her first love, Rupert of the Rhine. 'Mo Bhuicaill Donn', except that he wasn't dark; 'The Lowlands of Holland', except that it was so sad. And there were so few songs written for men. 'Shule Aroon', of course, but that was another sad one. She sighed, throwing onions into the pan, and, reaching for the green peppers, raised her voice in joyful lament:

> 'I'll sell my rock, I'll sell my reel,
> I'll sell my granny's spinning wheel,
> For to buy my love a coat of steel . . .'

'My God! Somebody strangling a cat?' Alison had wandered into the room.

Maureen jumped. 'You scared me.'

'Not half as much as you're scaring the neighbours. You left the door open. Keep on singing, though, it's a perfect burglar deterrent.'

'I'm fine, thanks very much. How are you?'

'OK.' Ignoring the sarcasm, Alison dumped a paper bag on the table, and threw herself into a chair. 'Let's get drunk.'

Maureen looked out of the window and shrugged: it was starting to rain. 'OK.' She opened the bag, and brought out a bottle of Jameson's, 'Oh, very nice.'

'Well, since you ask, I'd love some.'

Maureen found tumblers, and poured generous measures. 'Not going too well, huh? You and Clientman?'

'As well as can be expected. No, not too. Thanks. Cheers.' She drank and slumped back in her chair, stomach out, legs akimbo, managing, even in that position, a sort of awkward elegance. 'So what's up with you? You look happy.'

'Me?' She shrugged apologetically. 'Yes, I am, quite.'

'Aha.' Alison sat up slightly. 'I diagnose—who was it?—Daniel. Dan, Dan, the Dustbin Man. Right?'

'He's not a dustbin man,' said Maureen. She tried, and failed, to sound offended. She tried, and failed, to look aloof. She tried, and failed, to seem anything but one ridiculous, blushing, grinning, sheepish mess.

'I am right,' said Alison. 'Aren't I?'

'Well.' Suddenly, she felt sorry for Alison: were Maureen in her shoes, the news of another's good fortune, would be the last thing she would want to hear. On the other hand, Alison, more generous, clearly, than she, seemed genuinely and pleasurably interested; and besides, wasn't it the warmest feeling in the world to tell an old friend about a new love? 'Well, if you must know, yes.'

'*Aha!*' She raised her glass. 'Here's top o' the mornin' to Maureen Callaghan and Danny . . . What's his name?'

Maureen threw peppers and mushrooms into the pan with the onions and started to chop up sausage. 'Greenberg.'

'Oh. Interesting. Well, how many times have you seen him, anyway?'

'Three, I think.' For the sheer delight of it, she allowed herself to check. 'Yes, three.'

'Well, you seem pretty keen for three meetings, I must say.'

'Do I?' Was it so obvious? 'Yes, I suppose I am, really.'

'My God. Do you always move so fast?'

It was an awkward question, almost a stranger's question. And in many ways, it struck Maureen, they were strangers still. For all the wealth of intimate detail they knew about each other—birthdays, middle names, mothers' maiden names, who had been afraid of spiders and who of catching leprosy, who had spent four years in orthodontal braces, and who had not grown breasts until she was sixteen—when it came to grown-up matters, to falling in love, to behaviour when they were in love, there was still so much, each about the other, that was new to them.

Alison was right, though. Maureen did not usually feel so strongly so soon, had tended, until then, rather to be on the wary side. But of course, until then, she had never met Dan. She took the sausages, bought at the butcher's in Kilburn High Road, her people's food, not his, and threw them into the pan, watching them turn from pink to brown. He did not eat kosher himself, but his parents did.

'I suppose I don't,' she said, smiling a secret smile. Then she remembered that Alison was having her own problems. 'I suppose,' she added hastily, partly to make her feel better, partly as her own verbal touching of wood, 'it'll all end in a mess. But it's nice while it lasts, anyway.'

'Oh, don't say that. Look, if one of us is doing OK, that ups the average, doesn't it?'

Maureen grunted, added rice, stock, and wine to the pan, and set it to simmer. Then she sat down and gave her full attention to her friend. 'What exactly is happening, anyway?'

'About Adam?' She sighed. 'According to him, nothing. We get together, and we talk, and we have a good time—we have a smashing time, actually—and he's sending out signals to me, and I'm trying not to send signals back to him, which is all quite funny really because we both know what the other one's doing, and then he tries to push it just that little bit too far, and I tick him off, and he apologises very gallantly, and while I'm busy accepting his apology, he's sneaking another push in where I'm not looking.'

'Sounds charming.'

'Well, for instance, on Friday. He sent me this huge bunch of—beautiful—flowers, and I rang him to say thanks very much, but I'd really rather he didn't. So we met for me to explain, again, why I felt that, and he was frightfully apologetic, and then he took me for a—quote—friendly dinner, and after dinner, he tried quite hard to persuade me to invite him home for a drink. And of course, if I did that . . . So I ticked him off again, and he apologised again, and said he wouldn't feel forgiven unless I had dinner with him on Monday.'

'And you said?'

'That I'd have dinner with him on Monday.'

'You know, he doesn't sound very nice to me.'

'Oh, but he is, that's the problem. He just genuinely doesn't see why I'm so dead set against sleeping with him.'

She stopped, absent-mindedly poured herself more whiskey, and sipped, hearing his voice, seeing the mole on his cheekbone, inspecting a new idea, a suspicion born sometime last Friday evening, that, for all his careful casualness, she could, if she so chose, mean more to him than at the outset he had ever bargained for.

'I've been thinking about Mother Mary Berthe,' she said abruptly.

'Tough luck.'

'Remember how, if she found us eating sweets in the grounds, she'd made us throw them in the fish pond? "Eet ees a practeeze . . ."'

'"Forr ze grreat sacreefizes of life." Silly old bag.'

'You know, I've never actually not done something that I very much wanted to do.'

'*Haven't* you?'

'Well, have you?'

'*Yes.*' She searched her mind. 'I'm sure I have. Well, I always feel as if I have.'

'You know, I sometimes envy Catholics.'

'Ha.'

'I mean play-it-by-the-rule Catholics. You know, like your mum and dad. Even if they don't always do what's right, at least they always seem to know what right is.'

'Ha.'

'Did you go to Mass today?'

'Yes. Why?'

'I just wondered.'

'Oh, hey.' Maureen jumped up, peered at the rice, stirred it, and began to grate cheese into it. 'I have to tell you. Are you still coming to Aylesford?'

'As I recall, I didn't have too much choice.'

'Yes, well, sorry about that. Denis would never have spoken to me again.' Carefully, she bent over the saucepan. 'He likes you, you know.'

'So you say.'

'He's a nice guy, is Denis.'

'Maureen! Are you matchmaking?'

'Would I?'

'Yes.'

'Well, anyway, you're to be at Charing Cross at 9.30 *en punto* on Saturday.'

'OK.'

'Sorry. It shouldn't be too bad.'

'Believe it or not, I'm quite looking forward to it.'

Which was possibly going just a little far for politeness' sake, as the look Maureen gave her while she handed her risotto expressed. But it was not so far from the truth, either: she had never been to Aylesford and had heard that it was pretty; and as for the other members of the group, she had no objection whatsoever to spending time with them. In fact, and rather to her own surprise, she was actually finding herself—almost—enjoying them, had even—almost—been sorry to miss last Friday night's meeting. They were Catholics, after all.

And why should not a Catholic—even a Catholic to as limited an extent as was she—seek out the company of other Catholics? She finished her whiskey, and smiled at Maureen, who was trying not to smile to herself as she poured cheap Spanish wine.

'Here's to both of us,' she said.

Kate sat in her bedroom, watching the rain on her window, and carefully hoarding the last fifty pages of *Bath Tangle*. It was a useless endeavour, spitting in the wind of her desolation: try as she might, she knew she could not eke the book out for much longer than an hour, and what would become of her when the book deserted her, she shivered to think. She could take a nap now, postponing the moment: but since she had not risen until noon, and sleep, unlike sorrow, came only in limited quantities, that would leave the night wide open and wide awake. At least it was raining, however, at least the sky was weeping and the transient-trodden streets of grey South Kensington would be slippery with water and messy with mud. At least she had a reason not to go for a walk.

Through the closed door, she could hear Caroline and her girlfriend Linda, their voices lowered in confidence over tea and Battenburg cake.

'I don't know what to do,' Caroline was saying. 'Richard says I shouldn't get involved, and *she* says she's fine. But she's obviously not.'

'Maybe there's something on her mind,' said Linda's voice.

'Well, actually, I think there is.'

'*Really?*' Linda's voice had perked up. 'Don't tell me she's discovered sex at last? What's he like? Is he married? Is he a she?'

'No, nothing like that.' There was a pause, rich with embarrassment. 'I think she's having problems with her . . . you know. Her religion.'

'Her *religion?*'

'Yes. They have these problems, you know. Roman Catholics. My cousin married one. It was terrible. He was always going through a, well, he called it a crisis of faith. It was a bit like the change of life, except he never got over it. My cousin divorced him in the end, she just couldn't stand it. Honestly. It was terrible.'

'Lord.' Linda was sobered. 'Poor old Kate. Well, maybe it's for the best. I mean, if she gets out of it, maybe she'll start to lead some sort of normal life at last. Oh, listen, listen. *Guess* who I saw looking *very* cosy at Tuttons, and both turning *bright* red when they saw Yours Truly?'

Kate sat in her bedroom, watching the rain on her window, and reluctantly turned another precious page of *Bath Tangle*.

Denis walked up the Strand, not thinking about the weekend. It was not difficult for him: he was well practised, and this week, he had plenty else on his mind, Geoffrey to worry about, Aylesford to look forward to, Bob's crucifix to buy. He need not if he tried—and he always did try, and usually was successful—think about the weekend at all.

There were no developments with his mother or Kathleen. Nothing had happened that was significantly different from what had happened the month before, and the month before that, the situation lacked even the sick thrill of shock, was simply monotonous, a recurrent nightmare that did not rate a morning's recounting.

His mother had looked up when he had arrived, had smiled, and had muttered—because she knew and bitterly resented her madness —'Aha! One of the sane O'Learys,' and Kathleen, who did not yet know, had laughed loudly. They had eaten a splendid lunch of steak and onions, mashed potato and cabbage, apple pie and custard in silence, and then his mother and Kathleen had both retired for naps, leaving him to his own amusement of riffling through their library books and watching *Grandstand* with the sound turned down, because Kathleen demanded total silence while she slept. The two women had risen for a late, silent tea of scones and jam, soda bread, fruitcake, and cold apple pie. After tea they had sat in the dark lounge, and talked until bedtime.

On Sunday, they had gone, as always, to Mass at the convent, where the nuns, godly women, their senses crippled by charity, their lives condemned by their sex and their vocation to tedium and other women, had, as always, exclaimed over the saintliness of his mother and Kathleen, and made much of him. That, as always, had been their sole social contact of the weekend. They had returned to a silent lunch of roast beef and Yorkshire pudding, roast potatoes, carrots, and cauliflower in white sauce, followed by bread-and-butter pudding with cream, and afterwards—since he left in the early evening, they went without their Sunday nap for his visits—had sat in the lounge and talked until it was time for him to go. Denis never knew which he dreaded more, the silence or the talk.

It was all too attractive to shut off thoughts of those visits. He had felt himself starting to do it on Sunday as he had sat on the top of the bus home, chewing his nails, and removing himself with long-learned skill from what he had encountered. What else was there for him to do? It would not change, any of it, could not be resolved. All that might be achieved by his dwelling on it would be that he might lose his own grip, the grip that he had won so hard, that only he knew to be so tenuous, might be drawn back into the fold, the prodigal son returned at last to his natural home. And what would be helped by all three of them being mad? No, there was nothing to be gained by thinking about it.

He concentrated, therefore, walking up from Charing Cross to his office, on Geoffrey. He was worried about Geoffrey. What Geoffrey had said on Friday night was, though naturally unpleasant, not the problem. What worried him was the resolution with which the other had shut his mind to what Denis was trying to tell him. If even half of what Philip had said were true—and the number of telephone calls that Philip had made on Friday afternoon, and the expression on his face after each call, indicated that it was—then Geoffrey was in trouble. At best, it would be a nasty shock; at worst . . . well, if Francis were in it to the extent which at this stage it appeared, there seemed little limit to what the worst for Geoffrey, knowingly involved or not knowingly involved, might be. And now, when of all times he needed a friend, he seemed to be turning against Denis, his only friend. It was all very worrying.

He reached Lancaster Place, and caught a glimpse of the Thames, gleaming gunmetal-grey under Waterloo Bridge, flowing from his place of work to Geoffrey's, and beyond, almost to Westminster Cathedral, and the little repository where he absolutely must find time to go this week and buy the crucifix. There was one thing, at any rate, it seemed he need no longer worry about: Alison. Denis knew himself and his feelings about girls, and this battle was one he seemed, please God and blast it, to be winning. At least, she wasn't everywhere any more, as even a week ago she had been. He looked back to his state of mind on the previous weekend, and shook his head with the pitying detachment of one remembering a drunken escapade. Yes, it was definitely over, thank God and blast it, and he could regard her in the only way he could ever allow himself to regard girls, as a pleasant companion. If only he felt so optimistic about the situation with Geoffrey.

By the time he reached his office, he had put the weekend completely out of his mind.

By Monday, Geoffrey had his plan of campaign worked out. Saturday was the time, and Aylesford the place, where he would lay his claim on Alysoun. This nonsense with Denis had gone far enough. It was time for Geoffrey to make his move.

A pity, in a way, even to pay Denis the compliment of taking him seriously. In fact, for a while, Geoffrey had been tempted to drop out of the Aylesford trip altogether, leaving the field contemptuously clear, proving that even without competition present, one such as Denis could be regarded as no competition at all. But on further reflection, he had decided he would go. He would go, and he would return a conqueror. He had played Denis's game for long enough: time now to slap him into place, to show him, with his lies and his trickery and his blarneying scandalmongery, just who was the boss. And what better way to do it than to return from English Aylesford, in full view, tall and smiling, with Alysoun smiling on his arm?

Not, of course, that he was worthy of her, no one was. But if he pressed his suit, there among the old English stone covered with wet Kent greenery where quiet friars had prayed for knights at the crusades, and Simon of Stock had seen and spoken with Our Lady in the damp grass, how could she refuse? She was all things kind and gracious, she was Alysoun. She could not say him no.

'You look cheerful,' said Sue.

Geoffrey raised an enigmatic eyebrow. Poor cheap little Sue. If she only knew.

'He must be in love,' joked Nigel.

Geoffrey did not trouble to react.

They were both in early, though—Big Ben had barely struck the half-hour—and both, to Geoffrey's satisfaction, seeming on the nervous side. It had been a long conversation they had had with Francis on Friday afternoon, and both had returned, although they had tried to brazen it out, noticeably shaken. And high time, too, in Geoffrey's opinion. They had both taken the country's money for long enough, and given in return, God knew, little enough, and, inexplicably, got away with it so far: if Francis were beginning at last effectively to crack the whip, it was not, he thought, a moment too soon.

And if Francis were indeed cracking that whip, there was no question but that they would both feel it, and sharply. That was a thing Francis and he had in common: you could push them so far, and so far they would not waste their energy in resisting, but push them that inch, that one-tenth of an inch over the edge, and then watch out. As Nigel and Sue were apparently finding already, as that dirty little Denis would find on Saturday. Meanwhile . . .

'Simmonds! *Miss* Townsend!!' The office door opened, and Francis's huge head was thrust through. 'Shift your foul carcasses into my office on the double. Johnson, you might wipe that grin off your face, and—who knows?—even get on with some work.'

Meanwhile, he could look forward to a particularly pleasurable week of watching Nigel and Sue get precisely what was coming to them.

Anne always took Duty at Monday-morning break, walking the asphalt playground in solitary omnipotence while around her children swooped and shrieked, playing games that, had they known or cared, had likely been played by childish ancestors before the Normans conquered England. Her reputation was for vigilance, but today she was distant, even—had anyone dared to try her, which no one did—abstracted. She was enjoying her first full privacy of mind since the weekend, using it to turn over again and again the information that had been hers on Friday evening. That this coming Friday, there would be no group meeting, and Stephen would be out until late at an office party. That she would be, as Maureen had teasingly put it, a free woman. Free to do what she wanted, go where she wanted . . . meet whom she wanted.

Stephen—if she chose to go, and, going, chose not to tell him —need not know if she met Brian's friend Andrea. To deceive him would be simple, wretchedly, fatefully so. Friday was a school half-holiday, and she could all too naturally slip into town to buy some clothes for the coming spring. She could go in in the afternoon, stay until the middle evening, and the deception would be complete. Drinking late with his work friends, he would not even know.

At least, he would not know immediately. Soon enough, if she were to go, he would find out. Soon enough, as her imagination grasped the idea and soared, when her name was on every lip, her voice was heard everywhere, when princes sought to know her, and young girls dreamed of being her, when magazines interviewed her, and films were made of her life story, when she was a legend, a byword, was famous, famous . . .

She shook her head and laughed at herself. A woman of her age, a married woman, dreaming dreams that were better suited to her sister Michelle, sixteen in age, and, as Claire was fond of suggesting, little more in IQ. Even if she were to meet Andrea, which she wouldn't, she might well (as Brian himself, elephantinely machiavellian, had suggested) not even pass the audition for the show, and that would be as it should be, as it rightly should be.

But what if, asked the new, secret, unrecognisable Anne, just what if fame did find her? People, after all, did pass the audition, did appear on the show, were launched to new careers, new lives from it. Why not Anne? And if it happened to Anne, not the foolish dream but the actuality, how would Stephen react, how would he cope? She would have deceived him, and to achieve a result that would break his heart. Would she, having done that, find that his love for her had boundaries, after all, far-flung though they were? Or would she find that it just stretched on and on, like a recurring digit, like opposite mirrors? Which did she find more frightening? And how could she bear not knowing which it would be?

Two seven-year-old boys, fighting with the fury of best friends, cannoned into her knees, their twin expressions of absorbed rage turning to horrified realisation, painfully comic. She dusted them down, reprimanded them, sent them on their way with a friendly cuff across the head, and they ran off happily enough. They liked her. She liked them; she was a good teacher.

She was an even better singer.

It was better to be at work. Kate sat at her desk, sorting through the morning mail, grateful for five busy days ahead. Work was something you had to do, the perfect excuse not to think about anything else, not to think at all. Work was the answer, the more routine the better. She wished her desk were untidy so that she could clear it out. She wished it were Tuesday afternoon, so that she could file. She wished . . .

The telephone rang, and she reached for it hopefully. Perhaps it would mean more work.

'May I speak to Kate Waters, please?' said the voice on the other end.

'This is Kate Waters,' she replied.

'Kate. Hi. This is Maureen.'

Maureen! Kate covered the mouthpiece, her eyes darting furtively around the empty office. What should she say? What would she do?

'Hello?' said Maureen's voice. She sounded happy, but then most people sounded happier than Kate.

'Hello, Maureen.'

'How're you doing?'

'I'm fine, thank you. How are you?'

'Me? Oh, grand. Listen, we missed you on Friday. Was something wrong?'

Was something wrong. How could she convey to Maureen, who had spent a lifetime battling the Church, the chaos which had overtaken her?

'I had a touch of flu.'

'Oh, dear.'

'I'm better now.'

'Well, you take care, it's still bloody cold out. Listen, about Saturday.'

'Saturday?'

'Aylesford?'

She had completely forgotten.

'You are still coming, aren't you?'

How could she possibly go? How could she spend a day with Catholics, she who was, unthinkably, it seemed, no longer one of them? How could she look in the eye and wish happy birthday to the man whose colleague, whose spiritual brother, had pulled from under her feet the carpet which she had thought was nailed to the floor, was part of the floor itself? How could she possibly spend the day watching Denis watching *her*?

But then, having already agreed to go, what excuse could she possibly now make?

'Yes, of course I am.'

'Grand. Listen, there's no meeting on Friday, so be at Charing Cross at 9.30, and don't be late, or Denis will duff you up. Good. Well, I'll see you then, then.'

'Yes.'

There was a silent pause.

'It should be fun,' said Maureen's voice, hopefully.

'Yes,' said Kate. 'Yes, I'm looking forward to it.'

She put down the telephone, and continued to sort through the morning's mail.

After Midday Mass, Bob knelt in the sacristy for his private thanksgiving, today more fervent than usual. The relief that had seemed to begin on Friday had not, as a corner of him had feared, proved deceptive: rather, it had gained and strengthened over the weekend, until here it was only Monday, and he felt himself light-years removed from the man he had been the Monday before. Thanks, Pal.

A curious week it was, though, the last week of his young manhood. By the Monday to come, he would be thirty. Thirty. He prodded the idea, cautiously, stood back and examined it from different angles. The notion had been pushed to the back of his mind lately—chronology being a trivial matter in comparison with wrestling with demons—and taking it out again, he was surprised to find, as an unexpected bonus to his other blessing, that he was growing positively accustomed, almost even resigned, to the thought.

He had journeyed so great a distance in the last couple of weeks.

He had fought temptation, as Paul had fought it, and Jerome in the desert, and Christ on the mountain top; he had fought it, and by God, and thank God—thanks, Pal—he had won. He had broken through his runner's wall, he was God's athlete. A tough training, it had been, long days and merciless nights, for which now, looking back from the safe other side, he could even feel a sort of nostalgia—because the training had paid off. He had made it. And yes, he could even look forward with mild pleasure to seeing her on Saturday as he looked forward to seeing the others. She had no power over him now, now that he had—thanks, Pal—won. Hell, he deserved to be thirty.

He got up, dusted his knees, and prepared to go back into the church. Sister Martin had been in the congregation, and had had the unmistakable look on her face of one about to invite him back to the convent for her famous fruitcake. Well, it was Lent, after all. 'Thy will be done,' he said with a wink, squared his shoulders, and strode like a man approaching thirty back into the body of the church.

At least her tan was still holding up. In fact, Alison decided, peering into the mirror, she really didn't look too bad at all for someone who had downed almost half a bottle of whiskey just the day before. True, her eyes had been on the pink side that morning, but a brisk lunch-time walk had soon cleared that up. And at least she was still one of the few blondes in London in March who could wear white.

'But of course.' Sally sauntered into the room. 'The six o'clock hair fluff. As distinct from the 5.45 reapplication of perfume. And the 5.30 mascara check. And all for this extremely married man on whom she has not the faintest dishonourable design at all.'

Squinting at Sally's reflection behind her own, Alison decided to apply the ultimate silencer. 'Do you ever examine your conscience?' she asked.

Predictably, but satisfyingly nonetheless, Sally was thrown.

'Do I *what*?'

'Examine your conscience. You know, work out what sins you've committed lately. We were always doing it at school. We had great long lists in our prayer books of things we might have done. We had to go through them every night.'

'Good God.' Sally, she was delighted to see, was torn between disapproval, embarrassment, and a certain morbid curiosity. 'What if you thought you hadn't done anything?'

'Oh, that was the worst. Spiritual pride.'

'Good Lord.' She was actually bereft of speech. She shrugged herself into her coat, and picked up her bag. 'I'm going home. Good-night.'

As the door closed, Alison exchanged a snigger with herself in the mirror. Then she stopped laughing, as the strange loneliness rolled around her yet again. A joke was a sad joke if you could not share it, and this incident she would not be able to relate to anyone. Maureen, who had met and disliked Sally, would derive infinitely too much satisfaction from it, and no one else at the office would even begin to understand. Adam? Yes, oddly enough, Adam would understand, but she certainly was not going to give him the chance. The side issues that it would bring up would be far too complicated; and besides, the longer she knew him, the less, for some reason, she found herself wanting to expose to him even indirectly the wasting, dying thing that had once been her sturdy Faith. Poor Catholicism, she thought suddenly, not for her rooted in a rich tradition, like Maureen's, but a seed sprinkled on thin soil, to spring up quickly, and quickly to die.

But it was not gone completely, or else why did she have the nagging Mother Cecilia feeling she had, even as she checked herself in the mirror, that what she was doing was wrong? Was—here came Mother Cecilia again—a sin?

Of course, every reason in her body told her that it was not a sin. She was having dinner, just dinner, with a friend, who happened to be a man, who happened several years ago to have made a promise to a woman that neither had, since then, even pretended to take seriously. What in the world could be sinful about that?

But sin, as every convent girl knew, recognised no reasons, it sprang, not from the mind or the deed, but from the heart, from the—whatever that was—conscience, from the—whatever in heaven or hell *that* was—soul. Alison as a child had seen her soul as a roundish white blob lurking somewhere behind her ribcage. When she had sinned, the blob was splattered with dark marks like ink stains; when she had been to confession, or made a good act of contrition, the blob was clean again. Of course, she knew now that the soul, if she or anyone had a soul, was not so comic-book simple as that. But she still did not want to sin. She still based her image of herself on the assumption that, most of the time, she did not sin.

Was what she was doing tonight a sin? Assessing it, she decided that, in her terms, it was not. Were she to start an affair with Adam, however, that would be, again in her terms, and after all it was she who had to live with herself, not Adam and not Mother Cecilia, a grievous sin. Now if she could only rid herself of the uncomfortable little suspicion that tonight was, if not actually sinning, at least putting herself, culpably, into the occasion of sin . . .

She shook herself. Grievous sin. Occasion of sin. She was even beginning to sound like Mother Cecilia. It wasn't an occasion of sin, what she was doing, it wasn't any sort of sin at all, but no more nor less than thousands of young women all over London and all over Europe were doing at that precise moment: checking their faces in the mirror before going out to a flirtatious dinner with an attractive man who liked them. Granted, there were complications in this instance. And granted that she knew that, at some point in the not too distant future, she would have to sit herself down and sort out where her priorities truly lay. But until then . . .

Until then, she carefully wiped a minuscule blob of mascara from an eyelash, nodded at herself, her conscience, and the gaunt spectre of Mother Cecilia in the mirror, and ran down into Beauchamp Place to hail a taxi.

'The trouble with Jews,' said Daniel, setting down his glass in the beer puddle he had spilled earlier in the evening, 'is that they're too bloody clannish.'

'God,' said Maureen, 'Catholics, too.'

'Jews are worse,' said Daniel.

'You want to bet? Listen, when I was a kid, we lived next door to a Methodist family. Methodist, mind, not atheists or Satanists, or . . . Well, we used to pray for them every night, that they'd get converted to the true Church. You know, see the light. I mean, they'd have freaked if they'd known, and I can't say I'd blame them.'

'Jews are worse,' said Daniel. 'They don't even want converts. If you're not chosen from birth, then you're just not chosen.'

'And my church is worse than your church, so yah-boo.'

He laughed. 'I never thought I'd meet someone like you,' he said.

'Nor me,' she replied.

She never had. What a rare, what a one-in-ten-million chance it had been that had thrown them together. And how extraordinary it was that the chance should happen to her, who had never in her life won or expected to win a gamble or a bet or (unless you counted the framed postcard of Madonna Della Strada from the weekly school WEEF raffle, which she had won once in the second form) a prize of any sort. But it seemed that somehow, somewhere, her number had come up at last. And looking across the scratched wooden table at him, blinking at her in his troglodyte way over his beer puddle, she could not think of a way she had rather have it come.

The lights of the pub flicked off and on, and the barman shouted some words.

'Is that the time?' He brought his arm up and squinted at his watch.

She laughed, pointing at it. 'Don't tell me it's working again.'

'I think it is. I forgot my glasses, so I can't see.'

She took his wrist and looked. Eleven o'clock. 'Bugger. Closing time.'

'Really? I thought it was a lot earlier.'

'Me, too.' She studied her wine glass and tried not to blush, cursing her Irish skin. 'I've, uh, got some whiskey at home if you'd like?'

She looked at him through her lashes. He was not blushing, but he was looking into his glass. 'Actually, I've got a rather busy day tomorrow. If you don't mind?'

'OK.' What was surprising was that it really was OK. Such a reaction from, for instance, Jonathan, would have destroyed her, but Jonathan had been different. This was different. There was no pressure here, no hurry. It would happen when it happened, it would be however it would be when it did happen, and until then they could take it slowly. She bid me take love slowly, as the apples take the rain. Or however the song went.

'D'you feel like a walk by the river?' he said.

'It's a bit chilly, isn't it?'

'A bit.'

'OK, then.'

They walked down to the Thames and along the deserted Embankment, watching the cold white lights on the cold black water. Almost absent-mindedly, he dropped his arms around her shoulders, and she reached her own arm inside his coat and around his waist. It was not a hard body like Jonathan's, but slightly pudgy, the body of a man who did not exercise enough for his size. They walked in silence from King's College down to the Houses of Parliament, and Maureen, for all the lack of pressure, hoped it would happen very soon.

It was a nice crucifix, and well worth a couple of pounds' addition to the kitty, plainly traditional, in good wood, with a brass figure of Christ. Denis was pleased with it. A crucifix was not the most imaginative gift in the world for a priest, but then the advantage of unimaginative gifts was that it was difficult to go wrong with them. Of course, the imaginativeness or not of a gift depended largely on the recipient: he wondered what would be the reaction of Maureen, for instance, if he were to give her a crucifix for her birthday. Perhaps he would try it and find out.

He lifted the cross, solid and reassuringly heavy, from the repository shelf, and carried it past the jumble, familiar from childhood, of white-boxed prayer books, rosaries in clear plastic cases, and trays of cheap medals of saints, to the counter. The woman at the till was familiar, too, not personally but as a species, sweet-faced and close-mouthed, an Irish type he had known since, it felt, before he was born, and as he paid for and took the crucifix, they smiled at each other in silent recognition, two Catholics in a Protestant land.

He wandered out of the repository, through the back streets to the front of the Cathedral and sat down on one of the benches in the piazza, staring at the tall tower that had never looked quite in place against the London skyline. It was not a cathedral he associated particularly with London, anyway, but more with Europe, with standing amid a sea of wheelchairs for special pilgrim Masses before the boat train left for Lourdes, or himself stumbling in alone and travel stained on the way home from Gatwick. Doubtless he would feel differently if he worked around here, like the people hurrying in and out now. He would probably go in himself in a minute, might even stay for Mass if there were one starting.

Someone tall and fair crossed the piazza, walking with a familiar stride, his head held high. It was Geoffrey. Denis watched him, wondering whether it would be more politic to beard him and demand a further discussion, or simply to turn his head away and pretend that he had not seen him. While he was wondering, Geoffrey looked down, and their eyes met. Instinctively, Denis half rose. The other stared at him with hard eyes, and walked on.

Feeling both foolish and annoyed, Denis sat back on the hard bench. It was all so childish. But he could not find it in him to feel too much anger with Geoffrey, not with the *Sentinel* coming out tomorrow. It would be nasty, damned nasty. Philip had made sure of that. He had given it his all. He had spent the whole of Monday at his typewriter, his furious tapping interrupted by occasional wordless shouts of savage joy; he had spent this morning prowling the office like a cat on hot bricks; he was there now, at lunch-time, waiting for the early editions which would not arrive until late afternoon. Denis had never seen him so excited, and understandably so; in such a situation he would have been the same himself. It was a journalist's dream, a spy scandal delivered to his doorstep, a rattling good yarn that would expose corruption, send men to prison, topple a political party. What a pity that Denis was not only a journalist, but also Geoffrey's friend.

Poor Geoffrey. He had so little in his life, and it seemed that, of what little he had, so much would be taken away. 'God's a funny feller,' his mother had used to say, in the days when she was still capable of conversation. A funny feller, indeed. Denis suspected, however, that Geoffrey would not be laughing.

With Geoffrey in the church and ignoring him, Denis did not feel inclined to go in himself. Nor, on the other hand, did he feel any more inclined to go back to the office. The early editions would arrive any hour now, and, sorry though he was not to be able to share Philip's hour of triumph, he really did not feel he could face seeing them. On an impulse, he decided not to go back to the office that afternoon. He was due to interview an actress in Twickenham late that afternoon, and he could perfectly well fill in the time until then by researching her life story at the British Film Institute. The editor would not be pleased, but the editor could, in the editor's own words, do the other thing. The only problem was that it would mean humping this bloody cross with him all afternoon. Well, at least he was in good company there.

Wondering briefly how he would survive if he did not amuse himself, Denis picked up his cross and carried it.

*　　*　　*

It was almost spring. Anne had stopped on the way home from school to buy a bunch of blazing gold daffodils and white-as-purity narcissus, and arranged them in the earthenware jug to stand where the sunlight caught the table in the afternoon. She sat now, sipping a cup of tea—no biscuits, she had been good this week—and looking at them with pleasure. Almost spring.

She had not heard from Brian since Thursday, which was just as well. 'Just as well,' she repeated aloud, nodding her head approvingly; he would only have been bullying her to meet him and his awful friend Andrea on Friday, and she was so stupid she would probably have let slip that she would be free after all, and then there would have been no peace from him. No, it was just as well as it was, letting sleeping dogs lie, leaving her and her husband to live happy lives in obscurity, not, of course, that there had ever been any real chance of obscurity's lack in the first place, so that the disharmony that would doubtless have been caused would have doubtless have been caused for nothing and it was all just, just as well.

And then the telephone rang, and her heart jumped in her mouth.

She waited four rings before she answered it, not wishing to seem too eager.

'Hello.'

'Hello?'

And her heart plummeted to her shoes: it was a girl's voice.

'Can I speak to Sharon, please?'

'I'm afraid you have the wrong number.'

'Oh. Sorry.' The receiver dropped.

Anne sat for a moment, looking at the mouthpiece, listening to the dead dialing tone, examining the set of reactions she had just gone through. No reason for thinking it was Brian: she had been sure it was. No reason for disappointment that it was not he: she had been, granted just for a second, crushed with it. This was going beyond an idle daydream in the morning playground. She wanted—no, she needed—to talk to Stephen.

He answered at the second ring, his well-known voice a stranger's.

'Stephen Collins.'

'Hello, Stephen.'

'Oh.' His voice melted, became silly, he actually giggled. 'It's you. Hello.'

'Just wanted to say hello.'

'Well, that's nice.' His voice lowered. She imagined him swivelling his chair away from the rest of the office, talking close into the telephone's mouthpiece. 'Hello.'

'Hello.' A pause. She began to feel foolish. Why had she called him, anyway? Something cold pushed her to add, 'And to tell you we've run out of milk, so would you pick some up on the way home, please?'

'Lazybones.' He was delighted at the request, his voice did not begin to conceal it. 'Why don't you go to the dairy now?'

'Oh, I'm all in and unbuttoned.' She paused. 'Please.'

'So I've got to trek all the way to Muhammed's?'

'It's not that far.' It was a lie, the errand would add a good fifteen minutes to his walk home from the tube. 'Please.'

'Oh, all right.' He sighed in pure contentment. 'If I must.'

He would do it, there had never been any doubt about it. The coldness pushed her on, pushed her to push him.

'Are you still going drinking on Friday?'

'Well, yes. We did agree, didn't we?'

'Oh, yes.' Of course she had agreed; but even now, she had only to lift a finger, to breathe a word . . . And suddenly, she was saying other words. 'It's just I thought, if you're definitely going to be out, I might go up to town myself and meet Sarah.'

'Good idea.' His tone was as free of suspicion as a child's. 'We'll be one of those sophisticated couples with separate social lives.'

'Well, I'll think about it.'

'No, do it. I don't like to think of you at home alone, anyway.'

'I'll see.'

'OK.'

When he hung up, she did not, but continued to look at the telephone as she had a few moments before. It had all been so easy, so chillingly easy. And she had not spoken to her brother-in-law for almost a week, and what harm could it possibly do to find out exactly when and exactly where he would be meeting his friends? She put the receiver down, and went to look up his telephone number.

It was Wednesday morning, and the *Sentinel* had been out for several hours. So far, however, Denis had managed to avoid seeing it. He had done so simply by avoiding all newsagents and news-stands, denying himself even his *Guardian* to read on the train to work, and now, as he walked up the Strand to the office, keeping his head turned rigorously to the left, towards the traffic, and well away from all possible sight of newsprint. It was pointless, he knew, would not change a thing, but still, the longer he could keep himself from the physical confrontation of the fact, the longer he could cling to his foolish hope that something had happened while he was out of the office yesterday, that Philip's big scoop—tough luck for Philip, but those were the breaks after all—might have turned out, miraculously, at the last moment, to have been nothing but a great, embarrassing, catastrophic mistake. Foolish, unrealistic of him, but there would be plenty of time for realism later on. With the super-human effort that the Jesuits call custody of the eyes, he kept his gaze averted even from the news-stand at the entrance to the Temple —and it was *Private Eye* day, too—crossed Fleet Street, and went into the *Sentinel* offices. As he was slinking into the editorial room, he met the editor coming out.

'Ah, O'Leary,' the editor greeted him cheerfully enough. 'And a very good afternoon to you. So good of you to make time in your day to drop in.'

'As a matter of fact,' said Denis, 'I was out on the story until ten o'clock last night.'

'Of course you were,' beamed the editor. 'And as a matter of fact, you missed a rather good drink up we had yesterday evening to celebrate your comrade's little coup.'

And that was the end of his fantasy. 'Oh?' he said, slowly.

'Oh? Oh? Don't tell me you haven't seen the issue.' He snatched one from a pile, and thrust it at Denis. It would have been impossible for it to have been worse than he had feared. But it was fully as bad. 'We've had—let's see, Londoner's Diary called last night, and the *Mirror*, and the *Guardian*, and—get this—the *Telegraph* this morning, and that's only so far. I'm waiting for Scotland Yard, but maybe they're still stuck on the hard words. There's going to be trouble, anyway. Well, say something, man.'

'That's great,' said Denis. 'Really great.' The bugger of it was that for Philip, and the *Sentinel*, and the truth that should be told that the *Sentinel* tried to tell, it really was great.

The editor looked at him for a moment. 'Ah,' he said at last. 'Ah, I see. You *were* out on the story, weren't you?' With a careful hand, he guided Denis to his desk, and sat him down. 'I'll get Shirley to bring you an aspirin,' he whispered. 'Come and see me when you feel up to it.'

He tiptoed out, quietly closing the door behind him.

Left alone, Denis swung back on his chair, and put his feet up on his desk. He drew the triumphant latest issue of the *Sentinel* towards him, and glared at it.

Geoffrey could not tear his eyes from the *Sentinel*. It held him as the sight of a cat killing a mouse, a sight utterly repellent, irresistibly hypnotic. And to think that he had thought that Denis's last little exploit had rendered him pretty well unshockable. But that was before this, this lie, spread in dirty newsprint, clear across the country. Geoffrey himself was not mentioned in the lie, it was too clever for that. But Francis was. And Margaret Bellweather and the letters (how had Denis known about those? Geoffrey suddenly remembered seeing him outside the Cathedral the previous day: could he have taken to trailing him around London?), and even Nigel and Sue, not named but recognisable to those who knew them, all jumbled up in a cockamamie story of double agents and foreign powers. Were it not so sick, it would have been laughable.

It was clever, though, he had to admit it was clever. To fasten on a minor infringement of security, and blow it into something like this, and then not even to risk the repercussions of writing the article himself but to feed it to that chap Philip he was always talking about, making him his dupe, oh, it was very clever. And all to warn Geoffrey away from Alysoun. And that was extraordinary.

He continued to stare at the paper, and tried to imagine how one man could bend so far, dabble so deep in the muck of human potential. He failed, and he must be thankful for that. It was beyond outrage, beyond Geoffrey's ken. His frame of reference did not, thank God, simply could not encompass what his senses and the paper in front of him told him to be so. Something clicked in Geoffrey's brain, and shut off. It did not bear inspection.

It was not himself, of course, that he was worried about. He knew what was happening, knew what those lies in the paper meant, why they were there: what must Francis, who did not know, be going through at that moment? Francis, whose life was his country, to have his loyalty to his country called into question: what must he be thinking? Feeling? Terrible, terrible—and the most terrible of all was that it was he, Geoffrey, who had got him into this mess. Not that it was in any sense his fault: the fault, and such fault as the mind recoiled to acknowledge, lay squarely with Denis. But Geoffrey, innocent though he was, had been the cause of it all. Had he not stood so squarely, so tall and solid, between Denis and his Alysoun, all of this might have been avoided.

He must, naturally, explain it all to Francis at the first possible opportunity. The problem was finding that opportunity. Francis had been unavailable all morning, his motherly secretary turning from his door everyone from other secretaries to Cabinet Ministers, to —naturally—such of the raggle-taggle horde of Denis's colleagues as had made their way past the security guards at the gate. He was locked in his office now with, the secretary had told him, Nigel and Sue, talking, presumably, to his solicitor about the libel suit. Geoffrey would go to him as soon as he possibly could, and confess the whole sorry, sordid business to him. He hoped that Francis would understand and forgive him: he, after all, was thrown as much into the company of Denis's countrymen as was Geoffrey. But if he did not, then that was Geoffrey's loss, and he would simply have to live with it. There was a side of him that would even rejoice at the extra burden on Denis's already overladen conscience.

The door opened, and Nigel and Sue walked in. Both looked dazed, and the white March sunlight in the office showed up for the first time a puffiness in Nigel's cheeks, and little lines under the make-up around Sue's eyes.

'Hello,' said Geoffrey, feeling a wartime spirit of friendliness. Whatever else these people had done, they had never tried to trick him.

'Hello,' said Sue, wearily. Even Nigel nodded. Geoffrey wondered whether he should explain to them now—since they, too, after all, were affected—or wait until he had seen Francis.

'This,' he began, 'is a monstrous thing.'

'You know,' said Sue, 'I think that monstrous is quite a good word for it.'

There was probably the friendliest silence that the three of them had known.

'What happened with the lawyers?' said Geoffrey.

'Lawyers?' The two exchanged a quick glance.

'For the libel suit? You are suing presumably?'

'Oh, those lawyers.' Sue closed her eyes. 'We haven't been in touch with them yet. Francis is . . . is hoping it'll all blow over.'

That was like Francis. He would keep his dignity for as long as he possibly could. But then, maybe he was underestimating Denis's determination. And to think that Geoffrey had once thought of Denis as a friend. On a rare impulse, he decided to confide in his colleagues.

'I have a confession to make,' he said abruptly.

Nigel, who had been slouching in his chair, sat up and looked at him. 'Have you, now?' he said.

Geoffrey gritted his teeth. This was not going to be easy. But one thing the Church had given him was practice in admitting guilt. 'I am very much afraid,' he said, 'that, if you are wondering who to blame for the article, the answer is . . . me.'

There was a hard, cold pause.

'What exactly,' said Nigel eventually, 'do you mean?'

'I have a . . . an associate on that paper.'

The pause lengthened, froze into ice.

'And?' said Nigel.

'And.' And Geoffrey wished with all his heart that he had not started this. But they should know; they deserved to know. 'And this associate has a . . . grudge against me. And there are, apparently, few depths to which he will not sink to satisfy that grudge. With lies.'

Something had happened, the atmosphere had changed.

'Lies,' repeated Geoffrey. 'Calumnies. Libels. They're for my benefit, and,' he held his head high, 'I can only apologise to you—and Francis . . .'

'Libels?' said Sue.

'Calumnies?' said Nigel.

They looked at each other, and it was as it had always been, the two of them, banded together, laughing at him.

'Don't you know?' gurgled Sue. 'Geoffrey, don't you *know*?'

'I know,' said Geoffrey, 'the power of a lie. A malevolent lie.'

'Geoffrey.' She was laughing even harder. 'Geoffrey, darling Geoffrey, it's not a lie at all, it's all true. Look.' She came across to his desk, and pointed at the article. 'It's true. I don't know how they found out, but it's gospel every word.'

He looked up at her bending over him, and his eyes narrowed. 'Indeed?' he replied.

'You don't know the trouble you're in, Geoffrey, do you? Did you really think you were just taking harmless little letters to that bloody Bellweather woman? Because you weren't, you know. She and Francis have been in cahoots for years. And those letters weren't harmless, they were top, top secret. And she passed them on. And whoever she passed them on to, passed them on again. Francis has been selling secrets practically since he arrived here. And you've been helping him. So did Nigel and I, but the difference was that we knew, and that—that *shit* Francis never told you.'

'I see,' said Geoffrey. Jigsaw pieces fell into place, and it all became clear to him. 'I see.'

'How did you think I could afford to dress like this? Or Nigel —have you seen Nigel's car? We've been with him longer than you, Geoffrey. And what we're going to do now, and what Francis is going to do, and what you, poor Geoffrey, are going to do is—just . . . about . . . anybody's . . . guess.' She stopped, and doubled over, giggling.

Nigel stood up. 'I know what I'm going to do,' he said. 'I'm going to go across the road to the pub, and have several very large gins.' He looked over at Sue, and bowed from the waist. 'Will you join me, my lady?'

Still giggling, she swept him a curtsey, her expensive skirt floating to the floor. 'I will, my lord.'

After they had gone, Geoffrey sat looking out of the window. So that was how it was. Denis had recruited them to his side, too. State secrets passed on, indeed. She had shown him the Fra Angelico. It was clever of Denis, though. Not difficult, since they were both easily enough bought, God knew. But clever all the same. But how it all stank of spiritual putrefaction.

Geoffrey returned to his work—that no one else seemed to be working today was no reason why he should not—and by dint of heavy concentration managed not to think that, if anyone else had done this to him, it would be Denis he would immediately have discussed it with.

Maureen bought the latest *Sentinel* at the news-stand outside Tottenham Court Road station, and smiled to herself at the cover. Another spy scandal. She tucked the paper under her arm, her mind already whirling with sarcastic comments for Denis, wheeled her bicycle to a side-street, and chained it in a spot where, if it became necessary and the odds were with her, she could probably leave it unstolen until the next morning. If it became necessary and the odds proved against her, well, a bicycle would be a small price to pay.

She drifted towards Oxford Street and the Tottenham, her eyes already on the *Sentinel*, although she was expecting time enough in the pub to read it. She was a little early, and Daniel had said he might well be late, both of them, as it happened, having had the afternoon off. She had cycled to Notting Hill to buy sherry for herself, and *turrón* for him, since he said he had never tried it. He had been to Stamford Hill to take some books to his grandfather. There was something particularly attractive about a strong young man who was kind to an old one. She sent up a prayer—now that her prayers seemed, mysteriously, worthy of answer—that she would need to leave her bicycle overnight.

Outside the door of the pub, and below the paper, she heard a noise. 'Maureen,' it said. 'Maureen Callaghan.' She looked down. It was small, fair, immaculate, and carrying several shopping bags. It was Marianne Twomey from school, the nuns' favourite.

'Hello, Marianne,' said Maureen.

'Hel*lo*!' Unquestioning of her welcome, Marianne flashed small, pearly teeth. 'And where are *you* off to?'

Maureen did not like her tone at all. 'I am going,' she said firmly, 'into the pub. For a drink.'

'Oh, *good*. I'll join you. I hate sitting in pubs alone, don't you?'

Maureen's charity had been too deeply and painfully ingrained to allow her a reply. She led the way in, arms, legs, and torso bloating, as they invariably had in Marianne's presence, to roughly three times their usual size, gruffly ordered red wine for herself and sweet martini for Marianne, and manfully, Marianne followed in her wake, shouldered her way through the crowd to a table.

'So tell me,' she said, later, when they had discussed, briefly, Maureen's work, and, at length, the Bernadette problem, 'what are you doing these days?'

'Oh, don't you know?' She laughed. Maureen did not know: Marianne had always known more about other people's business than they had known about hers. 'I'm teaching domestic science and—would you believe this?—religious education!' She laughed again, seeing intense humour in the situation. 'Not at St Joseph's, of course. Can you imagine spending your whole life at one school? No,

I've gone over to the rivals, the Holy Name. I never know *who* to shout for at netball matches, it's hilarious. *And,*' she waved a ringed left hand in Maureen's face, 'I'm getting married next month, and you'll never *guess* who to!'

'I couldn't possibly,' said Maureen.

She leaned forward impressively. 'Tony Vittoria!'

A response was called for. 'I don't think . . .' began Maureen slowly.

'Oh, you remember Tony, of course you do! From St John Bosco's. We were all madly in love with him in the Fifth Form. Anyway, we started going out a couple of years ago, and . . .' She stopped, and spread her hands. Then she laughed again. 'I went all the way to Birmingham to teachers' training college, came back, and married the boy next door! Still, I always say, if the boy next door was good enough for Princess Di . . .'

She probably always did. Maureen sat looking down at her sausage fingers locked around her nearly empty glass next to Marianne's nearly full, and felt herself further from her own past than her grandmother, stumbling from the train into fifty-years-ago Paddington Station, had travelled from her salt-swept village in County Mayo.

'It looks as if your friend's stood you up,' said Marianne. 'Whoever she is.'

He *was* late. Maureen fought down the rising certainty that he had met on the tube and fallen in love with someone slim, blonde, and charming. '*He,*' she replied repressively, 'didn't say an exact time.'

'He!' Amusement and surprise warred on Marianne's face: Maureen had been famous at school for not having boyfriends. 'Well, he isn't very gallant. I should take him to task about it if I were you. Tony hates me waiting for him in pubs. He says he doesn't know what sort of trouble I'd be getting into!'

Maureen swallowed. 'He . . .' she began, when he arrived, tall and broad, shrinking her to normal size, reducing Marianne to a midget, a freak. He loomed over her, wearing his cleaner jacket, and kissed her on the cheek. He was breathless with haste, and had had a haircut.

'Maureen, darling, I'm sorry I'm so late! Have you been waiting for hours?'

He had called her darling.

'It was my grandfather. His heart, you know, he had an attack. God, it's all been frantic, I'm sorry!'

He had . . . his grandfather.

'Daniel, is he OK? What happened? Should you have . . .'

'Oh, he's fine now, he has them quite often. No, you're sweet, but don't worry. It was just a question of phoning aunts and waiting for doctors and stuff. Listen.'

'Oh. Marianne, this is Daniel. Daniel, Marianne.'

Marianne smiled her pretty smile. Daniel nodded unseeingly. 'Listen, can we go somewhere else? Somewhere quiet? I want to talk to you.'

'Sure.'

'If you're still speaking to me, that is.'

'I'll let you know. 'Bye, Marianne.'

As they left the pub, Maureen could see Marianne's neat jaw hanging half-way down her crisply pressed blouse. Daniel had ignored Marianne. He had called *her* darling. He looked utterly wonderful. And, oh yes, when he had told her about his grandfather, she had even proved to herself that she must be at least a reasonably good person by having, quite spontaneously, a considerate reaction. What is all this? she asked her saviour, as they wandered through the deserted streets of Fitzrovia. Are you catching up on your correspondence at last?

They walked past Maureen's bicycle, lurking disappointedly in the shadows, and she blew it a mental good-night kiss as she pressed Daniel's arm. He had called her darling, after all. He smiled, but did not return the pressure, seeming, now that the excitement of their meeting was over, preoccupied. Well, with the afternoon he had had, it was understandable. They found a dark little Cypriot restaurant, went in, and ordered mousaka and a bottle of icy retsina.

'So what exactly happened?' said Maureen. 'About your grandad?'

'Well, it was quite a shock, actually.' He began to blink hard. 'We were just sitting there, talking about the books I'd taken him, and he wanted to look something up in another book, which was on the top shelf of his bookcase. So he stretched up to get it, and the next thing, he was all over the chair, *blue*, and gasping for breath. All very dramatic.'

'God.'

'Yes. And he has these pills he's supposed to take, but *I* don't know where the hell he keeps them, and meanwhile, he's panting and wheezing, and—I *like* my grandfather, you know?'

'Yes, I know.'

'So I quickly phoned the doctor—who luckily lives practically next door—and he rushed round and did whatever it was he had to do, and we got him to bed. And when I left, he was grumbling at my Aunt Naomi for taking a taxi over from Hampstead instead of a bus. But it was a nasty ten minutes. I thought he was dying.'

'Jesus.'

A waiter brought hot pitta bread and germolene pink taramasalata, and he began to pick at it, clumsily.

'He was in a camp, you know, during the war. And he's hardly seventy, and it just seemed so stupid that he should go through all that and survive, and then die just because his moronic grandson didn't know where he kept his pills.'

'You didn't tell me he was in a camp.'

'Oh, yes.' He looked up at her. 'He was lucky. His whole village was wiped out. He never talks about it, ever. Oh, once my brother Bernard went to Poland, and brought back a book with lots of photographs in it of the village and the people he'd known. And he just looked at it—didn't say anything—and cried.'

Maureen was silent. He was so matter of fact in relating the century's horror story, his own race, wiped out, obliterated. She thought of her race's horror stories, of Cromwell's men, and the broken Treaty of Limerick, and the Famine. But they were all in the past, all safely tucked away in history books and sad songs around pub pianos in Kilburn. To have a genocide in living memory . . . she thought of her own plump grandmother, dead in her sleep on the feast of the Assumption, of her rambling, red-cheeked family, in London and Liverpool and Mayo and Galway, and her imagination balked. For the first time he seemed, truly, a foreigner.

'I'm getting very fond of you,' he said suddenly.

And that was sweet. She smiled and took his hand. 'Me, too,' she replied.

'It's all rather sudden, isn't it? I didn't . . . expect . . . this.'

'I'm not complaining.'

'I mean, I could get fonder. I could get very, very fond indeed.'

Sweeter and sweeter, but something was wrong. The words

did not, as they should have, make her heart leap and sing. Unconsciously, she withdrew her hand.

'The trouble with Jews,' he said, 'is that they're too bloody clannish.'

This began to be confusing: the conversation was doubling back and back on itself. 'So you say,' she said.

'You can understand why, I suppose. A threatened race, and so on. And it's always been like that. They've had to band together just to survive at all.'

'Well, that's understandable.' This part, at least, she could grasp, could show him she respected if she did not fully understand. 'I know how I feel about things that happened to my people centuries ago. I honestly cannot imagine having something so . . . horrible, so close.'

'No, you probably can't. . . . Well, Jews can be, really, quite unpleasant. I told you, didn't I, that I was expected to marry a Jew? Propagate the race?'

'Yes you did.' It had been a joke between them. Something was going horribly, heartbreakingly wrong here, and she grasped desperately at another joke for him. 'You also told me through a mouthful of ham and cheese sandwich, that you were expected to eat kosher.'

'Oh, yes.' But he did not laugh. Instead, he took a deep breath, and blinked at his wine glass through wide-set, slanting eyes. 'You know, Maureen, I realised something this afternoon.'

'Yes?'

'I realised that I expect myself to propagate the race, too.'

And the sun jigged drunkenly in the sky, and came crashing down around Maureen's ears. 'Oh,' she said.

'So I'm afraid I think that, given how we feel about each other already, there's really . . . not much point in our going on.'

'No,' she said. 'You're right. There probably isn't.'

'I could tell you all sorts of things. I could tell you it was seeing the number on my granddad's arm; I could tell you that when I looked in his pocket for the pills, I found a picture of his parents that he'd kept all the time he was in camp; I could tell you . . . lots of things. But, you know, they weren't . . . this afternoon wasn't really what was important. What is important is a feeling I have inside myself. It's a part of being Jewish, and I can't explain it, and I thought that if I ignored it hard enough it might go away, but I knew this afternoon that it wouldn't. Ever. And it's senseless, and it's counterproductive, and I hate it, and I—I *hate* the fact that it's hurt you, and it's . . . a fundamental part of me.'

'I see.' And of course, she did see. Knowing all she knew of the futility of attempting to ignore the irrational demands of a religion, how could she not see?

'You could,' she said, carefully, 'have thought of this earlier.'

'I'm sorry. You must believe I'm sorry. But it was all so sudden: you crept up on me.'

'Well, you sure as hell crept up on me.'

'Anyway, I've thought of it now. And I'm telling you now. Before we go any further.'

Despite herself, she smiled. 'Whoopee. Hey, cheers, mate. Thanks.'

He smiled, too. 'Um, Maureen? I don't suppose there's any chance we might stay . . . you know? Friends?'

'You have got,' she said, 'to be joking.'

'No, I thought not.'

'But listen.' She looked down at her own glass. It did not matter now if she blushed, if the scarlet of her Irish cheeks flooded the white of her Irish brow, the pug of her Irish nose. 'If you ever . . . if this feeling ever—by some fluke, freak, or miracle, changes . . . well, there's no obstacle in *my* mind. OK?'

'OK.'

'Look, here's my half of the bill—yes, go on, take it. If you don't mind, I think I'll find my bike and go home now.'

'You know what's so unfair?' he said. 'The reason I like you, one of the reasons, probably the main reason, is that you're almost the only non-Jewish person I know who'd understand all this.'

She nodded, and cocked a congratulatory eye at the ceiling. 'Bulls-eye,' she said, appreciatively.

They laughed, because it seemed the only thing to do, and neither had ever felt so close as in their parting.

'You finished it!' Adam looked at her with a respect bordering on incredulity.

She sat back with a satisfied sigh. 'I told you how I feel about rabbit.'

'Well, all I can say is, I don't know where you put it.'

'Don't you? I do, unfortunately.' She patted her stomach, flat

219

under the pale pink sweater she had worn for their first dinner together. It was a minor milestone in their relationship: the first time she had repeated an outfit.

'Haven't I seen that sweater before?' he asked.

'Not fair. Men aren't supposed to notice things like that.'

'Does this mean, my dear Ms Sexist Beck, that I have seen your entire wardrobe?' He smiled at her, eyebrows raised, gently but unmistakably nudging the conversation in the direction he wanted it to go.

She smiled, too, and, playing their game, as unmistakably nudged it back. 'I'm afraid that, until pay-day, it rather looks as if you have.'

'Dear me. Now, what on earth are we going to do about that?'

'Well, I wouldn't worry too much. Pay-day's tomorrow.'

'Excellent. In that case, I have a plan. You spend tomorrow lunch-time blowing half your salary on something absolutely diaphanous to wear, and tomorrow evening, I take you out somewhere particularly special to celebrate.'

'Oh, very likely.' She snorted. 'After all, what else do I have to do with half my salary? Anyway, I'm busy tomorrow. A reception at the Savoy. For—believe it or not—another client.'

He clutched at his brow. 'You mean there are other clients in your life? Well, how about this, then?' He leaned over the table with a Groucho Marx leer. 'You don't buy anything to wear, and on Saturday evening, we stay in to celebrate.'

'Oh, all right.' She opened her eyes wide, parodying *naïveté*. 'Maybe I'll bring my toothbrush, just in case I miss the last bus home. Anyway, I thought you spent Saturday evenings with—with Marcia?'

'Marcia,' he replied, looking at her directly, 'is going away for the weekend. With a friend. A rather good friend.'

'Oh.' She looked down at her wine. 'And don't you have any good friends you want to see?'

'Believe it or not,' he said, 'there's no one I much want to see but you.'

She was silent. But she believed him: he did not lie.

'And believe it or not,' he continued, 'I've never said that to anyone else but Marcia.'

She remained silent.

'How about Saturday evening?' he said.

'I don't think so.'

'Why not?'

'I just don't think so. I'll be out all day anyway, and God knows when I'll get back. And I just don't think it's a good idea.'

There was another silence.

'I said I wouldn't put pressure on you,' he said, at last.

'And I'm grateful for that,' she replied quickly.

'But.'

'But.'

'But I will say this. Ask this. You talk a lot about fairness yourself. How . . . fair . . . do you think it is, to you, and to me, that my wife goes away for the weekend with a lover, with my full knowledge and consent, and, merely because she is my wife, you and I are left sitting on opposite sides of the table, staring at each other like two prize idiots?'

She raised her eyes to his. 'It isn't fair at all,' she said.

'Oh.' He slumped his shoulders, in exaggerated relief. 'Oh, good. Well, thank God we've got that cleared up. Now what shall we talk about? Flower arranging? Origami? I suppose, by the way, you do want a brandy with your coffee?'

She grinned at him. 'Yes, please,' she said.

Anne never bought anything at Harrods, but a visit was a fundamental part of her shopping trips to the West End nevertheless. She wandered now, dreamily, through room after opulent room, through a world where long, slim, rich women did nothing but buy long, slim, rich clothes, where the air was sweet with expensive perfume and good leather handbags, where court heels clacked and silk scarves rustled, where for one glorious hour she could—provided she did not catch sight of herself in a mirror—imagine herself to be elegant.

After the hour, she would revert to type. She would catch a bus to busy, vulgar Oxford Street, would fight through the crowds at Etam, at Chelsea Girl, at Marks & Spencer, would buy a practical spring jacket, and a skirt in a larger size—it was becoming depressing, the way she seemed lately to be bursting out of her clothes—and possibly a pair of sturdy shoes. Solid, practical stuff, Anne stuff, not Harrods stuff at all.

After that, she would . . . resolutely, she refused to think what she would do. She knew where Brian was meeting his friends that evening, had not said she would be there, but had not said she would not, either. Nor had Brian, when they had spoken over the telephone, pressed her. In fact, he had been rather carefully offhand, trying to play it cool with so crystalline a transparency that her mouth twitched at the memory. But on the other hand, she was here, wasn't she, in London on a Friday afternoon when there was no group meeting? But on the other hand again, she did need new clothes, and even if she had not known he was to be here, she would very probably have come in this afternoon anyway. Wouldn't she?

She found herself at the hosiery department, and on an impulse decided to break the charm of inaccessability she had imposed on the shop—it was just a shop, after all—and buy something. She selected a, for Harrods, reasonably priced pair of tights in a slimming dark colour, and took them to the counter. In front of her was what she thought of as a typical Harrods girl, tall and blonde, wearing a full wool skirt and silk shirt, buying with the nonchalance of an habitual customer, not one but half a dozen pairs of tights in a frivolously light shade. The girl paid and turned around, and she and Anne both frowned for a moment before they recognised each other. It was Maureen's friend, Alison.

'Oh, hello,' said Alison. 'What are you doing here?'

'Just pottering,' said Anne. 'What about you?'

'Well, may you ask,' said Alison, darkly. She was flushed and wearing what on someone less pretty would have been called a scowl. 'My bloody boss made me wear a bloody skirt for a reception tonight, and then he had the cheek to complain about my tights. Look.' Schoolgirlishly, she lifted her skirt, to reveal a laddered nylon inexpertly patched with nail varnish. 'It always happens, I'm terrible with the things. So he sent me out for some more. Bloody cheek. As if I hadn't enough to do. As if . . .' Abruptly her face cleared. 'Hey do you want some coffee?'

'Sorry?'

'Coffee. I've damned well put the tights on expenses, and I think he can just jolly well take us out for coffee, too. Come on, do. I know a smashing place.'

'Oh . . . all right.'

There seemed no reason not to, so Anne paid for her own tights, and followed Alison out into Brompton Road. Alison flourished her green paper bag.

'Six pairs on the expense account,' she said. 'And it's pure venom, because I'll never use them, because I never wear skirts. I hate them, don't you?'

'I have to wear them for work,' said Anne. 'I'm pretty well used to them.' She did not add that her own legs were too short and too plump to fit even comfortably, much less becomingly, into trousers.

'Oh, well,' said Alison. 'It's all right for you. You've got good legs.'

'Me?'

'Yes. Calves and ankles. Look at me. Pure hockey stick.'

Deciding that Alison was, if a little overpowering, really extremely nice, Anne trotted beside her through the back streets of Knightsbridge.

The patisserie she led them to was small, dark, and well established, a place where iron-backed Knightsbridge matrons ate melting pastries served by iron-jawed French waitresses.

'We absolutely must,' said Alison in a tone that admitted no argument, 'have the chocolate éclairs. They do the best chocolate éclairs in London. Or they used to. I haven't been here for years, you know. An aunt of mine used to take me in school holidays.' She contorted her face into an expression of pained puzzlement, and raised her voice half an octave. '"They're *French*, y'know. Simply *frightful* people, but simply marvellous cooks."'

Anne laughed. 'I'm half French,' she said.

'Are you? Oh, Gawd. Sorry.'

'That's OK. I'm used to it.'

The éclairs arrived, and they both agreed them to be still the best in London.

'I like France,' said Alison. 'I lived in Paris for a year, and had a marvellous time. Which part are you from?'

'Les Landes.'

'I've never been there.' She wouldn't have, thought Anne. She was a Paris type, Paris and the Dordogne or the South in the summer. She would not know the flat middle-class expanses of Anne's mother's home. 'Do you get back much?'

'A fair bit. We're going this summer; I have to introduce Stephen to the family. I think he's a bit nervous about it.'

'Hasn't he met them?'

'Well, we were married in a bit of a hurry.'

'Oh.'

There was a silence.

'Have you been married long?' said Alison.

'Just since Christmas.'

'Newlyweds! Do you like it?'

'Oh, yes.' But then, Anne was not the sort of person who would ever want to go to Paris for a year. Was she? 'Yes, I love it.'

'That's nice. . . . It's a funny thing, marriage, isn't it?'

'How do you mean?'

'Well.' Alison paused, stirring grainy brown sugar into her coffee; naturally, she would not have to watch her weight. Then she seemed to come to a decision. 'Can I ask you a question?' she asked.

'Sure.'

'I mean, tell me to shut up if you like, but . . . I've got this friend who's having marriage problems, and . . . How would you feel if you knew Stephen were having an affair?'

'What?' It was the last question in the world she would have expected Alison to ask her.

'Sorry, rude question. Forget I spoke.'

'No, that's OK. It's just . . .' It was just such a surprise. 'It's just that I can't imagine Stephen doing any such thing.'

Alison's eyes, blue and intense, were on her. 'Can't you really?'

'No.' She thought; she tried. *'No.'*

'But hasn't it ever entered your head? My friend says . . .' Her eyes dropped, and her cheeks pinkened; what an extraordinary conversation, thought Anne, this was. 'OK,' Alison continued. 'OK. Just suppose Stephen came home tonight from work, and said "Anne, darling . . ."'

'As a matter of fact,' after their conversation about legs, the least she could do was to confide this, 'as often as not he calls me Chubbo.'

'OK. He comes home, and says, "Chubbo, I love you, you're my wife, I want to spend the rest of my life with you. But I think you should know I'm having an affair with . . . another woman." How would you feel?'

And Anne's world shattered and splintered and crashed around her, as Alison looked up from her coffee and the look in her eyes was one of pure and knowing guilt, and Anne knew that Alison and Stephen were lovers.

For perhaps a second they stared at each other, the betrayer and the betrayed, the murderess and the murdered, and then Alison laughed.

'If you could *see* your face ... That bad, huh? Well, you've obviously got a marvellous marriage, and here's to it.'

She lifted her coffee-cup, and the world set itself to rights again.

Anne sat back as the warmth of what she had, and Alison had not, flooded every nook and cranny of her being.

'Your friend,' she said, 'hasn't got a good marriage, then?'

'No,' said Alison. 'No, in fact, it's a bit of a mess, the whole situation.'

'Well, that's a shame.' It was a shame, too, a sad shame for Alison, who was so nice and so pretty and who was not having an affair with Stephen. 'I hope it works out.'

'God, so do I,' said Alison. 'And so does my friend, of course ... Well, where are you off to now?'

'Oxford Street. I've got to buy some clothes.'

'That'll be fun for you. All those lovely crowds.'

'Actually, after school, it's quite nice to be among people who come higher than my waist.'

'I hadn't thought of that.'

They left the patisserie, and parted on Brompton Road.

'Thanks for the coffee,' said Anne.

'Oh, don't thank me, thank my bloody boss. Well, say hello to Stephen for me.'

'I will. And ... good luck. With the tights. I mean.'

'Thanks. I'll need it.'

Anne watched her striding, long-legged and jaunty, across the road and down Beauchamp Place, and then turned and walked towards the bus stop. She sat on the bench, waiting for the bus, thinking of Stephen, and wanting at the same time to laugh for the love she had, and to cry for what she now would never have, what she now could not contemplate ever wanting to have. The bus came, and she climbed to the top and sat, looking down over London, and all the lovely lonely girls like Alison, and wanted to cry again, with pity for each one of them. Maybe she should introduce Alison to Brian. But she had a feeling that it might be too late to introduce Brian to anyone. She looked at her watch. Four o'clock. In two and a half hours Brian and Siobhan would stroll from the television station, and would sit, arguing or laughing about Brian's ridiculous driving, until the door would fly open and there would be Andrea, glossy haired, glossy teethed—but very nice, Brian had assured her, in person—to be greeted with kisses and affectionate ribbing while the whole wine bar tried not to stare at the celebrity who had just entered. And they would drink and laugh and gossip about famous friends while drinkers at the next table would try to appear not to listen in, they would forge for themselves, the three of them, a charmed circle, a golden circle. A circle which they had specifically invited her to join. Anne got off the bus at Marble Arch. Before she started shopping, she found a telephone and called her husband.

'Anne! Where are you?'

'In Oxford Street, it's a madhouse here. Listen, I don't have much change. Sarah can't meet me. Can I meet you, later on, just for a quick one, before you go off with your mates?'

'Can you . . .' The sun rose in splendour in his voice. 'Well, that'll be a nice example for Roger. Me three months married and henpecked to hell.'

'Well, otherwise I won't see you all evening. Go on, please.'

'Oh, all right. Just a quick one.'

'Well,' he said, later, when it became apparent that he was never to make Roger's stag night. 'So much for our plans to be sophisticated, young open-marrieds.'

'Yes,' she replied. 'So much for them.'

Bob woke early to a childish excitement. It was a special day. His birthday. St Patrick's day.

'And aren't you a lucky boy,' year after year the nuns had exclaimed at junior school, and his mother at home, 'to have a day like that for your birthday?'

Bob at the time had not agreed. Birthdays, as every spring child knew, were days when you alone were excused the Lenten resolutions that everyone was excused on St Patrick's day: had he had the good sense to be born just a few hours earlier, or just a few more hours later, that would have been two days, instead of the one, when he was allowed to eat sweets. On the other hand, it was undeniably pleasant to have his birthday as a day of universal celebration.

He lay in bed for a few moments, sniffing hopefully, if hopelessly early, to see what Mrs Herlihy was burning for breakfast, and wondering whether he had received any birthday cards. Then he jerked himself upright. He was thirty. Thirty. Patrick Robert Aloysius Power—Pongy Power, Power Major, Tyrone, Father Bob —was a man of thirty. He didn't feel any different. He wondered how he looked. Feeling ever so slightly ridiculous, he got out of bed, crossed the room, and looked at himself in the mirror. Then he sighed with relief. He looked exactly as he had looked the night before. His eyes were no more sunken than then, his jowls no more pendulous, his white hairs no more plentiful—and he had been thirty for a full seven and a half hours. He smiled at himself in the mirror, instantly looking, despite the faint lines forming around his eyes, some five years younger. He was thirty, and it was going to be all right.

Anyway, it was his birthday, was and would always be, no matter what the number of years, a special day. And what better way to spend a special day, even if no one but he knew just how special a day it was, than making a pilgrimage to Aylesford with a group of young, intelligent Catholics? And Alison. And that was the best of all: in the last forty-eight hours, he had scarcely given Alison so much as a thought.

'Thanks, Pal,' he muttered as he began to shave for the early Mass.

It was going to be a good day.

The alarm woke Kate from the deep sleep which lately never seemed to be enough for her. She shut it off, and sat up in bed, blinking in puzzlement. She could have sworn that today was Saturday. Then she remembered.

Aylesford. Father Bob with his group of the loud, the confident, the Catholic. Aylesford which, not two weeks ago had seemed, in prospect, like a bliss beyond earthly imagining, and which now ... Aylesford. Bob. Denis. And *her*.

Of course, she did not have to go. She could lie here for five minutes, and then for five minutes more. And if she lay for enough five minutes, it would be late, and then almost too late, and then actually too late. She could lie here all day.

But she had said she would go. They would be waiting for her.

She got out of bed, padded to the dressing table, and took the roller from her hair.

She had no one to pray to to see her through the day.

Maureen had dreamed that it was all a dream; she had woken to find it was all true. She lay in her narrow bed, thinking about it, trying to force it from her heart to her brain, as if it were no more to her than an old romance found in a yellowing book, or a caoine half heard in the night. She was taboo.

Taboo. A barbaric word—from the Tonga Islands, her dictionary had told her, awakening in her mind vague, semi-comic pictures of cannibals in a ring dancing around a missionary in a large stew pot, of overlush jungles populated by Wopsy the black guardian angel from the story-books, and the poor little black children whose souls Mother Jeanne d'Arc had taken up a collection every Lent to save. A word that applied, in her terms, to seducing priests, or taking communion less than an hour after she had eaten; and in his terms, to any member of the human race who could not help him propagate his own race. To her.

It was a curious sensation to be taboo. In a sense, it was almost a comfort, absolving her from all personal responsibility for what had happened. But what had happened, had happened. And she would never know for sure that if she had been (been what? Prettier? That did not matter. More agreeable? But she had never been anything but agreeable, not with him) different somehow, she had no means of knowing how, more important to him, more worthy of his love, that taboo might not have been, somehow, overthrown. But she had not. And it had not. And no thinking about it could ever change that.

She got up, because there was no reason not to, pulled back the curtains, and looked out over the roofs of Kilburn. Of course, it would have to be sunny today, it was always sunny for St Patrick's day. Too sunny, now she thought of it, for the rainbow-striped wool sweater she had planned to wear. Which left, as the only suitable clean garment, the black shirt. Jonathan had never liked her in black; Daniel had never seen it. Well, she would wear black, it was a good colour, a Catholic colour, a colour for elegant women mourning dead Kennedys in Boston, for toothless crones leading donkeys along Mediterranean mountain passes. Yes, she would wear black.

She plodded to the bathroom, and looked at herself in the mirror. Ruddy cheeks under springy black hair, a healthy face for St Patrick's day. Her eyes met her own in sorrow: then, since mocking her sorrow was as traditional to her race as was the sorrow itself, she drew back her lips in a grimace, and waved her fingers menacingly at herself. 'Taboo,' she hissed, and laughed.

She would, after all, have to put on a more or less cheerful face for Bob's birthday.

It was going to be a good day, Denis decided, waking to the instinctive cheerfulness he always felt for St Patrick's day. His shamrock had arrived yesterday, a great moist lump of it, in a green and white box. It came from Grandma Dunmore, arriving faithfully ever year, no matter where he happened to be living, and was the only acknowledgement she ever made of his existence. Some would have arrived for his mother and Kathleen, too. His mother was probably even now pinning a sprig onto her coat, on her way to early-morning Mass. They did themselves well on St Patrick's day, she and Kathleen, sausages for breakfast, ham and champ for lunch, and potatoes again at supper-time, potato cakes, crisp on the outside, fluffy inside, eaten piping hot from the oven, with lashings of butter. After supper, they would sit down with a bottle of whiskey, and drown the shamrock. Probably, they would sing: when she was young and well, his mother had had a beautiful voice. He hoped they were happy: he prayed they were. It was all he could do for them.

Geoffrey, now, that was another matter. Denis was really becoming extremely worried about Geoffrey. He had rung him at work several times over the last few days, only to be told by the switchboard operator that his line was busy; from the home number, he had received no answer at all. It was obvious that Geoffrey was avoiding him.

And that was where Geoffrey was a silly ass. The mess his party was in had been filling the newspapers and television news shows for three days now, and Geoffrey had to choose this time to avoid his only friend. Perhaps he was embarrassed. Silly ass. Well, Denis would talk to him today, clear the air a bit. Anyway, he was determined himself to have a good time. He wandered into the bathroom, ran the water, and began to sing 'Hail Glorious St Patrick.'

It was going to be a good day.

He would not know, gloated Geoffrey, what had hit him.

Oh, he had been clever, his little plan working out with a success, probably beyond his wildest dreams. He had intended to cause trouble to Geoffrey: he had caused, temporarily, chaos to the entire party. Everyone, it seemed, was being questioned, from Francis downward. His own turn would come on Monday, and he would be glad of it. He had, God knew, nothing to hide, and the sooner this thing was cleared up, the sooner he and Francis and the party —minus, at last, Nigel and Sue—could go about their own business, the country's business. His only hope was that, when the truth came out, Denis's part in it would come out too. But it probably would not. He had probably covered his tracks too efficiently for that. Well, he would get his just desserts one day.

But for his own personal vengeance, Geoffrey would have it today, and would take it, oh, so cleverly, and enjoy it, oh, so well. It was all worked out. He would wait. Bide his time. Watch, with a secret smile, while the little whipper-snapper fawned around Alysoun's ankles, and then, at the last moment, when he fancied himself a winner, if nothing else, by default, Geoffrey would step in, tall and English, and take her hand under the tall, English sky. And dirty Denis, hopelessly outclassed, could do nothing about it.

He licked his lips, savouring already the sweetness of his day of triumph.

Anne was never sick. She had crammed herself with chocolates, eaten five-days'-opened tinned salmon, crossed the English Channel in force nine and ten gales, and all without a tremor. Nothing could make Anne sick. She was sick now, tears pouring down her face, as she retched what felt like her very entrails into the small bathroom hand-basin.

Large, useless, and terrified, Stephen hovered over her.

'I'll sue them,' he said. 'I'll report them to the health authorities. We're never going there again.'

On the way home last night, they had stopped at the local Chinese take-away. But Anne knew deep inside her that what was making her throw up was nothing that she had eaten. Clutching the edge of the basin, she looked wearily at her husband.

'I can't make it to Aylesford,' she said. 'You go. Go and get dressed, or you'll be late.'

'You're joking! Go with you ill!'

'I'm not ill, just sick. Well, go and phone Denis, then, tell him we're not coming. Now, before he leaves.'

Stephen disappeared into the living-room. Anne looked at herself in the mirror over the basin, eyes red, cheeks hanging flabby and chalk-white, and many things became clear. Slowly, hand to stomach, she crept back to the bedroom, lay down on the bed, and, very quietly, began to sing a berceuse.

Alison had been awake for some time, lying in that ridiculously big bed, counting the possible outcomes, but she counted again anyway, in the hope against hope that there might be one she had overlooked. There were, so far as she could make out, three. Number one was that she stop seeing him; number two, that they start an affair, and he remain married; number three, that they start an affair and he eventually leave his wife for her. All of them, as far as she could see, were impossible. Number one was, of course, unthinkable. Number two she had considered for a while, had almost been tempted into, seeing it as one way of keeping both their relationship and her conscience intact; but that was before she had had that extraordinary conversation with Anne, had seen the terrible, stricken look that had crossed her face at the mere suggestion of Stephen's possible infidelity. Granted that Marcia was clearly no Anne. . . . But it was a grim prospect, that of being the other woman, a prospect stretching out for years of growing smart and hard and brittle, of living elegantly in a beautiful flat for one, of watching, in not so very many years' time, friends' children, and wondering, before it was too late, whether you had the strength to bring up a child alone. No, the role of the other woman was not what she was cut out for. Which left number three, that she break up the marriage. And what was so very terribly wrong with dealing the final blow to a marriage already so buffeted, so fragile as Adam's? But if that were true, what sort of world was it where even 'till death us do part', once it became inconvenient, was considered as no more binding than a lunch date? Less—Alison never, if she could help it, broke lunch dates. No, number three was not on at all.

Which left number one, which was unthinkable, which left number two, which . . . Alison's head began to reel. She needed help, guidance. She needed to talk to someone who knew, yet was detached, someone who was sympathetic, yet with firm views, someone who . . . She suddenly opened her eyes wide, and blinked at the ceiling, as the glaringly obvious solution flooded in upon her. She needed to talk to Father Bob.

As soon as she had thought of it, she could not imagine why she had not thought of it earlier. Bob knew her, but not very well. He was a priest, but he was young and informal. And despite all that Maureen said about him, he could not—doing the job he did, in the parish he did it in—but be up on the ways of the modern world. And she was seeing him that very day. 'Bob,' she muttered to herself. The perfect person.

Without warning, there flashed into her mind the sudden image of Mother Cecilia, tall, pale, and ascetic on the speech-day rostrum, gesturing with proprietary pride towards squat, whiskey-reeking Father Brown, and urging in inimitable tones that were nevertheless imitated throughout the school, 'The very instant, my dears, that you find yourself caught in a moral dilemma, you must immediately seek recourse to one of God's holy priests,' and she let loose a hiccough of laughter at the sheer incredibility of the fact that that was exactly what she was planning to do. Feeling—unreasonably enough, God knew—optimistic, she leaped out of bed, and stood in front of the mirror, wondering whether she needed to wash her hair.

On balance, she thought she would. It would not do to approach the day of truth with the greasies.

Denis was the first to arrive at Charing Cross. He stood alone for a few minutes, trying to make as inconspicuous as possible the bulkily wrapped crucifix—perhaps one of the girls would have a handbag he could hide it in—and reading the station notices. The line was up at Rochester, which, annoyingly, meant that the service was cut. Then he turned, to see Kate standing quietly next to him.

'Kitty, me darlin',' he greeted her. 'And the top of the mornin' to you this fine St Pat's day, and isn't that the grand piece of shamrock you have on your own coat fastened?'

'Hello,' said Kate. As always, she failed quite to meet his eye. 'Yes, my aunt sent it from Galway.'

'Did she so? 'Twas me own white-haired oul granny sent mine from County Tip.'

There was a silence. Kate never started a conversation.

'No one else has arrived,' he said. 'Plenty of time, though, I think we're a bit early. Oh, Stephen and Anne aren't coming, Anne's got some stomach bug. And the line's up at Rochester, so we'll just have to try to keep you sober this lunch-time.'

She blushed, and smiled faintly. Denis never quite knew whether she disapproved of him or not. He glanced at her handbag, but it was far too small. Maureen's, as far as he recalled, was bigger.

'What time do you make it, anyway?' he asked, just as the silence became uncomfortable. 'Look, there's Maureen. Hey, Callaghan, over here! Jesus, call yourself an Irishwoman? Where's your sham-rock?'

'It'll arrive on Monday,' said Maureen. She looked tired: probably been out on the batter with the new boyfriend. 'It always does. Lousy sense of time in my family. I spent my whole school career scrabbling around with bits of mustard and cress.'

'It's no life for a girl, is it? Here, have some of mine—and while you're about it, shove this in that great rucksack.'

'Thanks'. She took the shamrock and the cross, smiling briefly.

'Well, we can't have people thinking you're English, can we? And speaking of the English . . .'

Geoffrey and Alison arrived at the same time, Geoffrey from the tube, Alison from the taxi rank.

'Have some shamrock,' said Denis.

'Thank you,' said Alison.

'No, thank you,' said Geoffrey.

'Suit yourself,' said Denis. 'Get it?' He pointed at Geoffrey's jacket. '*Suit* yourself? Oh, well. Where's Bob?'

'Probably heard your last little effort and went home,' said Maureen.

'So what do you expect at this hour, Oscar Wilde? No, there he is.'

And there he was, smiling, not knowing that they knew his secret, and, laughing, yawning, carrying the styrofoam cups of British Rail coffee to which Denis insisted on treating them, they all jostled into the train and settled down for the journey. It was all, Denis decided, going very well.

The train pulled out of the station, crossed the river, and jerked past Southwark Cathedral into the endless, anonymous suburbs.

'Do you know,' said Denis, 'how the top Irish brain surgeon got to be the top Irish brain surgeon?'

'No,' said Alison. 'How did the top Irish brain surgeon get to be the top Irish brain surgeon?'

Denis tapped his forehead. 'Kidneys,' he said.

'I must say,' said Bob, 'I'm looking forward to this. I've never been to Aylesford.'

'Haven't you?' said Maureen. 'The nuns were always dragging us there. There or Concarneau, or *The Sound of Music.* God, I had a lousy childhood.'

'Who was St Patrick, anyway?' said Alison.

'Jesus,' said Maureen. 'She's not with me, folks. Didn't they teach you anything at that posh school?'

'Well, they were French, too. Now, if you ask me about St Therese of Lisieux . . .'

'St Patrick . . .' began Bob.

'St Patrick,' said Geoffrey, 'was an Englishman.'

'Did you hear about the young nun,' said Denis, 'who went to the Reverend Mother, and said, "Reverend Mother, I've got a terrible problem, I'm pregnant?" So the Reverend Mother says, "Go into the kitchen, mix the juice of a lemon with three tablespoonfuls of vinegar, and drink it." So the young nun says, "Why, will that cure my pregnancy?" And the Reverend Mother says . . .'

'"No,"' said Bob, '"but it'll wipe the grin off your face."'

'How're you doing, Kate?' said Denis.

> 'O-oh, Kitty, me love, will ye marry me, marry me,
> Kitty, me love, will ye go-o?
> Kitty, me love, will ye marry me, marry me,
> Kitty, say yes or say no.'

'She probably was fine,' said Maureen, 'till a minute ago. Hey, Kate, are you over your flu?'

'Yes, thank you,' said Kate. 'I'm fine.'

'Are we nearly there?' said Bob. 'It's a bit like the train to Lourdes, isn't it? I feel we should round a bend, and everyone rush to the window to see it.'

'And the train fall half-way off the tracks,' added Denis. 'I like Lourdes. It's the only place I know where you feel a bit of a freak if you're not on crutches or in a wheelchair.'

'I shouldn't imagine you have much difficulty in feeling a freak anywhere,' said Maureen.

'Did you hear about the little old man,' said Denis, 'who was sitting up in heaven and crying? So Jesus goes up to him, and says, "What's the matter? This is heaven, you're supposed to be happy." So the little old man says, "Well, you see, on earth I was a carpenter, and I had just the one son, who I loved very much and lost, and I don't expect I'll ever see him again." So Jesus says, "Father! Father, how could you think you'd never see me again?" So the little old man leaps up, flings his arms around him, and says . . .'

'"Pinocchio!"' said Maureen.

They arrived at last, got off the train—'a motley crew,' commented Bob—and straggled down the country road to the Friary.

'Hats *on*, girls,' said Alison. 'And I do *not* wish to see Eileen Fitzgerald walking with Martina de Rosa, is that clear?'

'I'm glad I didn't go to a girls' school,' said Denis.

The Friary was just over a mile from the station, an old stone building with lush lawns around it, and the River Medway running behind, all smiling in the pale yellow sun.

'But it's beautiful,' said Alison, looking around. California, China, or France had held nothing she could love as she could love this. 'Just beautiful. A real piece of old England.'

'Of old English Catholicism,' agreed Geoffrey. It was as it would have to be: before the day was out, she would be his.

'The way it used to be,' snapped Maureen, who had been pleasant for as long as was right or fitting, 'before old English Henry VIII.'

They walked through stone cloisters where monks had walked before the dissolution of the monasteries, where now at last, over four centuries later, monks were walking again, and into the airy modern chapels around the new piazza.

'Now, this is more my style,' said Bob. The day was going better and—thanks, Pal—better. 'The new look.'

'To go with the old rules,' said Maureen.

'Do shut up, Maureen,' said Denis. 'Hey, Geoffrey, come and look at this.'

Geoffrey turned, strode into a chapel, and knelt to pray. Were he truly charitable, he could pray for Denis, his enemy; but, being merely an imperfect human being, he simply knelt, a knight keeping vigil before a quest, and offered to his God his day and his love. At least he had the cleanliness of heart that could do that.

Denis looked at him, and gritted his teeth: Geoffrey really was playing silly buggers. If only he himself were not so aware of what the other must be going through.

'Don't tell Geoffrey,' he muttered to Bob, 'but have you noticed how everyone else in the Chapel of the English Martyrs is wearing shamrock?'

'On the other hand,' Bob pointed out, 'Geoffrey is at least using the Chapel for what it's meant for.'

'Look.' Unabashed, Denis nudged Maureen, and pointed behind an altar. 'Your pal Teresa of Avila. If this is how you treat your friends.'

Maureen said nothing. She dropped to a bench and stared at the representation. She did not pray, she did not think: she simply sat, heavy and unmoving, and felt tired as Teresa, riding her horse through rainy nights, with mud on her habit, fever in her head, and no light to show the end of the journey, had surely felt tired. But Teresa had had her God to talk to and to joke with; Maureen was alone.

Everyone seemed to be busy: now, perhaps, was the moment for Alison to speak to Bob. 'Bob . . .' she began, looking around for him. But she was just too late: he was praying in the Chapel of St Anne. After a few seconds, she followed him, and knelt down beside him. She had prayed more in the last few weeks than in, probably, the half-dozen years before that: she had a feeling that, in the time to come, she might be praying more still. Which would, had Mother Cecilia known about it, have surprised her, infuriatingly, not in the least.

They met outside the piazza, and walked around the quiet garden of Rosary Way.

'I always liked the rosary,' said Alison. 'The joyful mysteries first, and then the sorrowful mysteries, leading to the glorious mysteries. It made a nice flow, somehow.'

'I always lost mine,' said Maureen, who was pleasant once more. 'Had to count on my fingers. I was always pleased when I got to the second hand, because it meant it was half over.'

'Bob . . .' began Alison again.

But Bob, again, was praying. This quiet word with him would apparently be more difficult than she had thought.

At the end of Rosary Way was the shrine to St Simon Stock.

'Well, Geoffrey,' said Bob. 'This is where it happened. Your friend Simon Stock saw Our Lady.'

Geoffrey smiled, and said nothing.

'What utter bollocks,' said Maureen. She could not be pleasant about that, dear God, not about that.

'Maureen!' said Alison.

'Well, it is,' said Maureen. 'People don't see visions. They don't now, and they didn't then.' She drew her brows down in a frown. 'They don't,' she repeated.

In the village of Aylesford was a peaceful riverside pub. They sat outside, drinking beer and eating sandwiches, looking over the gun-grey waters of the Medway, and the green fields of Kent beyond.

'Well, this is all just lovely,' said Alison. 'You forget how lovely England is in London, don't you? But it was things like this I really missed when I was in the States.'

'We're glad,' said Bob gallantly, 'that you came back.'

Denis kicked Maureen: it was time.

'By the way, Bob . . .' he began. Maureen opened her bag, and drew out the parcel, she, Denis, and after a moment, Alison, joining in an approximate rendition of 'Happy Birthday to You'.

'Oh,' said Bob. 'Oh, I say.' He actually blushed. 'How did you know?'

'They don't,' said Denis, 'call me Digger O'Leary for nothing. Well, go on and open it. Here's a clue: it's not a tie.'

He opened it, touched and pleased. Better and still better the day was going: the sun was shining, she posed him no threat, and here a group of his friends had conspired in secret to buy him a birthday present. The paper fell away, and he looked at the symbol of the suffering that would lead to the glory.

'Oh, I say,' he repeated.

'You've probably got a million,' said Maureen.

'But you probably can't have too many,' added Denis.

'Well, thanks,' said Bob. He looked around at their smiling, well-wishing faces. 'I think I'd better buy the next round, hadn't I?'

'Certainly not,' said Denis. 'Not on your birthday, my God. No, the next one's on Geoffrey and me. Come on, Geoffrey.'

Silently, Geoffrey rose and followed him into the dark interior of the pub. He laid a five-pound note on the counter, and, without a word, turned and made for the men's lavatory. Denis, being not like other people, was generally careful not to allow himself the self-indulgence of anger. But where Geoffrey was concerned, it was sometimes extraordinarily difficult.

He caught the barmaid's eye, ordered, and the drinks arrived as Geoffrey returned. Silently, they each picked up half their round, and, silently, returned to their party.

'Well, *slàinte*,' said Denis. 'Here's to the birthday man in front of us, and the great saint above us.'

'And here's to a jolly good day,' added Bob. Thanks, Pal, for the day, and for the decade. Thanks.

Maureen scowled into her Guinness. It might be a jolly good day for the rest of them, but she had had enough of pretending it was one for her, too. And as for the wishy-washy, fairy-tale rubbish they had talked about Simon Stock . . .

'What would you say, Bob,' she asked suddenly, 'if you met Simon Stock and his vision today?'

Alison caught her tone, and sighed in exasperation.

'Interesting question.' said Bob. 'Do you know, I don't know? What would you say, Kate?'

'I don't know,' said Kate.

'Really,' persisted Maureen. She was onto it now, demanding a reaction, prepared to worry the subject like a dog with a bone you would swear had no meat on it. 'Supposing someone came to you, not a monk, but someone ordinary, a, a teacher, or me, or anyone, and said, "Look, Father, you can call me mad if you like, but I swear I've seen Our Lady? Or an angel? Or whatever?"'

'I just can't imagine it,' said Bob. He could not. His faith dealt with discussion groups, with teenage pregnancies and Sister Martin's fruitcake, not with visions.

Alison decided to inject some humour into the conversation. 'I met a man in Mexico,' she said, 'who everybody said had seen an angel. It turned out he was the town drunk.'

Geoffrey laughed, himself and Alysoun and Simon Stock banded together against foul-mouthed Maureen and the Mexican drunkard. 'But Simon Stock wasn't a drunk,' he pointed out.

'Do you really believe,' demanded Maureen, 'that he saw Our Lady?'

'Oh, yes,' said Geoffrey.

Maureen slapped down her Guinness. 'I don't see how you can possibly believe that. Not really.'

'Perhaps,' said Denis, 'people really do see visions.'

'Rubbish.' The anger that had so long been inside her was fomenting, was coming, at last, to a blackly boiling head. 'Of course they don't.'

'Do you have to be quite so dogmatic?' inquired Alison.

'Perhaps,' put in Bob, pacifically, 'it's like the poem says, "there hath past away a glory from the earth."' He had studied Wordsworth at school, and the phrase had stuck with him. 'Perhaps people used to see visions, but these days, for some reason, they don't.'

'I don't see that that's any answer at all.' Maureen was pink in the face now, and her brows were thunderous. 'In fact, I think it's a complete cop-out. To say—wrap up, Denis—to say that people *did* see things once, but *don't* now, well, that's just skirting the issue. If you want to know, the whole idea of, of visions, is just sick.' She stopped; fire such as she had never known was raging inside her head. 'Sick,' she repeated. 'Sick, neurotic, and disgusting. And it doesn't make it OK if they . . . *happened* five hundred years ago.'

'Maureen . . .'

'Wrap *up*, Denis. Sick, I said. And any philosophy that countenances them is sick, too.'

'Congratulations, pal. You've just written off the entire history of organised religion.'

'Sod organised religion.' She had said it before, many times before, in schoolrooms and pubs and living-rooms and church halls; but this time was different. This time, she meant it. 'Organised religion,' she raked her mind for its foulest words, 'it stinks. It—it

sucks. It means war, it means chaos, it means madness, it means . . .
Look at us.' Her black gaze swept the table, seeing all of them as in a
fairground mirror, distorted, their worst sides grossly exaggerated,
nervous Denis, and selfish Alison, and blind Bob, and lonely
Geoffrey, and . . . and Kate. Kate, poor, mousy, little nothing-of-a-
thing; Kate, scared to speak, with nothing to say, scared to be, almost
non-being. 'Look,' she said finally, purposefully, pointing to her, 'at
her.'

'Maureen!'

'Don't Maureen me, Denis. *Look* at her.' Maureen, the new
Maureen, looked; and spoke with knowing cruelty. 'She's had the
life sucked out of her by the Church, and she's got fifty years to live,
probably, and she'll spend them going to Mass every Sunday, and
confession every first Saturday, and kneeling down to pray twice a
day, and in between times, just, just floating in a sub-zero nothingness, and she'd just better hope there is a heaven, because she sure as
hell isn't getting anything good, or bad, or, or anything at all on earth.
And you tell me—you dare to tell me—that organised religion is not
sick.'

'Jesus Christ, Maureen . . .'

'Keep your Jesus Christ. I mean it.' She stood up, leaned over the
table to the crucifix, and, deliberately, spat on it. 'And I mean that,
too.' She stood for a moment, looking down on them. 'Why,' she
asked finally, 'can't people just be *good*?' She turned, and stormed out
of the pub.

There was a stunned silence around the table. Denis punched
Kate lightly on the arm. 'What the hell,' he said, 'has bitten her?'

'Don't ask me,' said Alison. She finished her drink, taking the
opportunity, as she did so, to glance at her watch. It was clearly not a
good moment to take Bob away. But then, time was passing all too
quickly, and she simply had to speak to him before she returned to
London. Besides, she was damned if she'd have her life ruled by
bloody Maureen's tantrums.

'I hate to break up this merry gathering,' she said, 'but there's
something I'd really like to talk to Bob about in private. Can we walk
back to the Friary, Bob? Now?'

Surprised, Bob picked up his cross and followed her out. When
they had gone, Geoffrey sat for perhaps half a minute. Then he, too,
rose and left.

'I think,' said Denis to Kate, 'that you deserve another drink.'

When he returned from the bar, she was pale, and suspiciously puffy around the eyes.

'You OK?' he said.

She nodded.

'No, you're not. No one could be.' He sat down and looked at her in concern. Maureen was really the end. 'Listen, she's the pits, Maureen, we all know that, but she doesn't . . . I really don't think she knew what she was saying. Doesn't excuse it, of course. Jesus, d'you want a handkerchief? Here.'

She took it with a watery smile, the constraint that was between them quite washed away in Maureen's storm.

'The stupid thing is,' she said at last, 'that I haven't actually been to Mass for two weeks.'

'*What?*' He must have misheard; Kate was like him. She would never miss Mass.

'That's why I wasn't at the meeting last week. In fact,' she choked back a hysterical little laugh, 'I don't really think I'm a Catholic at all any more.'

'Hang on.' This was moving too fast for Denis. 'What are you talking about, haven't been to Mass? Not a Catholic?'

'A priest told me not to be.'

'*What?*'

'He told me to leave the Church. I did know about the, the sub-zero nothingness, and I asked him, and he said, leave the Church. So I did, and it's no better outside, in fact it's much, much worse, and now I don't know what to do.'

'Look, just hold on a tick, will you?' There was clearly a problem here, which the poor old sausage had apparently been trying to cope with all alone; it suddenly occurred to him to wonder why he had never before thought to worry about Kate. 'Do you want to slow down, take a deep breath, blow your nose—that's better—and start again from the very beginning?'

Alison and Bob left the pub and walked up the lonely lane towards the Friary.

'I hope you don't mind,' said Alison, 'me taking you away like that. I've just got a . . . problem I'd like to talk to you about.'

'That's what I'm here for,' said Bob. What is all this? he asked.

You take the temptation away, *and* You trust me to talk about her problems? It looked as if it might be an interesting decade.

'You see,' said Alison, 'there's this man.'

This, not talk of visions, was Bob's territory. He smiled sympathetically. 'There often is.'

'Is there? Yes, I suppose there is. Anyway, he wants to sleep with me, and I,' she glanced at him rather uncertainly, 'I want to sleep with him, too.'

'They did tell me about sex,' said Bob, 'at school.'

'Yes, of course, sorry. Well, the problem is that he's sort of married, and . . .'

'Now, hang on.' Yes indeed, his foot was on his native heath here. 'You say he's married?'

'Well,' she grimaced. 'You see, he . . .'

'But you do know, Alison, that to sleep with a married man would be wrong?'

'You see, it isn't like that. He's married, yes, and he lives with his wife, yes, but neither of them even pretends to take the vow at all seriously . . .'

'But they have made the vow.'

'Well, yes.'

'Well, haven't they?'

'Well, *yes*.'

'And do you think that their not, apparently, taking it seriously absolves you from your responsibility to take it seriously?'

There was a pause. 'No,' she said at last, reluctantly. 'No, it doesn't. But it does just seem unfair that while she—his wife—is off doing exactly what she wants to do without a second thought, he and I can't do . . . what we want to do.'

'Alison, when was life ever fair?'

'Well, that's true.' There was another pause, and she set her teeth. 'So you think it would be wrong for me to sleep with him.'

'The important thing is that *you know* it would be wrong.'

'OK.' She grimaced, ruefully. 'OK, I know it would be wrong. OK. Now, the thing is, I see him sometimes. Socially, you know. And we . . . we don't *do* anything, because I won't let us, but we talk, and we have a good time, because we like each other. Do you think that's wrong?'

'Do you?'

'I don't know. I mean, I can't put my finger on anything actually wrong with it, but . . .'

'But?'

'But what?'

'But do you think you can carry on not *doing* anything?'

'No.'

'Well, there's your answer.'

'So what you're telling me is . . .'

'What I'm telling you is what you know.'

'Yes, but what you're *telling* me is, the right thing to do is, not to see him again.'

'If you want to put it like that. Yes.'

'OK.' Slightly to his surprise, she seemed to be, if not accepting this, at least considering it seriously. A rum old world You made, he said, where a beautiful—and make no mistake, she was still beautiful —sophisticated woman consults Pongy Power the celibate Priest about her sex life.

'It's sort of a relief,' she said suddenly. 'I mean, it's bad news, but at least I know what the news *is*.'

They walked for a while quietly, two weary athletes, two battle-scarred warriors limping home.

'It's bloody bad news, actually,' she said then, and he shifted his crucifix to the far hand and moved closer to put a friendly arm around her shoulders. As he did so, a ray of March sunlight struck her shining hair.

And suddenly, he was on her, the crucifix tossed on the grass, his clammy hands everywhere, his wet mouth and inexperienced tongue fastening on hers, his breath coming hot and smelling of cheese and Guinness. She struggled, but he was strong, arms of iron pinning her, broad body pressing on hers, crushing her.

She knew what to do, and she did it. She brought her knee up fast and hard; he released her immediately, and doubled over in pain. Not stopping to look or think, she ran down the road until she saw another human being. To her unspeakable relief, it was someone she knew, Geoffrey.

Head well back, gulping at the clean air, Geoffrey strolled through the little village of Aylesford. It was all going quite remarkably well.

Alighting from the train, she had looked at him and smiled; in the Friary, they had had words; there in the pub, they had even shared a joke. She would be his before the day was over, it was as inevitable as the roses blooming in the rainy English summer.

She had left him for the moment, true, gone off with Father Bob, but that was all right, there was no hurry. The time would come when the time would come; meanwhile, perfectly pleasant it was to walk the old cobbled streets in the soft spring. Besides, he liked to think of her so near, walking with the priest, golden head bent, eyes downcast, talking of things spiritual. She had mentioned the Friary: perhaps he would turn his steps in that direction, perhaps catch a glimpse of her from afar.

He was half-way up the grassy lane and deep in his thoughts when it happened. She was there, not his Alysoun, but a girl, a girl with messy hair and face an unbecoming scarlet, pawing at his jacket, and screaming unintelligibly about Bob and the road.

Geoffrey turned to stone. This was not supposed to happen; it was not supposed to happen at all. She looked a fright; she was causing a scene; she must be stopped immediately.

'What on earth,' he demanded, hoping to shame her into seemly behaviour, 'is the matter?'

She continued to scream, shaking his arm, here in a public place, with no thought of dignity or self-restraint. Geoffrey saw with sudden disgust that the button of her fine silk shirt was undone, that he could see her skimpy brassière, could see, if he wanted to, which he did not, even more.

'For God's sake,' he told her icily, 'button yourself up.'

She dropped his arm at that, she stood back, and stared at him with eyes that he could see were quite wild.

'Fuck you,' she screamed at him, bawled like a fishwife. 'Fuck you, fuck you!'

Without a word, Geoffrey turned, and strode away from her towards the station.

She stood, staring after him for a while. 'Fuck you,' she said, finally, softly. She buttoned her shirt, smoothed her hair, and made her way, purposefully, towards Aylesford's other pub.

Geoffrey's day, of course, was ruined, and more than his day, his dream. How could he dream now of Alysoun when she had shown herself to him in such a light, standing half-dressed in the road, cursing him at the top of her shrill female lungs? She was no better than Sue had been that day outside the House of Commons. It just went to show that women were all the same. St Paul had been right not to trust them.

Walking back to the station, he saw with crystal clarity the mess into which she had led him. Acting like an idiot, turning his back on his friends—and to think he had actually been so deluded as to blame old Denis for the mess at work. Geoffrey of all people should know what it was like to work with unscrupulous colleagues. And Denis, Irishman, journalist, and all, was such a nice chap, too. Geoffrey would have a word with him before they got back to London, apologise, perhaps even offer a friendly word of warning about Alison. Women, he decided, were nothing but trouble.

Maureen left the pub, and strode away from the Friary, through the village, and along the country road to the station. She felt good, wickedly good, better than she had for days, the good anger burning through her system like a fever, leaving her cleansed, refreshed, renewed.

It also left her, this time, free. Because this time she had done what she had never done before, what she thought that only devilish people darkly hinted at by nuns did: she had spat on the crucifix. She had gathered up her spittle, and had sent it, age-old symbol of her contempt, at the 2,000-year-old symbol of constriction, of possible life through certain death, possible victory through certain defeat; she had locked herself out of the old, cold darkness that was the Church, and left herself, for the first time in her life, irrevocably outside, truly free.

'Free,' she said aloud, the word tasting sweet on her lips. Free from the Church, from the old rules and the glorified mortification of the flesh, free from Bob and poor, nothing Kate, free from falling in love with Daniel, free above all and forever from the dully beaming spectre of Miss Feeney, who couldn't possibly—'yah, Feeneybats!!' shrilled the triumphant eleven-year-old inside her—have seen an angel, because the good truth was that there were no angels, and if there was a God, and he was good, and he had made the world, then the world must be good, and she was free to be like Jonathan, or Alison, or all the rest of the world. Watch out world, she was coming.

She walked on down the road, dancing a little, her hips swivelling. This was a good world, if you approached it the right way, there was no reason to look outside it. No reason in the world. As if in agreement the sun came out, and squinting up at it, she felt suddenly, euphorically, langorously lazy. She wandered off the road into a field, sank down on the ground, and ran her fingers through the fat grass, while she stared up at the blue March sky, and thought about everything in the world, and nothing in the world.

After a few minutes, she got up, and strolled towards a copse of trees. There was plenty of time still before the train left, and she might as well enjoy this warm day that she had thought would never come, when the buds began to show on the black old bark, and life began again. And oh, she was enjoying it. She stretched her arms to the sky, and then stooped, picked up a stone, and for the sheer joy of her life, flung it high, high into the clear air.

There was a scream, a raucous cry of agony, and almost on top of her, it fell out of the sky. Wings, huge, beating, catching in her throat like a feather duster, choking her. Yards and yards of cloth, fanning over her face, smelling of mothballs, and old chests, and nuns' habits. A huge hand, a mammoth foot, damp looking and pale.

The thing landed face down and turned over, crushing its wings behind its back. It tossed its head from side to side, its outspread limbs jerking, like a gargantuan insect caught upside-down in the shower. Down one side of its face, past closed eyes and stony lips sneering in pain, ran a slow trickle of blood. It lay there, screaming and flailing for a few moments, and then it died.

Maureen screamed.

She woke up screaming, shivering with cold and sticky with sweat, and sat bolt upright on the grass. 'It was a dream,' she told herself. 'A bad dream. A dream.' She sat there for some time, shivering, and repeating, hopelessly, over and over again, the words whose comfort she knew she could never in all her long, lonely life now accept. 'It was a dream, that's all. Just a dream.'

The train was almost due, but Geoffrey was still the only one from the party at the station. The others would have a two-hour wait if they missed it: it would be their own stupid fault if they did, but Geoffrey hoped they did not. He had been neglecting his friends from the group lately; and besides, he wanted to have that word with Denis.

The first to arrive was Alison, who naturally would not put herself to the inconvenience of a long wait at a draughty station. She was neat and composed, looked at him with hard eyes, and went to stand far away from him. Geoffrey could not blame her: knowing what she knew about her, he knew he would have expected no other behaviour.

Then, happily, Denis appeared. He was deep in conversation with Kate, which was in itself a surprise, but then Denis did pick up the most unlikely lame ducks. They were talking so hard that they appeared to notice neither Geoffrey nor Alison, and sat on a bench near the station entrance.

Geoffrey went and stood over them.

'I want a word with you,' he said to Denis.

'What?' Denis looked up. 'Oh, hello, Geoffrey. Be with you later, OK?' And he returned to Kate.

The train was almost due; and Geoffrey liked to get his apologies over with as quickly as possible.

'Come over here,' he said, jerking his head. 'I want a word with you.'

Denis looked up again: he seemed almost annoyed. 'I'll talk to you later, Geoffrey. I'm talking to Kate now, and it's quite important.'

'This is important, too,' said Geoffrey, and to emphasise the point, he bent down and shook Denis by the shoulder.

Denis had been so involved in his conversation that he had hardly noticed the walk from the pub to the station. What a poor old sausage Kate was indeed, describing to him, quietly and without a hint of Maureen's rhetoric, a dark night of the soul such as Maureen —Maureen—whom Denis currently rather disliked—could surely only guess at. But Denis, while never having experienced it himself, could understand and imagine it with no difficulty. They spoke the same language, he and Kate: it was as absurd as it was sad that they had never properly spoken before.

They were fathoms deep in their talk when Geoffrey appeared, interrupting them. Denis looked up, remembered briefly that aeons ago, he had been annoyed with Geoffrey, and politely told him to buzz off. But Geoffrey would not go. He hovered over them, a smile on his face, an expression Denis could not or did not trouble to read in his eyes, and tried to persuade Denis to leave Kate and talk to him.

It struck Denis that he was enjoying talking to Kate in a way he had never enjoyed talking to Geoffrey.

'I'll talk to you later,' he said at last, firmly. 'I'm talking to Kate now. It's quite important.'

His tone was meant to be squashing, but Geoffrey was unsquashed.

'This is important, too,' he said.

Damn Geoffrey—who for Christ's sake, had *seen* what that bitch Maureen had done to Kate in the pub—and his whingeings! Denis rose to tell him, in no uncertain terms, precisely where to go. As he did so, the other bent down and actually shook him, shook him rudely by the shoulder, and the shoulder next to Kate too, so that the back of his large blunt hand, catching her, carelessly jostled her. And for a second, Denis saw the monumental selfishness of Geoffrey; and for a second it mattered.

And quite without warning, the world turned red and boiling hot, and his fist felt something harder than wool but softer than stone, and he was fighting, Denis the sane O'Leary, was striking out as the mad Dunmores were known to, Denis, freed like his family from shackles of civilised behaviour, was punching another human being, punching savagely and with full intent to hurt.

He had not, of course, a hope of making an impression. Geoffrey, half a head taller and two stone heavier, merely, it seemed, put out a hand, and Denis was reeling back with a hand to his eye, while at the same time, the train was arriving, distracting the attention of the other passengers from the fight that was over almost before it had begun.

'Jesus,' said Alison, feeling sick to the pit of her stomach. 'Jesus Christ.' She turned from the scene, and found herself face to face with Maureen, who was watching it all with close attention. 'You're mad,' she said. 'You're all mad. All Roman Catholics are mad.'

Maureen looked at her for a moment, then moved up the train to an empty carriage and got in. Alison followed.

'Come on,' said Kate. 'It's leaving in a minute. Hurry!' She opened the nearest door, climbed in, and held out her hand to Denis. 'Come on!' Still staggering from Geoffrey's blow, he allowed her to help him up.

Geoffrey looked in at them through the window. 'Sorry, Denis,' he said. 'But I did try to warn you. Don't get mixed up with women:

they're trouble.' He walked down the train and as far away as he could. When the guards began to shut the doors, he climbed in.

As the train was pulling out, a figure in a black suit, undog-collared, but unmistakably a priest, ran alongside it, and hauled himself in. It was Father Bob.

Denis fell into the darkness of the guards' van, and sat on the floor.

'Let me see your eye,' said Kate.

'God,' said Denis. 'I hit him. God.'

'Let me see it,' she said.

'I hit him. I haven't hit anyone since I was twelve years old. God.'

'Let me see.' Surprisingly skilful, she looked at it. 'I think you need some ice,' she said. 'I'll get some from the buffet. Don't move.'

He sat back and shut his eyes, the world whistling around him, and in the embrace of an almighty pain in the left side of his head. But he did not feel bad. On the contrary, he was rather exhilarated: anger which had been building up, bottled inside him for years, had let itself fly in that short flight, and now that it was over, he felt refreshed. Sane.

Sane. He opened his good eye. He felt sane. He had acted like a mad Dunmore, and yet he was still sane. Hastily, he checked: yes, he remembered all that had happened during the day, his opinions were the same as they had been ten minutes earlier, nothing had changed, *he* had not changed. He could allow expression to the Dunmore in him without its necessarily taking over. It was a revelation.

And now, here came Kate, back quickly from the buffet, carrying an improvised ice pack, which she applied expertly to his eye. It felt good.

'You obviously know what you're doing,' he said.

'I know black eyes,' she told him.

'Do you? How?'

She paused, blushed, and shrugged very slightly. 'My family fight a lot.'

'Do they?' Quiet little Kate in the middle of a battling family? It was a day of revelations.

'I mean, my father and brother do. We're quite used to this sort of thing.'

'*Are* you? Don't you get scared?'

'Oh, they keep me pretty well out of it.' She paused, smiled, and for the first time in her life, let loose an uncharitable comment. 'I think they want to keep Florence Nightingale in good shape.'

He laughed, slightly to his own surprise, and then stopped.

'Must be rough on you, though.'

'Well, every family has its problems.' She paused again, blushed scarlet, and looked at him with eyes which, he had never until now noticed, were really rather pretty. 'Doesn't yours?'

'Doesn't mine?' Denis gave up all effort to make any sense whatsoever of the day, and, sitting in the dusty guard's van of the London train, began, for the first time, fully to tell another human being about his family.

Poor Denis, thought Geoffrey, looking comfortably out of the window at the Kent fields. To have escaped the clutches of one woman—since he had apparently seen through Alison at some earlier point which Geoffrey, locked in his own madness, had not noticed—only to fall into the clutches of another. Who would have thought, though, that mousy Kate would have turned out to be like all the rest of them after all? Who, on the other hand, would have thought it of his Alysoun? Women. Geoffrey had had it with them. There, on the lane to Aylesford Friary, had been revealed to him the nature of the entire sex, and it had sickened him. There would be no more women in Geoffrey's life, and he was the better man for it.

Denis, however, was clearly not so enlightened. Poor Denis. An hour had set him well in Kate's thrall, and look where it had got him. A hand raised in anger against his best friend, and a black eye to show for his trouble. Geoffrey would really have to talk to him. Not, of course, now, not with that Kate around, but later in the week, after the trouble at work had been straightened out, he would give him a call, and they would go out together for a drink, just like in the old days. Between Denis's Philip, and Geoffrey's Nigel and Sue, they would have plenty to talk about.

Geoffrey stretched out his legs in front of him, and reflected that it would be good to have Denis back in his life again.

Alison and Maureen sat on opposite sides of their compartment, frozen into the uncomradely silence that only the oldest of friends can achieve. They both looked out of the window at the gathering dusk over the spreading suburbs. As the night fell, their reflections in the glass became clearer, and occasionally the eyes of the reflections would meet, only to turn, sharply, away. By the time they reached Charing Cross, the empty compartment had become full; but since none of the other passengers had seen them boarding together, none of them could possibly have guessed that they had even been introduced.

Down at the very rear end of the train, Bob stood in the corridor, unmoving in his black suit, staring out of the window at the sights Alison and Maureen had stared at a split second before.

Alison and Maureen were the first through the ticket barrier. They stood for a moment, looking at each other.

'Do you want a drink?' said Maureen, coldly.

'I don't know,' said Alison.

'Where's Bob?' Denis and Kate had joined them, Denis with the beginnings of an impressive black eye.

Maureen shrugged. 'Did he catch the train?'

'Maybe he didn't. Well, happy birthday, Bob, wherever you are.'

At that moment, Geoffrey passed. He stopped, nodded to them all, and laid a hand on Denis's shoulder. 'Sorry about that,' he said. 'But I'll phone you in the week and explain. Good night.' He nodded again, jovially, and marched towards the cavernous depths of the tube.

'Now that bloke,' said Denis, 'is strange. Well, *slàn libh*, all. Kate and I are off to drown the shamrock. Bye, Alison.' His voice chilled. 'Bye, Maureen.'

'Goodbye,' said Kate. 'Happy St Patrick's day.' To the surprise of everyone, she reached up to kiss first Alison, then Maureen, on the cheek. 'It's been a lovely day.'

'Well?' said Maureen, as they left. 'Do you want a drink?'

'No,' said Alison. She smiled a smile that had a new, hard edge to it. 'No, I have to phone Adam. I'll see you next week, though, OK?'

Maureen shrugged. She herself did not need to make a phone call to go where she was going. She knew Miss Feeney would be at home, alone, with nowhere to go and no one to go with, even on Saturday, even on St Patrick's day. Maureen could stop off at the off-licence for a bottle of whiskey, and they could drown the shamrock together. And this time, she knew, she would ask outright about what had happened in Trent Park, and this time, she knew, Miss Feeney would answer her.

Maureen sighed a sigh so deep it seemed to start in her womb. 'Shit,' she said. And again, 'Shit.'

And turning so that she failed to see the black-clad figure of Father Bob scuttling from the ticket barrier and out into the sin-ridden London night, she stumped wearily towards the tube train that would take her to the terrible, joyful, inevitable, outstretched arms of Holy Mother Church.

FOR THE BEST IN PAPERBACKS, LOOK FOR THE

In every corner of the world, on every subject under the sun, Penguin represents quality and variety – the very best in publishing today.

For complete information about books available from Penguin – including Pelicans, Puffins, Peregrines and Penguin Classics – and how to order them, write to us at the appropriate address below. Please note that for copyright reasons the selection of books varies from country to country.

In the United Kingdom: For a complete list of books available from Penguin in the U.K., please write to *Dept E.P., Penguin Books Ltd, Harmondsworth, Middlesex, UB7 0DA*

In the United States: For a complete list of books available from Penguin in the U.S., please write to *Dept BA, Penguin, 299 Murray Hill Parkway, East Rutherford, New Jersey 07073*

In Canada: For a complete list of books available from Penguin in Canada, please write to *Penguin Books Canada Ltd, 2801 John Street, Markham, Ontario L3R 1B4*

In Australia: For a complete list of books available from Penguin in Australia, please write to the *Marketing Department, Penguin Books Australia Ltd, P.O. Box 257, Ringwood, Victoria 3134*

In New Zealand: For a complete list of books available from Penguin in New Zealand, please write to the *Marketing Department, Penguin Books (NZ) Ltd, Private Bag, Takapuna, Auckland 9*

In India: For a complete list of books available from Penguin, please write to *Penguin Overseas Ltd, 706 Eros Apartments, 56 Nehru Place, New Delhi, 110019*

In Holland: For a complete list of books available from Penguin in Holland, please write to *Penguin Books Nederland B.V., Postbus 195, NL–1380AD Weesp, Netherlands*

In Germany: For a complete list of books available from Penguin, please write to *Penguin Books Ltd, Friedrichstrasse 10 – 12, D–6000 Frankfurt Main 1, Federal Republic of Germany*

In Spain: For a complete list of books available from Penguin in Spain, please write to *Longman Penguin España, Calle San Nicolas 15, E–28013 Madrid, Spain*

A CHOICE OF PENGUIN FICTION

Monsignor Quixote Graham Greene

Now filmed for television, Graham Greene's novel, like Cervantes's seventeenth-century classic, is a brilliant fable for its times. 'A deliciously funny novel' – *The Times*

The Dearest and the Best Leslie Thomas

In the spring of 1940 the spectre of war turned into grim reality – and for all the inhabitants of the historic villages of the New Forest it was the beginning of the most bizarre, funny and tragic episode of their lives. 'Excellent' – *Sunday Times*

Earthly Powers Anthony Burgess

Anthony Burgess's magnificent masterpiece, an enthralling, epic narrative spanning six decades and spotlighting some of the most vivid events and characters of our times. 'Enormous imagination and vitality . . . a huge book in every way' – Bernard Levin in the *Sunday Times*

The Penitent Isaac Bashevis Singer

From the Nobel Prize-winning author comes a powerful story of a man who has material wealth but feels spiritually impoverished. 'Singer . . . restates with dignity the spiritual aspirations and the cultural complexities of a lifetime, and it must be said that in doing so he gives the Evil One no quarter and precious little advantage' – Anita Brookner in the *Sunday Times*

Paradise Postponed John Mortimer

'Hats off to John Mortimer. He's done it again' – *Spectator*. A rumbustious, hilarious new novel from the creator of Rumpole, *Paradise Postponed* was made into a major Thames Television series.

The Balkan Trilogy and Levant Trilogy Olivia Manning

'The finest fictional record of the war produced by a British writer. Her gallery of personages is huge, her scene painting superb, her pathos controlled, her humour quiet and civilized' – *Sunday Times*

A CHOICE OF PENGUIN FICTION

Stanley and the Women   Kingsley Amis

Just when Stanley Duke thinks it safe to sink into middle age, his son goes insane – and Stanley finds himself beset on all sides by women, each of whom seems to have an intimate acquaintance with madness. 'Very good, very powerful . . . beautifully written' – Anthony Burgess in the *Observer*

The Girls of Slender Means   Muriel Spark

A world and a war are winding up with a bang, and in what is left of London all the nice people are poor – and about to discover how different the new world will be. 'Britain's finest post-war novelist' – *The Times*

Him with His Foot in His Mouth   Saul Bellow

A collection of first-class short stories. 'If there is a better living writer of fiction, I'd very much like to know who he or she is' – *The Times*

Mother's Helper   Maureen Freely

A superbly biting and breathtakingly fluent attack on certain libertarian views, blending laughter, delight, rage and amazement, this is a novel you won't forget. 'A winner' – *The Times Literary Supplement*

Decline and Fall   Evelyn Waugh

A comic yet curiously touching account of an innocent plunged into the sham, brittle world of high society. Evelyn Waugh's first novel brought him immediate public acclaim and is still a classic of its kind.

Stars and Bars   William Boyd

Well-dressed, quite handsome, unfailingly polite and charming, who would guess that Henderson Dores, the innocent Englishman abroad in wicked America, has a guilty secret? 'Without doubt his best book so far . . . made me laugh out loud' – *The Times*

A CHOICE OF PENGUIN FICTION

A Fanatic Heart   Edna O'Brien

'A selection of twenty-nine stories (including four new ones) full of wit and feeling and savagery that prove that Edna O'Brien is one of the subtlest and most lavishly gifted writers we have' – A. Alvarez in the *Observer*

Charade   John Mortimer

'Wonderful comedy . . . an almost Firbankian melancholy . . . John Mortimer's hero is helplessly English' – *Punch*. 'What is *Charade*? Comedy? Tragedy? Mystery? It is all three and more' – *Daily Express*

Casualties   Lynne Reid Banks

'The plot grips; the prose is fast-moving and elegant; above all, the characters are wincingly, winningly human . . . if literary prizes were awarded for craftsmanship and emotional directness, *Casualties* would head the field' – *Daily Telegraph*

The Anatomy Lesson   Philip Roth

The hilarious story of Nathan Zuckerman, the famous forty-year-old writer who decides to give it all up and become a doctor – and a pornographer – instead. 'The finest, boldest and funniest piece of fiction which Philip Roth has yet produced' – *Spectator*

Gabriel's Lament   Paul Bailey

Shortlisted for the 1986 Booker Prize
'The best novel yet by one of the most careful fiction craftsmen of his generation' – *Guardian*. 'A magnificent novel, moving, eccentric and unforgettable. He has a rare feeling for language and an understanding of character which few can rival' – *Daily Telegraph*

Small Changes   Marge Piercy

In the Sixties the world seemed to be making big changes – but for many women it was the small changes that were the hardest and the most profound. *Small Changes* is Marge Piercy's explosive new novel about women fighting to make their way in a man's world.